Philosophy's Higher Education

Philosophy's Higher Education

By

Nigel Tubbs

King Alfred's University College,
Winchester, U.K.

KLUWER ACADEMIC PUBLISHERS
DORDRECHT / BOSTON / LONDON

Library of Congress Cataloging-in-Publication Data

ISBN 1-4020-2347-2 (HB)
ISBN 1-4020-2348-0 (e-book)

Printed on acid-free paper

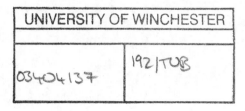

DEDICATION

*I dedicate this book and the thoughts within it to the memory of
Derek Brown.*

TABLE OF CONTENTS

TABLE OF CONTENTS

PREFACE

At about the age of 13 I began to realise that my formal education was separating itself off from my philosophical education. Of course, at the time I did not know it in this way. I experienced it as a split between what I was being taught and my experience of what I was being taught. It was, I now know, the philosophical experience of formal schooling. It was not until beginning the study of sociology at 16 that I came across the idea of dualisms—pairs of opposites that always appeared together but were never reconciled. In sociology it was the dualism of the individual and society. The question most asked in our classes was always regarding which aspect of the dualism dominated the other. The answer we always leaned towards was that both were mutually affected by the other. The answer seemed to lie somewhere in the middle.

It was only at university, first as an undergraduate and then as a postgraduate, that I came across the idea of the dialectic. Slowly I began to recognise that the dualisms which plagued social theory—I and we, self and other, good and evil, modernity and post-modernity, autonomy and heteronomy, freedom and nature, truth and relativism, and so many more—were not only dialectical in being thought about, but also that the thought of them being dialectical had an even stranger quality. It was the same experience as being at school. I was thinking about what I was experiencing and experiencing what I was thinking about. Yet still I couldn't find any recognition of this circle in the literature. My frustrations led me to an MA in *Sociological Studies* at Sussex University and thereafter to a PhD. It was there that I read a book which finally spoke to the experience of my experiences. This book was Gillian Rose's *Hegel Contra Sociology*. There I discovered that the thinking of thinking which I had been aware of since school was what Hegel called 'philosophical experience'. *Philosophy's Higher Education* is a testament to what I have since learned *from* philosophy *about* philosophy.

One has to search very hard to find any recognition that philosophy knows such things about itself. But if, like me, you have often felt that there must be more to dualisms than either the mere assertion of one side over the other, or a despairing scepticism in the face of their return to each other, then I hope you will find yourself somewhere in what follows.

Nigel Tubbs
Chandler's Ford
February 2004

ACKNOWLEDGEMENTS

This book has been in progress for the last six years. In that time it has been my privilege and my pleasure to work with the many students on the Education Studies programme at King Alfred's College, Winchester, who have been prepared to suspend their disbelief in philosophy and join me in trying to express our philosophical thinking. They have all risked philosophy's higher education and in doing so, many have produced work of a quality beyond their expectations. This only goes to show that when the content of your degree really matters to you and in some cases *is* you, then so much can be achieved in a short time. I want to acknowledge these students, and in particular those who have worked with me on their dissertations. They have been my university. I hope that in some way their higher education is sustaining them in the difficulties of their lives and contributing to its joys.

Two colleagues in particular have always supported my attempts to retrieve the educational significance of philosophy. Josh Cohen and Howard Caygill, both at Goldsmiths College in London, have, in different ways, inspired me with the rigour and the excitement in and of their work, and their commitment to the truth of philosophical experience. I will need them again, but I thank them now.

Special thanks go to Anne Judd. As a Subject Administrator she has embodied the spirit and the truth of the Education Studies degree for each student on an individual basis. Her care and wisdom are their own higher education. As a friend, well, she knows I could have done none of this without her.

Finally, my thanks to Julie. She has changed my life and continues to do so. She is my teacher in the things that I have been slow, all too slow, to understand and to feel. As I write this, we are in mourning, but it is an inaugurated mourning, and is the beginning, slowly, of a new life together.

INTRODUCTION

'This is probably the sort of book whose significance will take some while to sink in...'
Anthony Giddens on Gillian Rose's *Hegel Contra Sociology*.
It is beginning...

Few will disagree that philosophy is educational, or that at the root of philosophy lies the struggle to understand ourselves, or, even, that this struggle is formative for us. The real disagreement begins regarding the nature and import of this learning. In the following pages I will challenge philosophical experience to recognise the notion of the absolute that lies hidden within the struggles and contradictions of its educational substance and activity. And if the absolute is another way of saying God, then I will be arguing that God is currently masked within the illusions of social relations, but can be known in and as philosophy's higher education.

The term 'philosophy's higher education' carries two immanent connotations. It is both the higher education that philosophy can offer to other disciplines about themselves, and it is the higher education of philosophy by itself. As Kant recognised in *The Conflict of the Faculties*, higher education in general needs philosophy in order to know why and how it is 'higher'. But in order to achieve this, philosophy itself, the so-called lower faculty, must find within itself the truth of the education that it then offers to other disciplines. Kant's three *Critiques* in this sense act as the work required for the former, and as the pre-requisite for the work of the latter.

However, philosophy is often ill equipped or ill prepared to recognise the absolute significance of the higher education that it can gain from itself about itself. In what follows I will offer examples of how this higher education can be re-cognised in some of the most important European philosophers of the modern era. Necessarily, the implications of this re-cognition of philosophy's higher education mean that teachers of philosophy must again become its students. If, for example, we see Nietzsche only as the death of philosophy, or philosophy as the death of a tightrope walker carried to the forest to be buried by an untimely free spirit called Zarathustra, then we miss the inscrutable and rigorous logic and substance of the eternal return of the will to power. Alternatively, if we see only the abstract systems of Kant and Hegel, we miss the struggling, aporetic yet learning individuals whose lives are committed to the spiritual trials and the necessity of negative subjectivity. Further, and absolutely to the point, if we do not see, for example, Nietzsche *and* Hegel struggling with philosophy as its own higher education then we comprehend neither the system nor the subject. At root both are witnessing the truth of their thinking by opposing everything

xiii

in philosophy that falls short of its own necessity, a necessity which is present in and for itself as *learning*.

Here, then, is to be found the crux of my argument regarding philosophy's higher education. I will state it here, boldly, and all-too-boldly. Learning is the immanent condition of its own possibility in and as experience. As such, philosophy's higher education is the philosophy of experience experienced as philosophy. The absolute is realised and known not only by education, but as education.

'That was a way of putting it—not very satisfactory,' as T.S. Eliot wrote in *The Four Quartets*. Such abstract assertion may get you a degree (in philosophy as in other subjects), and most likely gets you published, but only the negation of such abstraction realises a genuinely higher education. Philosophy's higher education is realised when philosophy itself is not only abstractly about the negative, but is the work of being the negative. For example, it is suppressed unless and until its students are able to think about thinking, that is, to begin philosophy again, but this time in the truth of the experience of doing it. This means thinking negatively, thinking about contradictions through contradictions. It means saying things that on the surface cannot make sense. It means making abstract claims for philosophical truths in order that they inevitably undermine themselves. It means saying 'yes' to negative truths and remaining within their contradictory logic. All of this is already implicit within the work and the experiences that the students are having, but so often remains unre-cognised by and within their programmes of study, and worse still, by their tutors. Too many students pass through higher education never being given the space in which to pursue the necessity of their own doubts as the substance of their degree.

At stake, then, in philosophy's higher education, is our coming to learn differently about philosophy, from philosophy, and therein, also differently about its forms and contents. Philosophy, in this sense is both teacher and student to itself. For Socrates there was no distinction between philosophy and education. To engage in dialectical thinking, or to rigorously follow the path of one's doubts, was to do philosophy and to be learning at one and the same time. The learning may have appeared negative, but it was the positive formation and development of philosophical consciousness, or knowing that we don't know. Such a philosophical education is now at least 2,500 years old in the West. It has changed its form and its content continuously over that time but, in its various speculative guises, it has in some way always retained the relationship between thinking and education. Yet perhaps it is still Plato that provides the clearest attempt to explicate this relationship between philosophy 'and' education in terms which are faithful to both partners. The dialectical journey of the philosopher to and from the cave, the divided line, the conditions of possibility represented by the sun, and the struggle between reason, spirit and desire, all bear testimony to the

oneness of philosophy as learning and learning as philosophy. Since Plato, it is harder
to find such unashamed and explicit witness to the unity of this chiasmus. (This can be
explained according to the property relations predominant in any particular historical
period but such an account must be the subject of a future study.) However, as I will
argue at various points below, modern bourgeois property relations ensure that the
relation between philosophy and education is masked in and by misrecognitions of
subjectivity and substance. In this misrecognition their relation is distorted in many
ways, not least in that there is a discipline of the *philosophy of education* which
misrecognises their separation precisely in asserting the relation. But even within
philosophy itself, education is rarely analysed.

Let me put this another way. If the negative is our philosophical experience, then
how the negative is to be known depends upon philosophy's understanding of itself.
The paradox is that philosophy requires to know the negative in order to understand
itself! The very thing that should make education possible regarding the negative
stands in need of its own negative education. As such, and with Kierkegaard, we can
enquire whether we know not-knowing any differently now than Socrates did in
Athens? Just as Marx asked, how do we now stand in relation to the Hegelian
dialectic, so we must also ask, what is our modern relation to the negative and how do
social relations affect our understanding of it? Are we any nearer to knowing its
absolute necessity, and our unforgiving contingency within it, or are we still ironic
regarding its totality and just arrogant and bourgeois in our masterful judgements upon
it?

It is part of philosophy's higher education to realise that we have moved on from
Socrates. We do 'know' more about Socrates than he knew about himself. We are in
receipt of a higher education from philosophy than he was. *How* we are different from
Socrates is one of the underlying themes of this book. Kant, Hegel, Heidegger,
Kierkegaard, Nietzsche and Rosenzweig, in differing ways, are all philosophers of the
negative. They are all philosophers who attempt to learn the truth of the negative
without importing presuppositions about it before it has been learned. Yet, at the same
time, they recognise that such a project is only possible because the negative is always
already presupposed. What marks out their work from so much other philosophy is
their fortitude in working within the aporias that constitute the conditions of
possibility. At the very heart of the following study lies the ways in which each of
these philosophers presents his negative thinking as something 'and' nothing.[1]

To achieve this, each chapter looks at the way philosophy's higher education is
contained within a particular dualism that characterises the substance and subject of
the philosopher's work. With Kant we draw out philosophy's higher education from
the relation of formation and finality that constitutes reflective judgements; in Hegel

the master/slave relation is explored as a template for philosophy's higher education and as the subject and substance of the notion; in Heidegger being and time are argued to be a somewhat careless treatment of the necessity of learning within and by doubt; with Kierkegaard we look at recollection and repetition and the significance of their relation for faith and formative, upbuilding education; in Nietzsche eternal return and will to power are read as an educational relation *contra* their interpretation by Deleuze; and finally, in Rosenzweig, the fire and the rays of *The Star of Redemption* are read as an educational relation, one that enables a retrieval of the philosophy of history and world spirit as bearers of philosophy's higher education. The significance of the 'and' that carries the relation of learning within these dualisms is also examined in this final chapter.

The chapters are placed between two other brief essays. *What is Philosophy's Higher Education?* acts as an abstract statement of the structure and logic of the experience that is self-determinative of philosophy's higher education. It introduces several of the key concepts that are central to this education—dualism, contingency, law, truth and learning—but in a way that does not presuppose the relationship within each chapter that provides them with their actual content. The book ends with an essay on *The End of Culture* which takes up several provocative statements made in the opening sections of the book. It argues that recent developments in philosophical thinking mark a new form of the domination of the absolute.

But the deeper we pursue philosophy's higher education, the more intriguing its implications become. Not only is it a realisation of the absolute within modern social relations, it is also a retrieval of our contingency within the philosophy of history. On a smaller scale, but exactly the same learning, philosophy's higher education retrieves the oldest form of enquiry of all, 'know thyself'. What gradually emerges in the book is that one of the most significant manifestations of philosophy's higher education is in the relation of self to self and to the other. What it teaches us is difficult, and negative, but universally true in its negativity: *I am already other and the other is not me.* This is implicit and explicit at different times in the text and is directly discussed in the final chapter. This is more than just symbolic. It is placed in the chapter in which philosophy's higher education is moved onto the stage of world spirit. It explores the relation of the eternal people and the historical peoples within the world historical relation of the philosophy of history, and argues that reason itself is diasporic. The chapter is on Rosenzweig 'and' Hegel, but the relation of reason to the other that it evokes has implications beyond that between the Jew and the Gentile. Our higher education in philosophy is our rethinking of *all* of the appearances that this relationship to self and other takes, re-presenting as they do prevailing social and political relations. Astonishingly, in our hopes that we can repair the relations between self and other that threaten the world, the most important thing we learn in philosophy's higher education is not to overcome the broken relation between them, but to sustain it in its educational truth.

Here, then, is the absolutely intriguing truth of philosophy's higher education. Each of the philosophers explored below not only tries and fails to produce the magic synthesis, the magic third way, that will unite theory and practice, subject and object, freedom and necessity—*they re-cognise the law of the failure in the experience of failure*. Thus, as we will see, the (failure of the) synthesis of the transcendental *a priori* in Kant is the law of contingency within reflective judgement; (the failure of) mutual recognition in Hegel is the law of spirit; (the failure of) thinking in Heidegger is the law of Being as Dasein; (the failure of) faith as doubt in Kierkegaard is the law of recollection and repetition; (the failure of) Zarathustra in Nietzsche is the law of eternal return; and (the failure of) the philosophy of history in Rosenzweig is the law of *The Star*. In each case, law is realised within the desire of the ordinary natural consciousness for a healing of division, and it is realised as the education of the misrecognition of this natural consciousness. The universality of this contingency draws a dramatic realisation. Not only is this our education regarding law, it is also the law of this education. Law and learning are each the necessity of the condition of the possibility of the other. Together 'and' apart, they are philosophy's higher education, and they are the absolute.

Perhaps one might object that such a notion of philosophy's higher education is merely a Hegelian reading of Kant, Nietzsche, etc., finding determinate negation in their work. To the dissembling thinking that is refusing to learn *of* learning *from* learning, this would offer a retreat from the risk and the truth of law. If philosophy's higher education can be reduced to the application of a system then it is rendered arbitrary and optional. But philosophy's higher education is not Hegelian, any more than it is Kantian or Nietzschean or whatever. They have expressed the truth of its education in their work, and in each case, as I will try to show, this has been done in full recognition of its necessity in and as their thinking. Commentators so often fail to bring out this necessity within the work of philosophers. But as Nietzsche said, usually this is more about the weaknesses of the interpreters than the philosophers themselves. The thinking of our selected philosophers has a rigour and an integrity that must be honoured, even and especially when their work reaches its most difficult moments. That the rigour lies in their learning of necessity and their trying to do justice to it, is masked by the dissembling thinking which refuses the beauty of the eternal difficulty that *is* philosophy and education. Aporia in our experiences is not only the difficulty of thinking; it is the truth of thinking. Moreover, as we will see, it is reason's teleology and it is modernity being modern.

Obviously the book could have been written very differently. Instead of working in such detail on educational readings of particular philosophers, it could have followed the more usual model of abstract assertion about the merits of an idea, in this case philosophy's higher education, providing the community of academic scholars, as Hegel would say, with further dead bones to pick over. Such assertions are anathema to philosophy's higher education which is realised only in the actuality of the learning individual whose thinking becomes its own content. It is in treating such work with integrity and in finding its own logic and necessity from within itself that we retrieve the absolute significance of the work. Therefore, in the main I will not be dealing with commentaries, but only with the work itself, to reveal the way philosophy's higher education constitutes the learning of the thinker. Each chapter explores dualisms within the work of the selected philosopher, drawing out the higher education that is contained within their formulations. In short, I am arguing that whilst the differences between Kant, Hegel, Heidegger, Kierkegaard, Nietzsche and Rosenzweig are interesting, of much greater significance is the educational necessity that their thinking shares. When we see not only that they are all wrestling (Rosenzweig) with the same difficulty of knowing that which is not known, and with the conditions of the possibility of there (their) being thinking at all, but also that, in different ways, they all struggle with the integrity of this impossibility, then what they have in common and what they share is philosophy's higher education. They are all modernity; they are all the re-cognition of reason's misrecognition. Their differences are in the way each of them is the learning individual of philosophy's higher education. The significance of the differences is not that they are different, but that these differences are the infinite become singular.

On a personal note, I have to recognise that the book is underpinned and fuelled by, at worst, an anger, and, at best, a deep frustration. This frustration, in different ways, has carried me for some twenty five years now through different and various kinds of educational milieu—the family, schooling, teaching, the erotic, and most recently higher education. This anger/frustration is related to the difficulty of truth. It reveals itself when faced with those who try to refuse the work of our continuing education and opt for the safety of arbitrary way-stations. Such resignation is often accompanied by desperate self-justification, but the latter only betrays the true nature of the former and is formative of hypocrisy and, at times, wilful mastery. In important ways *Philosophy's Higher Education* issues from witnessing this refusal and this resignation, both by those in higher education who avoid the philosophical, and then, in philosophy itself, by those who eschew the subjective substance of the difficulties that are immanent in philosophical thinking. It is against such practitioners, as against my own failures, that I offer this re-education of the relation between philosophy 'and' education.

However, as I end the book, now, I note that the anger and the frustration are changing. Partly, but not exclusively because of the book, [2] I am now angry at the anger. It has made much possible that otherwise would not be, but equally, to use the most ancient of philosophical models, it has not been in proportion with other elements of desire and reason. Now I feel a change, one perhaps implicit in the reading of the philosophers below, but largely unrealised closer to home. Still love's work, but now a more forgiving and a more generous spirit makes itself known out of this sublation of anger by itself.

NOTES

[1] Contra Heidegger (1987) who asks why there is something rather than nothing?
[2] And also in large part because of J.

REFERENCES

Eliot, T.S. (1969) 'The Four Quartets,' in *The Complete Poems and Plays of T.S. Eliot*, London, Book Club Associates.
Heidegger, M. (1987) *An Introduction to Metaphysics*, New haven, Yale University Press.
Kant, I. (1979) *The Conflict of the Faculties*, Lincoln, University of Nebraska Press.

WHAT IS PHILOSOPHY'S HIGHER EDUCATION?[1]

'It is not at all the intention of the new teaching to be new, it wants to remain the old
teaching, but a teaching grasped in its absolute sense,' (Buber, 1967, p. 46).

My thesis is this: philosophy is thinking; thinking is negative; negativity is experience; and experience is learning of experience as negative, in thinking, and as philosophy. The circle is philosophy's higher education, and all concepts, all philosophical work, all identity and all truth, are this circle. The only term not to appear twice in the formulation is *learning*, but this is deceptive. Learning is not only the 'return' of the circle, its soul or immanent self-movement, it is also already the beginning and the end of the circle, but importantly—in its domination by abstract thinking—it is not seen as such. This is the most significant aspect of philosophy's higher education, that philosophy is already its own misrecognition. When philosophy examines the conditions of its own possibility, it does so in and as the illusion that those conditions exist for it as its object. This illusion is the misrecognition of the circle of experience by itself. The misrecognition is therefore the necessity of the conditions of possibility. Knowing experience as this necessity is knowing the truth of illusion. Such a knowing is the necessity of its own possibility as learning and as education. Learning the truth of this education from Kant, Hegel, Heidegger, Kierkegaard, Nietzsche and Rosenzweig is the subject of this book.

Or, again, philosophy is the relation to the object. More precisely, philosophy is the relation of the relation of thought and object. As such, it is the question of objectivity and it is object to itself, both as the result of its enquiry and as the enquiry. Each of these appears to undermine the other. The enquiry already has its object, thus the object of the enquiry collapses. This is the truth of the illusions that determine philosophy. The contingency of philosophical enquiry is self-defeating, yet is also its own self-determination. The contradiction is not optional; it is philosophy's own law. It is, for us, the necessity that underpins philosophy's conditions of possibility, a necessity that also underpins the conditions of the possibility of experience and of objects of experience. The most powerful illusions within this necessity are that the law is empty, or is optional, or is only other. Illusion constitutes the relation of the relation between experience and law, and is itself the law of doing so. It is part of that law that illusion be posited as thinking 'and' object.

It is from within this misrecognition of the relation of the relation that assertions are made about contingency which abstract them from contingency. It has become *de rigueur* to use contingency against the absolute, against subjectivity and against the philosophy of history. Used *against* truth, this is merely a positing of contingency by that which does not recognise itself as the illusion which *is* absolute contingency. The real test of philosophy's higher education, therefore, is to know the experience of thinking as an education within the circle of its necessity, and not to prejudge the 'result' of that experience with concepts or scepticisms that assert some kind of immunity from this necessity. Such prejudgements lack the courage for the absolute contingency that returns again and again in conformity to itself. This latter is philosophy—the relation to the object—which knows its self-determination within and as illusion, and which knows this as the necessity of its own conditions of possibility. It lies within philosophy's higher education to learn of this necessity as learning. As such, in philosophy's higher education, illusion is the social and political foundation of the absolute.

1. PRESUPPOSITION OF EDUCATION

Philosophy's higher education is immanent within the logic of negative experience. Equally, it is the necessity, the law, of doubt's own possibility, and, as such, it is reason's own self-formation and finality. It is suppressed, however, because even when philosophy works negatively and with doubt, one concept within reason always remains immune from its own necessity, and that is 'education'. Judgements within and upon philosophy inevitably do not work with a philosophical notion of education, and it is from within this misrecognition of education that the understanding of *what is* is traduced into imperatives about *what ought to be*.

In fact, a presupposition of the concept of education is hidden within and masked by judgements that are made regarding the import of philosophy. This presupposition takes two forms. It is present in the notion of enlightenment as 'overcoming,' where the positive, i.e. what has been learned, is always given sway over the negative or what was not known. Equally, it is present in the critique of this notion of enlightenment, a critique which also presupposes a knowledge of education, this time as non-result. All philosophical work which has ultimately fallen back on one or other of these abstractions of education sells its own work short, as it sells modernity and reason short. It allows the negative to think itself in regard to everything except the immanent nature and necessity of its own notion of learning. Realising this learning from within the negative and as philosophy, is the whole of philosophy's higher education and is the true nature of modernity known to itself. When pursued rigorously and passionately the negative not only teaches us what to unlearn, it also teaches us how unlearning is formative and substantial. This is the higher education pursued below, finding in each of the selected philosophers an educational necessity at the heart of the logic and the content of their thinking, and in their being philosophical.

2. DUALISM

The logic, the necessity and the immanent notion of higher education within negative experience lies in the relation that is 'dualism'. The illusion of all dualisms is that they contain only two partners. However the determination of a dualism is relation being thought as separation. Our natural consciousness appears on the scene too late to see this work of separation being performed, and is faced always by the immutable separation of contradictory opposites. Taking the world at face value, and as the beginning of thinking, our natural consciousness conceptualises education in the same way, as a dualism of activity and result. Each time it employs education to overcome or repair a dualism, or to assert that their separation cannot be repaired, it merely employs a concept of education (as overcoming or not-overcoming) which is imbued with the same dualistic structure as that which it seeks to comment upon. Dualism meets dualism, and scholasticism is given its head.

What the abstract notion of education misses is that a notion of education already lies within dualisms. Indeed, dualism *is* our education; it is just that we misrecognise the significance of what we are being taught by it. Education is present in the dualism as the work, the work in which being known is also not-being-known. More simply, the work is present as doubt. When doubt is misrecognised as merely not-knowing, then dualism is aporia without educational significance, without its own truth. But neither knowing nor not-knowing, on their own, are the truth of what the negative is teaching us. It appears so because our abstract consciousness presupposes the truth of education dualistically. It uses as a tool for judgement that which has the very structure that awaits judgement. To retrieve the educational significance of our experience of this presupposition is the work and the truth of philosophy's higher education.

How is this to be done and what is to be learned? Philosophy's higher education involves an immanent critique of doubt—of dualism—by itself. It knows that doubt manifests itself as dualism, where what is known is negated in being known and produces its opposite. But its relation to the dualism is also dualistic for it negates the dualism as something known and now has that as its contradictory opposite too. This education is doubt being rigorously and necessarily turned against itself, and is already present in its being known. It is an education present as contradiction, not just the contradiction of dualism, but the contradiction that is produced in trying to know the contradiction. This education, this experience, is the relation of the relation. What lies ahead is our learning from our selected philosophers how and what to learn from within this relation of the relation.

What has reappeared for us now, which was previously masked, is the immanent work that determines dualism. In the relation of the relation is the work of the work. That which was suppressed in the appearance of dualism is now present in the relation of the appearance to itself. What kind of experience, what kind of knowledge is this now for us? It cannot be positive and abstract, for that would be to impose from without upon the work itself. Equally, it cannot be nothing at all, for it is our (philosophical) experience, we 'know' of the work because it is what our experience consists of. So what do we learn in this experience of negative experience? We learn precisely what we have just said: that the experience is of the work—abstraction—and is the work—negation. If our philosophical experience is about thinking and is thinking, if it is the formation of itself as content, then this is philosophy's higher education, for here philosophy experiences itself. This does not presume the identity of what philosophy is or is not. Rather, it allows philosophy to learn of itself from within its own presuppositions but without importing new ones. The difference now between this higher education and merely dualistic misrecognitions is that we do not judge the experience as *either* true *or* false, i.e. dualistically, we judge it only according to itself, bringing nothing to it except that which is necessarily already within it. As contradiction, it is its *own* truth.

Philosophy's higher education therefore shares the same triadic structure as Rose's notion of the broken middle, for both are the same knowing of not-knowing, the same something that is the knowing of itself as not-known, the same negative result. The broken middle is a suspension of philosophy in, for and by philosophy. But the truth of the broken middle, the broken middle in and for itself, is learning. It is to learning that we must look now, if the broken middle and the realisation of the absolute are to be comprehended as the one project *to think modernity*.[2]

3. SELF AND OTHER

This truth of the relation of the relation inheres in all dualisms. One of the most persistent forms of misrecognition however is that of the relation of self 'and' other. The dualism of the relation of the relation of self and other constitutes the positive reconciliation of and the negative incommensurability of their difference. The former is often centred around a notion of mutual recognition, the latter around varieties of pluralism. Put another way, the former is the recognition of each as the other; the latter is the recognition of each as not the other. Both are misrecognitions of the relation that is already the work of self 'and' other. As with the misrecognised notion of education referred to above, a posited dualism is already the condition of the possibility of the relation. That is, what is claimed in the meeting of the two self-consciousnesses, that they are or are not each other, is already presupposed by the meeting. Positing is the hidden and prior work of the dissembling reflective consciousness which takes at face value the meeting of self and other, but misrecognises its own determination in and by that positing. This misrecognition is relation only in and as the aporia of the relation of self and other. Either 'we' are other to each other and therefore the same or 'we' are not each other and are therefore different. The 'we' is the necessary presupposition for such judgements, but it appears as if the 'we' results from the judgement.[3] Judgements for or against mutual recognition or difference are therefore already the relation of self and other but as illusion.

Illusion here has a logic and a substance of its own that is realised in philosophy's higher education. Self, by definition, is not other. The relation of self 'and' other that is the condition of the possibility of self as not other is suppressed in the appearance of their opposition, or their dualism. The relation of the relation appears only as a *sollen*, as something that ought to be realised, in this case, the mutuality or the difference of each other. But the *sollen* is not only the misrecognition of the 'and' that is the relation of the relation, it is also a highly dangerous misrecognition for it legitimates a political agenda. It demands that we repair relations between others either by intervention or by forbearance. But the demand fails to recognise how its own conditions of possibility are the same as those of the appearance of self 'and' other. The political 'ought' for and against communities must lead to domination and terror, for repair will have to be forced against its own conditions of possibility. What remains, however, is a higher education regarding this relation of the conditions of possibility to themselves. This 'self-relation' is one of self 'and' other, but is present only in and as the illusion that is already their opposition. This re-cognition of itself as misrecognition does not mean that the illusion is 'overcome.' Its conditions of possibility cannot overcome themselves, for their necessity demands that all such illusions learn, again, of their absolute contingency. Thus, in philosophy's higher education, self and other are not the same or different, they are both. But 'both', here, means the truth that I am already other and the other is not me, or, somewhat bluntly, I am that which I am not. The contradiction is the movement of the abstract statement. It is at rest, or is itself, when and because the negative is the condition of its possibility. The truth of the relation of self and other is carried within the 'and' of self and other. The 'and' is already the illusion of the relation of self and other and is, itself, the site and the significance of our education regarding the relation that is the relation of self and other.

Philosophy's higher education, therefore, is formative and re-formative of modern subjectivity. In it and through it we become what we already are. Revolution seeks to make us different by changing our social and political predetermination, whilst reformation seeks to make us different within existing social relations. It sounds neither revolutionary nor reforming to suggest that philosophy's higher education makes us more of what we already are. However, given that we are, already, *not* what we are, there can be no more transformative education than into the nature of this negative identity. To become what we are is to gain a mind of our own, and 'apprehending itself in this way, it is as if the world had for it only now come into being' (Hegel, 1977: 139-140). Here, philosophy's higher education is the actuality of who we are, the modern version of the ancient 'know thyself'.

There are important political implications here. Visions of the unity of mankind that see all as one do not liberate us from difference, they dominate it. Similarly, pluralistic visions of mankind which see one as all do not understand difference. By retreating from the necessity of the condition of the possibility of difference, they render it socially, politically and spiritually meaningless. What we learn in and from philosophy's higher education is that otherness is not determined merely in a relation of one to an other, it is determined in and as a relation to itself. If I 'know' or do not 'know' otherness, either way I have failed to learn of myself as the illusion that is absolute contingency, and refused its difficulty and its education which teaches that I am already other and the other is not me. This is the self-relation of otherness, or its own necessity, its own law. Such an education does not overcome the other in a vision of what he should be, nor fetishises the other in a misrecognition of what he is. It learns that the relation of the relation of self and other is my education, and that in my education otherness speaks its own truth. For the abstract consciousness that treats all relations as dualisms, this relation of the relation can only be suffered in its incompleteness. But our philosophical experience of the necessity that lies suppressed within this ordinary experience teaches us that there is a completeness here, although according to a law unlike any that we have been prepared for.

4. LAW AND PRIVATE PROPERTY

Modernity carries its own version of this relation of self and other within the illusion of its social relations. Modern bourgeois social relations, or universal property law, are already the positing of the relation of the relation of self and other as a relation of equal persons to that which is other as 'nothing'. The 'already' is present to us as the political status accorded to the self who is not other, and to the other who is other than the self. In modern bourgeois property relations, the self who is not other is the property owner, and the other who is other is a thing. But within this misrecognition of self and other the thing has the last laugh, for it therein also determines relations between people as relations between things. Marx's insight still stands here. The thing is what is left when all the significance of 'otherness' as a relation is usurped by the self in terms of universal property rights. The owner has gained himself at the expense of any relation of otherness. This victory is his defeat of human relations, or is where the relation of the relation, as Adorno feared, is wholly objectified. All owners are other not to other men, but to things. Therefore, as other, they are as things to each other. As such, philosophy's higher education becomes indifference.

But, as always and everywhere, the misrecognition of the other within particular social relations contains the seeds of its higher education. As a property owner I am dependent upon the thing for my status. I am already therefore like the thing, for I am also nothing in my own right. This is a critical re-education for the master regarding his objectivity, for now he is no longer the self who is not other. Now he too is like the other, like nothing, and is not himself. This philosophical, spiritual and political experience, this re-cognition, is actual as contradiction. He re-cognises that the owner was always already of the relation of self 'and' other, but that this self (and its objects) were another misrecognition of that relation. He was therefore always already other to the relation that is now his own truth. Thus, he is already other, and the other is not him. We can learn the truth of the untruth of bourgeois social relations, and we can learn of the law and necessity of this self-determination. But the universality of the higher education is also the universality of property relations. And the universality of the former, or 'the other', is the work of education that we engage in against the universality of the latter. In relation to (or in the relation of) absolute ethical life we are already other and the other is not us.

Modernity is thus far more complex than its supporters or detractors allow. Its abstract model of enlightenment as overcoming is taken to mean a vision of market relations and private property governed by a self-reproducing democratic system of personal freedoms. Taken across the world, this is the ubiquitous culture of globalisation. *Post* this crude imperialistic modernity, the non- or anti-enlightenment vision is of a modernity that knows its limitations, respects that which is not (or is post) modernity, and encourages tolerance. Modernity, properly understood, is neither of these abstract models. The truth of modernity is philosophy's higher education. Its universality is that it is already other and that the other is not it. In other words, its own universality and truth includes the untruth of this relation to itself, and learns from that untruth of the truth of its relation to the other and as the other. In this sense it is the very essence of reason to be at home not in globalisation but in the diasporic.[4] Modernity learns about the truth of the other through its own educational work. The inner law and necessity of modernity is that reason always seeks to learn from itself, wherever it meets itself and in whatever guises and social relations it appears. It therefore protests against itself as globalisation, for there it only meets the untruth of itself. Yet, paradoxically, its diaspora from the world is also a return to the world. The truth of modernity is not its homogenisation of the world but its repeated losing of itself to itself as otherness. Similarly, it cannot 'sanction' pluralism. Tolerance freely given is the worst form of insidious imperialism, and absolutely does not understand the self as other, nor therefore does it respect the other who is not me. Pluralism has the same presuppositions as mutual recognition; it assumes that which it then seemingly negotiates. It is in the struggle of self and other, and the struggle of self with self as other, that reason comes to recognise itself as already the other, in a manifold of different forms and guises. But always, in being the other, the other is also not me. It is when the relation of these truths is suppressed that reason ceases to learn, and the bombs continue to fall.

5. TRUTH

However, the most ubiquitous form of this suppression is that which asserts the unknowability of 'truth', or truth as other. Assertions regarding truth, and scepticisms regarding (the impossibility of) truth are borne of the same illusion. Both suppress the necessary and absolute contingency of knowing that truth is not known in favour of the less difficult path, the one which presupposes truth as other in order, then, to make such judgements about it. Philosophy's higher education regarding truth lies in the experience that negates both of these paths, recognising the illusion of the relation to be the truth of the relation to truth. If we call this 'learning', then the dissembling thinking will play master and make autonomous judgements about the dualism of such a concept. *Either*, it will assert, learning is a process that goes on all the time, and is not in itself a result, but just a movement. Here, for the master, learning is mere slave, nothing in itself. *Or*, it might assert that learning is a something when it is a moment that produces a result.[5] Here the master simply frees the slave to be master in his (the master's) own image. In both cases, dualism is judged by that which fails to recognise its own necessary misrecognition of itself as relation. It is for philosophy's higher education to learn about its own immanent law (as learning) from the experience of this domination of learning without suppressing that law by importing ingenious new forms of domination, or ingenious third ways that will synthesise and heal where doubt always fails. What makes philosophy's higher education 'higher' is not that we do or do not come to know truth, but rather that we come to know the truth of the untruth of the dualism within which the assertions regarding our capacity to know the truth or not are made. As we will see with each of our philosophers, to know the untruth of dualisms is to learn of truth's own self-determination. It is here, as philosophy's higher education, that we find the truth of our selected philosophers' most difficult ideas.

Of course, looking for meaning and truth (and redemption) in suffering, in difficulty and in struggle is nothing new. Religion is the culture of this deepest desire of the human condition. But it re-presents this suffering and its meaning figuratively in ways that empower the dissembling understanding to take it or leave it, as it wishes. As a culture, religion is always re-formed by itself, and this experience of re-formation is (potentially and philosophically) its own higher education. This is explored in the final essay of the book. Faith is the positing of a suffering consciousness which knows the despairing implications of positing to be separation from the true, but does not know that faith stands opposed to the truth of positing. Faith is already the misrecognition of philosophy's higher education, and has to die to itself if it is to realise its own truth. Faith's negativity is absolute. Thus faith *is* part of the re-formation of religion, and part of our higher education into the meaning of suffering and struggle, but not the unreformed faith that, against its own nature, stands opposed to the recognition of its absolute negativity. Kierkegaard is our guide to this form of philosophy's higher education in chapter 4. (We will see at the end of chapter 1 that the same logic applies to the idea of 'hope'.) Re-formed faith is the work of philosophy's higher education, a faith in its own truth, and a faith not just in learning, but *as* learning. A fair question with which to end this introduction might be what difference does a re-formed faith make over against unreformed faith? It makes all the difference because it is the law of difference contingent upon itself. It is the difference in which faith is possible, but also in which learning is the necessity of faith's own possibility, and as such, its truth.

Is it 'safe' to be using the term 'truth' so freely here in regard to philosophy's higher education? In fact, it is unsafe not to. The work of being thought, or thinking, now exercises its (un)truth of everything else upon itself. This is self-determination, and this is freedom, but in a manner and of a kind that only the negative can achieve. Only the negative can work upon itself in the same way that it works upon everything else. It can do this because it starts from a different place than everything else. The positive starts in illusion and the negative therefore is already of illusion. Only the negative enjoys this diasporic truth of philosophy's higher education in and for itself, separated and related, and independent in its dependence.

What are we to call this negative self-work? We are to call it learning, for learning is the in and for itself of the negative. Learning is the relation of the relation. Learning is the form and the content of our philosophical experience of contradiction. Learning is the freedom of the negative, an end without end but also, precisely, the end in itself. Learning is the truth of illusion as self-determination. Learning is the circle whose movement and return is its own experience of itself. It is a whole, but one in which we learn to know the meaning of the concept of 'the whole' differently. Philosophy's higher education, in sum, is that we learn of the absolute to be the law of learning and the learning of law. And if God should therefore be present to modern consciousness in and as learning, so be it.

NOTES

[1] We will see in the following chapters that philosophy's higher education is not only about the absolute nature of contingency, it is also contingency absolutely determining itself. An abstract statement can be made regarding philosophy's higher education prior to those chapters precisely because the education is absolute. As such, we can speak of its logic as its content. This is briefly set out now. Much more compelling, though, is to explore the ways in which its content is its logic. This is the absolute method that is employed in each chapter of the book, where content is the thinking of the selected philosopher, logic is the movement of that content, and together they are the work, or the relation, that *is* the philosopher.

[2] *The Broken Middle* is the title of a book by Gillian Rose, published in 1992. However, an earlier book, *Hegel Contra Sociology*, (1981) has been much more the inspiration for my finding philosophy in (and as) the education of my own thinking. It is to that most difficult of books that I recommend you go if you want to explore further the idea of the broken middle!

[3] Rose (1996: 4) refers to this as part of the new ethics that characterises post-modern outlooks, with their positing of new communities of gender, race, etc.

[4] We will rehearse this in greater detail below in chapter 6.

[5] We will explore the problem of learning as a moment with Kierkegaard and Nietzsche below.

REFERENCES

Buber, M. (1967) *On Judaism*, New York, Schocken Books.
Rose, G. (1981) *Hegel Contra Sociology*, London, Athlone.
Rose, G. (1992) *The Broken Middle*, Oxford, Blackwell.
Rose, G (1996) *Mourning Becomes the Law*, Cambridge, Cambridge University Press.

CHAPTER 1

KANT: FORMATION AND FINALITY

Kant's philosophical higher education lies in the relationship between the three *Critiques*. The first *Critique* misrecognises the relation between the conditions of the possibility of experience and the conditions of the possibility of objects of experience in and as subsumptive judgement. The second *Critique*, even more ambitiously, seeks to reveal the categorical imperative of the relation between will and its object as the condition of the possibility of freedom. The third *Critique* is Kant's higher education regarding the truth of these misrecognitions. Philosophy's higher education is to be found here in the structure of reflective judgements. Judgement (power) learns of and from itself that it is already the immanent work of formation and finality, or is the relation of the relation of the conditions of the possibility of experience to the conditions of the possibility of objects of experience. If the *Critique of Pure Reason* (1968) is the misrecognition of mutual recognition, and the *Critique of Practical Reason* (1956) is the misrecognition of the master and the slave, then the *Critique of Judgement* (1952) is the re-cognition of these misrecognitions. The relation between all three is judgement's own higher education regarding its immanent educational truth.

1. CONCEPT AND INTUITION

One of the central problems in Kant's *Critique of Pure Reason* is the relationship between the ability to conceptualise or to think about the world and the objects in the world at which this thinking is aimed. From the start this is far from straightforward because in trying to think about this relationship, certain things are already before us, certain things appear to have already happened, the most important of which is that, in thinking about this relationship, the relationship, somehow, already appears to be established.

Kant's analysis of this pre-existing relationship states that it must be the case that certain conditions pertain in order for us to have thoughts about the world in the first place. There are two such conditions, the transcendental aesthetic and transcendental logic. The former concerns the necessary preconditions for there to be objects of experience. Objects first come to our attention through what Kant calls our 'sensibility', a capacity in which we are able to 'represent' to ourselves our 'intuition' of any particular manifestation of the manifold of material. A representation registered through a particular sensation is empirical and *a posteriori*. What an object might be apart from our intuition or representation of it

1

'remains completely unknown to us' (1968: A42/B60). But pure intuition, separate from all particular or empirical intuitions, is the possibility of sensation *per se*, or is '*a priori* sensibility' (1968: A21/B35), and this is the transcendental aesthetic, constituted by time and space. Time and space are the pure forms of intuition and are the transcendental conditions for the possibility of all intuition and representation.

The second condition which must be in place before we can think about the world refers to 'concepts' used by the understanding. As with time and space, Kant reasons that there must be *a priori* conditions to understanding which are themselves not dependent upon the understanding but which, rather, make understanding possible. These conditions are met by pure reason which, again like time and space, is transcendental and, for human understanding, unknowable in itself. As intuition is contingent upon its own possibility—pure intuition—so concepts are contingent upon their own possibility—pure reason.

What happens, then, when these dual faculties of understanding and sensibility are brought together? How, in our experience of the world, is sense made of the manifold of intuition? What is the relation between the dualism of concepts and intuitions such that we can understand intuitions rather than merely be aware of them? How, in other words, are thoughts (ideas) and objects (material) related in such a way that each is added to by the other to give both a shared meaning? Kant's answer is that they are synthesised into human meaning and understanding by 'judgement'. A judgement brings together 'various representations under one common representation' (1968: A68/B93), that is, 'in every judgement there is a concept which holds of many representations' (1968: A68/B93). But the concept is not the intuition, nor is the intuition the concept. They are not in an 'immediate' relation with each other. They have been brought together by a 'third party'. This third party—judgement—is what relates concept and intuition. As Kant famously remarked, 'thoughts without content are empty, intuitions without concepts are blind' (1968: A51/B75). Judgement, we might say, ensures that the mutual dependence of each upon the other is continuously upheld. Through judgement *something* is understood and something is *understood*. This leads Kant to conclude that objectively valid judgements express the mutual dependency of concept and intuition. Consequently he is able to state that 'the conditions of the *possibility of experience* in general are likewise conditions of the *possibility of the objects of experience*, and that for this reason they have objective validity in a synthetic *a priori* judgement, (1968: A158/B197).

There are two ways in which Kant interprets these synthetic *a priori* judgements, as subsumptive and as reflective.

2. SUBSUMPTIVE JUDGEMENT

2.1 Critique of Pure Reason

Although Kant's formula implies an equal relationship or dependence between the conditions of the possibility of experience and the conditions of the possibility of objects of experience, nevertheless it becomes clear that there is a one-sided domination here. Caygill raises this issue in his *Kant Dictionary* (1995).[1] He notes that Kant himself saw judgement as the solution to the question as to how the understanding is 'to construct for itself entirely *a priori* concepts of things, with which the things are necessarily in agreement' (1995: 103); that is, adds Caygill, how the understanding can generate principles 'which both agree with and are yet independent of experience?' (1995: 103). If the principles of the understanding are independent of experience then experience, and consequently the objects of experience, must conform to that prior independent set of rules. Thus it gives to the understanding a dominion over sensibility where synthetic *a priori* judgements work for the understanding over and against the intuition of imagination. The 'agreement' reached between understanding and sensibility is one which is always decided in favour of the understanding. Suddenly, the open relationship between concept and intuition, kept open by and expressed as judgement, becomes a pre-judged relationship where the dry, logical, mechanistic understanding and employment of pre-existing categories is always lord over the fluid, creative, imaginative, immediate intuition. The latter lacks any 'rules' to which the understanding must conform and is therefore dependent upon the understanding, or is its 'slave'. Intuition is subsumed under the inflexible and pre-given rules of the understanding by what can now be recognised not as a judgement of mutual dependence, but a subsumptive judgement in which the universal law or principle of understanding subordinates the particular in nature. What Kant calls the 'schema' in the *Critique of Pure Reason* facilitates this subsumption for it is the 'tool controlled by the understanding' (1995: 360) by which concepts are 'applied' to intuitions. Even though schematism, as Caygill points out, prepares both intuition and concept for their agreement in judgement, a preparation which is 'concealed in the depths of the human soul,' (1995: 361) nevertheless that 'mutual' preparation always involves applying categories to appearances and never appearances to categories, for the category is precisely that which cannot and must not be dependent upon any empirical experience.

There is another way of describing what is at stake here between concept and intuition, this time in terms of freedom and necessity. Looked at in one way, the theoretical reason of the *Critique of Pure Reason* reveals that, through subsumptive or determinant judgements, it is the concept which enjoys a self-mastery and therefore freedom or self-determination. It is the rules of the understanding or pure reason which are free from any outside or heteronomous influence or determination. It is they that are autonomous for even though they are made real to us through experience, they are not dependent in themselves upon that experience. Kant argues that freedom is constituted by this sort of autonomy and self-determination. Further, the enemy of freedom is any sort of heteronomy where the principle of self-determination is threatened by contingency upon something from without. Therefore theoretical reason is free, autonomous and grounded upon its own independent necessity. However, the cost of its freedom is the subjugation of nature under the schema of judgement. As concept dominates intuition in subsumptive judgement so reason dominates nature. Nature is not protected either by the need of concepts for objects, nor by the way synthetic *a priori* judgements are the condition of both objects of experience and experience itself, for in both cases judgement is the free work of reason following its own necessity over and against nature, and, indeed, against the feelings and emotions which accompany our intuitive representations of nature.

In subsumptive judgements, then, the mutual dependence of concept and object, and therefore the objective validity of *a priori* synthetic judgements, is itself subsumed by the prior validity granted to the understanding by pure reason. The truth of this mutual dependence is really the truth of master to slave. Nature is subordinated to the understanding through the schematism of experience, a schematism that binds concept and intuition together in a one sided relation of domination. Here the master is the truth of the slave. It is in the *Critique of Practical Reason*, however, that Kant tries to work out the truth of this master as independent, autonomous and free.

2.2 Critique of Practical Reason

In theoretical reason, then, pure reason dominates nature by being independent of it. In pure practical reason this independence becomes the basis for the objective conditions whereby moral and political freedoms become possible. As theoretical reason provides objective validity for what is, so practical reason, for Kant, must provide objective validity for what ought to be. In the *Critique of Pure Reason* the conditions of experience and objects of experience are held apart from any particular end or purpose other than the purpose immanent to reason itself, that of subsumptive judgements or understanding. This is both its strength and its weakness. Its strength is that the conditions—of experience and of objects of experience—although conditional upon each other, are never conditional upon anything from outside. The conditions are autonomous, not heteronomous. But its weakness is that pure reason cannot directly legislate in the kingdom of knowledge. Pure reason does not provide 'pure' knowledge, because all knowledge is already (mutually) dependent upon intuition. When pure reason seeks to legislate directly, Kant calls this a transcendental or constitutive employment, and is a 'misemployment' (1968: A669/B697) which claims, wrongly to know things in themselves. All that pure reason can do in trying to express its own totality is to work within the conditions of possibility, and that means according to 'ideas'. Its ideas of the absolute, therefore, are God, soul and the world, but they work only 'as if', or by analogy, and are regulative but not constitutive.

> I do not seek, nor am I justified in seeking, to know this object of my idea according to what it may be in itself. There are no concepts available for any such purpose; even the concepts of reality, substance, causality, nay even that of necessity in existence, lose all meaning, and are empty titles for (possible) concepts, themselves entirely without content, when we thus venture with them outside the field of the senses. I think to myself merely the relation of a being, in itself completely unknown to me, to the greatest possible systematic unity of the universe, solely for the purpose of using it as a schema of the regulative principle of the greatest possible empirical employment of my reason (1968: A679/B707).

Practical reason enjoys all the advantages of autonomy but it does not share the weakness of having to rely on nature. Pure practical reason legislates directly in the realm of desire in a way denied to pure reason in the realm of knowledge. It is in practical reason, therefore, that the conditions of the possibility of experience and of the possibility of objects of experience become a fully sovereign, self-determining, independent and autonomous experience, an experience which is free and which is freedom. We might say that Kant's definition of freedom is that the conditions of morality in general are likewise the conditions of the possibility of moral action, or of what ought to be done. This is the same as saying 'act only according to that maxim whereby you can at the same time will that it should become a universal law' (Kant, 1990: para. 437, Caygill, 1995: 100). [2]

The reason that practical reason can be free in a way that theoretical reason cannot is that where the latter is mediated by ideas, the former is totally independent of the natural conditions of sensibility. It can act not 'as if' it were another, but only as itself. This correspondence, rather than lack of correspondence by analogy, is the will that wills itself, or is freedom. Here, then, in practical reason, Kant is offering a different kind of mutual dependence to that of the Critique of Pure Reason. Where the latter was a mutual dependence between the a priori and nature in their separation, the former is a mutual dependence in their self-relation, a spontaneous unity that is the will's free self-determination. Here mutual dependence is the equality of the will with the object of the will, and that equality is freedom. Kant calls this freedom the categorical imperative, and its mutual dependence is both freedom from any misconceived judgements based on 'human feelings and inclinations' (1995: 102) in regard to any particular objects, and it is also freedom to be dependent upon oneself. The claim is therefore that in the categorical imperative, desire is both master and slave.

The direct freedom and autonomy that theoretical reason lacked can be said to reside in the will as the freedom and autonomy of practical reason. This is achieved by the will of each person being treated 'as if' it were universal. The test to be applied here is that in deciding what a person ought to do, something passes the test provided that one acts 'as if the maxim of your action were to become through your will a universal law of nature'[3] (Kant, 1990: para. 421, Caygill, 1995: 100). This 'as if' must be qualitatively different from the 'as if' of theoretical reason. In practical reason the 'as if' of freedom is between the universal and itself, not between the universal concept and the particular object. But this presupposition is also the weakness of practical reason and its not so hidden subsumptive structure. The 'as if' of universal self-relation is still separated 'as if' it were a dualism of universal and particular. What the categorical imperative seeks to deny is its own necessary and dualistic positing of itself. [4]

If an action conforms to this rational test of universality and freedom and is consistent with it, then the will is a free expression of its own truth, or is at one with the imperative of its own categorical self-realization. Freedom here is to be equated with duty, for it is our duty to conform to the universal against our own particular and capricious desires which are aimed at only particular ends or objects. Only in duty will we find freedom and autonomy for only in duty will we be free from dependence upon particular objects. The heteronomous will which acts for particular ends is unfree in the same way that subsumptive judgements in theoretical reason are not objective if they are dependent upon empirical experience. As the accord of judgement is prior to and independent of objects in theoretical reason, so the accord of the will with duty through the categorical imperative is also independent of particular desires. The final part of Kant's argument here is that in treating the human will of each person as a phenomenon in its own right, and independent of heteronomous influences, then the will is being treated as an end and not merely as a means to an end. This now adds to the formula of the categorical imperative the demand that one act 'in such a way that you treat humanity, whether in your own person or in the person of another, always at the same time as an end, and never as a means' (Kant, 1990: para. 429, Caygill, 1995: 101). Caygill sums up the translation of *a priori* categories into moral principles as 'the maxims of common human understanding, "think for oneself", "think from the standpoint of everyone else", and "always think consistently"' (1989: 353).

Equally the mutual dependence of the will and nature in freedom, or in the categorical imperative, underpins Kant's notion of enlightenment. Famously he defined enlightenment as

> man's release from his self-incurred tutelage. Tutelage is man's inability to make use
> of his understanding without direction from another. Self-incurred is this tutelage

when its cause lies not in lack of reason but in lack of resolution and courage to use it
without direction from another. Sapere aude! "Have courage to use your own reason!"
– that is the motto of enlightenment (1990: 83).

—or in terms of mutual dependence, become the freedom that lies in being one's
own teacher, or master, dependent upon oneself but upon no other. This definition
of enlightenment is itself often treated as the template by which subsumptive
judgement is turned into modernity's educational manifesto. In its abstract form,
as a domination of reason over nature and imagination, it is only implicitly
philosophy's higher education. But equally, the *Critique of Judgement* would not
have become necessary if Kant had not first illuminated the subsumptive nature of
freedom's educational imperative and then turned its illusions back on itself.

3. THE NECESSITY OF THE THIRD *CRITIQUE*

Caygill notes that there are many interpretations as to why Kant needed to write a
third *Critique*: perhaps to 'close' the critical philosophy; perhaps to reconcile
nature and freedom; perhaps to explore judgement as the means by which the
faculties of knowledge and desire realise their *a priori* categories; perhaps to add a
third faculty, that of pleasure and pain; or, finally, perhaps to add aesthetic
judgements to the theoretical and practical judgements already examined (1995:
139). Caygill's own view is very clear. He worries most about the treatment given
to nature particularly in the *Critique of Practical Reason*, but also in the *Critique
of Pure Reason*. His own work in *Art of Judgement* (1989) is (partly) an
interpretation of Kant's third *Critique* as doing the job that the *Critique of
Practical Reason* set out to do but failed to achieve. The second *Critique* sought to
embody the mutual dependence of concept and intuition as an immanent self-
relation in desire, taking categorical judgements to be both the condition of the
possibility of morality *per se* and the condition of the possibility of moral actions.
In other words, freed from mutual dependence upon objects, and dependent only
upon itself, practical reason is independent. But at the heart of Caygill's critique
lies the problem of what has happened to nature and to the imagination in practical
reason. The object, or nature, has been completely suppressed by a notion of
freedom which holds that in its purity it is free from any dependence upon nature.
Caygill gives several reasons why we should be worried about the domination of
sensibility implicit in subsumptive judgements and about the implicitly dualistic
misrecognition that underpins this domination.

One of Caygill's criticisms in the *Dictionary* is the way in which, particularly
in the *Critique of Practical Reason*, the relation to the heteronomous object is so
easily dismissed and overcome by pure practical reason. The immediate relation to
objects, for Kant, comes through the faculty of representation which resides in the
imagination. This faculty has little or no role in Kant's practical philosophy, and is

a role subsumed by the faculty of knowledge in theoretical reason. Caygill notes wryly that 'according to the reader's temperament, the absence of imagination from the *Critique of Practical Reason* may be regarded as the saving grace of Kant's practical philosophy, or as good reason for seeking his practical philosophy in the pages of the first and third *Critiques'* (1995: 249).

Caygill is also critical of the way in which the intuition of objects for Kant is subsumed by the categories via the understanding. This becomes a triumph of reason over feeling and reduces understanding to the role of conforming to pre-given rules. Caygill, in *Art of Judgement*, takes up this challenge on behalf of the imagination, trying to retrieve its importance in the whole picture of human understanding by showing how, in the *Critique of Judgement*, intuition is not only an immediate sensation but also a mediated appearance. The double nature of intuition will be seen below to be an important constituent of reflective judgements and of philosophy's higher education.

A third doubt arises regarding the relationship of the first and second *Critiques* around the themes of nature and freedom. It is clear that in the second *Critique,* when freedom is achieved at the expense of nature, it is also at the expense of all aesthetic relationships to the world and its objects. Caygill notes that in the *Critique of Practical Reason* Kant not only maintains this dualistic tendency, he takes it 'to an unwholesome extreme' (1995: 143).

Caygill's fourth point, found in *Art of Judgement*, is that in the *Critique of Judgement* Kant is forced to rethink the relation between logical and aesthetic judgements. The latter, produced within the faculty of 'feeling', always fares badly against the former, produced in and by the faculty of knowledge. This reduces aesthetic judgements to being always mediated or known through logic or through the *a priori* synthetic judgement which subsumes the manifold under a pre-given category of unification. Put more simply, this means that pleasure and displeasure, the common ground of all 'feelings', can be neither autonomous nor independent. They cannot just be 'felt'. They have to be known. This inequality subscribes to part of the *Critique of Pure Reason* in which the imaginative schema serves the understanding and which, in turn, leads to the embodiment of that domination in the *Critique of Practical Reason*. But it does not subscribe to the way in which the understanding is also dependent upon imagination and nature.

It is to retrieve the importance of nature and its representation in intuition and the imagination that Caygill turns to the *Critique of Judgement*. Against the one-sided interpretations of experience practised by the understanding and personified by reason, Caygill argues for a more speculative appreciation of the transcendental condition of possibility, central to which is a speculative interpretation of reflective judgement. Caygill notes that to begin with Kant tried to reassess the relationship between logic and feeling by maintaining aesthetic judgements as subsumptive. This says Caygill, was the 'only way of keeping such judgements within transcendental philosophy,' (1989: 301) for if the objective validity of aesthetic judgements lay not in reason but in the objects themselves, then that validity could never be known by us for no *a priori* synthesis independent of the object would be possible. One opinion would be just as good as another. As always, Kant was desperate to avoid the pernicious implications of such empiricism but, Caygill argues, he was forced to admit the unavoidable difficulty of an argument which required subjective pleasure to be predicated on objective principles. Pleasure and displeasure seemed to offer a new and exciting way of exploring disinterestedness as an end in itself, and one which avoided the heavy handedness of subsumptive judgements and the relativism of merely subjective judgements.[5] In the light of this, and through the *Critique of Judgement*, Kant pursues 'another, more radical possibility' (1989: 301). Caygill notes that instead of trying to include the aesthetic within a subsumptive model, Kant would 'extend the notion of judgement to include both forms of judgement' (1989: 301). This 'more generous notion of judgement' (1989: 301-2) not only shifts Kant's transcendental philosophy into 'that of outlining a general technic or art of judgement,' (1989: 302) it also, as we will see below, makes possible a speculative reading of Kantian transcendental philosophy.

Caygill can turn directly to Kant in support of this venture. In the *Preface* of 1790 Kant notes that it is in and through judgement that the *a priori* principles of understanding and reason are established. But judgement itself, which stands between knowledge and desire, has not been the subject of a critique. Kant asks, 'has it also got independent *a priori* principles?' (1952: 4). If it has then this, says Caygill, will have implications regarding '"the greatest difficulty" of reconciling freedom and necessity,' (1989: 300) and for us it will mark the re-cognition by Kant of judgement as its own higher education.

4. BENJAMIN'S KANT

Before exploring Kant's notion of reflective judgement, we will briefly look at the relationship between the transcendental and the speculative that underpins Caygill's interpretation of Kantian re-cognition, or higher education. This is interesting not only in itself as a sophisticated re-reading of the self-relation of the conditions of the possibility of experience and their objects, but also because of the conclusions regarding the nature of hope and possibility that Caygill draws from it. I will examine Caygill's speculative treatment of Kantian reflective judgements first from his interpretation of the relationship between the transcendental and the speculative in Benjamin and then, in the next section, from *Art of Judgement*.

Caygill argues that Benjamin throughout his work tries to retrieve Kant's model of theoretical, practical and aesthetic philosophy but, at the same time, to rework Kant's concept of experience and its basic assumption that there is a

distinction between concept and intuition. Crucial to Caygill's reading is that
Benjamin also introduces an absolute into Kant's concept of experience,
something that Kant himself, says Caygill in the *Dictionary*, was careful not to do.
Benjamin tried to show how *a prioris* are already present in intuitions and
concepts, that is, that time and space are not only transcendental but also
speculative or part of the configuration of the experience of objects. The
speculative strand of his argument is that Kant has conflated the concepts of
'experience' and 'knowledge of experience'. 'For the concept of knowledge,
experience is not anything new and extraneous to it, but only itself in a different
form; experience as the object of knowledge is the unified and continuous
manifold of knowledge' (1996: 95).

Caygill, in *Colour of Experience* (1998), offers a number of examples in
Benjamin's work of how transcendental conditions of possibility and speculative
objectification of those conditions co-exist. The first example is from the fragment
entitled 'On Perception In Itself' (1917). For Caygill this fragment[6] states that the
transcendental conditions of legibility are themselves also dependent upon the
surfaces which frame legibility. The significance of this is that the transcendental
conditions of possibility are themselves known within and by the configuration of
a particular surface. Here, then, is the mutual dependence of concept and intuition,
or understanding and sensibility, which Kant was unable to preserve in his first
two *Critiques*. In place of a schematic judgement, Benjamin 'situates the
particularity of the transcendental condition of experience within the speculative
context of the infinite configuration of surfaces' (1998: 4). Mutual dependence is
sustained here because the transcendental is dependent upon surfaces for its
configuration, but surfaces are themselves dependent upon the conditions of
legibility *per se*. In this mutual dependence there is a 'double infinity' (1998:4):
'the transcendental infinity of possible marks on a given surface... and the
speculative infinity of possible bounded but infinite surfaces or frameworks of
experience' (1998: 4).[7] It is in Benjamin, then, rather than in Kant's first two
Critiques that 'the conditions of the possibility of experience in general are
likewise the conditions of the objects of experience' in that both are infinite and
both are conditioned by the infinity of the other. Time and space, in this
interpretation, are themselves only modes of configuration which are open to
change, and are 'one among many possible configurations of experience' (1998:
5).

Caygill's second example of Benjamin's reworking of Kantian experience as
transcendental and speculative is in terms of colour. Just as legibility is not what
is written but is already conditioned by the surface which conditions what is
written, so, colour is not what is 'on' the surface, it is the whole experience of
each particular surface. As there is reading without writing, so there is colour
without art. This for Caygill is the colour of experience where the speculative
configuration is both 'folded into and exceeds the particular surface of legibility'

(1998: 4). The conditions of the possibility of experience are already coloured (or configured) by the particular surface on which colour, then, appears. This does a great deal of philosophical work for Caygill. The implication of his argument is that the colour of experience is both immanent in its experience, its speculative nature, and yet is not the whole experience, for the experience is always of both its own possibility and therefore of possibility in general, or its transcendental nature.

The third example is taken from Benjamin's essay 'On Language as such and on the Language of Man' (1916), where language, like colour, is another transcendental surface speculatively configured. If Benjamin is to hold the mutual dependence of the transcendental surfaces and their speculative configuration then he needs to avoid falling into two dogmas: that there is an ineffable surface beyond the speculative configuration and that this speculative infinity closes down the infinite possibility of transcendental surfaces. For Caygill this means Benjamin has to distinguish between 'the infinity of possible contents which may be communicated *through* a language, and the infinity which communicates itself *in* a language' (1998: 16). 'A' language, which serves as the condition of communication, is already configured speculatively by the 'spiritual essence' (1998: 16) which is communication. The mutual dependence of the relationship is maintained as in reading and colour, in that language is both an infinite number of possible expressions on an infinite number of configured surfaces. Against the dogma of the ineffable Benjamin argues that in communication what is communicated is language itself, and, against the dogma of closure, he argues that the speculative infinity of surface is not the condition of configuration *per se* and is not therefore 'the speculative condition of all other languages' (1998: 19). This latter, he says, is the creative word of God.

Caygill's criticism of the way Benjamin tries to hold mutual dependence in a reworked Kantian notion of experience leads us now to his interpretation of reflective judgements. Caygill argues that in 'On the Programme of the Coming Philosophy' Benjamin adds that philosophy needs to be subordinated to theology but also states that experience be seen as the uniform and continuous multiplicity of knowledge. This 'formal idealism' on the one hand and material empiricism on the other is, notes Caygill, a 'characteristically Kantian tension' (1998: 26). Benjamin responds to it not with a dogmatic absolute but rather by trying to express the precarious balance between them. Or, put another way, Benjamin seeks to show the colour of this experience of itself without either dominating the surface with eternal ideas or letting configuration loose from its transcendental conditions and free to nihilism.[8] Instead Benjamin concentrates on the negativity of the experience of mutual dependence, tracing 'the removal of the absolute through the warps, distortions and exclusions of a bereft experience' (1998: 26). It was in the decay of one type of experience that Benjamin saw the double infinity of surface and configuration open up to new possibilities, new truths and new experiences, or as Caygill says, out of passive nihilism came active nihilism

(1998: 30). On either side, then, of the strategy to hold the mutual dependence of Kantian experience together, lays 'the danger of lapsing into either a redemptive idealism or the melancholic endless task of the collector of scattered fragments' (1998: 26). But in the danger lay the infinite possibilities of the double infinity. The hope of new freedoms was announced 'in the distorted, comical and even terrifying patterns of modern experience' (1998: 32).

5. REFLECTIVE JUDGEMENT

Caygill's interpretation of Benjamin is very similar in important ways to his own interpretation of Kantian reflective judgements in *Art of Judgement*. Central to Caygill's reading is that what the *a priori* synthetic judgement achieves is the representation of a representation. An object in intuition is always already an imaginative or affective representation. A concept is a function of the 'spontaneity of thought' (1968: A68/B93) which unifies 'various representations under one common representation' (1968: A68/B93). This unification is judgement, and is the knowledge yielded by understanding. But, *contra* the somewhat blunt subsumptive structure seen earlier, Kant notes here that,

> since no representation, save when it is an intuition, is in immediate relation to an object, no concept is ever related to an object immediately, but to some other representation of it, be that other representation an intuition, or itself a concept. Judgement is therefore the mediate knowledge of an object, that is, the representation of a representation of it (1968: A68/B93).

The mutual dependence of the conditions of the possibility of experience and of objects of experience is expressed here in that judgement is the representation of a representation. Neither side can be totally determinant of itself or of the other because no side can take itself to be independent of the other. Neither side can claim immediacy, for each is contingent upon the other. It is in this relation of absolute contingency that we learn of philosophy's higher education.

To begin with we can see that this resembles closely the double infinity found in Benjamin's reworking of Kantian experience. Objects as surfaces are the condition for experience, but all objects are already configured surfaces. The accord of surface and configuration, or intuition and concept, is the judgement in which an object is known, subject to these 'mutual' conditions. Judgement here is not closure, for the possibility of new experiences—new surfaces and new configurations—are held open in a non-dogmatic relationship.

If there is 'necessity' accompanying this infinite possibility, it is clearly not of the subsumptive kind found in the first two *Critiques*, for subsumptive judgements do not uphold mutual dependence or the representation of representation.[9] What kind of necessity is there in the relation of the representation of representation, or in the shared conditions for experience and objects of experience?

As seen above, in the third *Critique* Kant moves from subsuming nature within concepts to the more 'generous' notion of judgement which includes both subsumption and aesthetics, or taste. This shift, says Caygill, indicates a wider relation than just the relation of particular and universal required for subsumption. Now determinate judgement 'is extended into a notion of reflective judgement which replaces the unification of the manifold with the search for analogy and proportion within the manifold' (1989: 302). This move enables Kant, through the *Critique of Judgement*, to expose the necessity of the conditions of possibility of judgement itself as *formation and finality*. This relation of the relation of judgement is philosophy's higher education in Kant.

Caygill anticipates some of the key distinctions that Kant makes in the *Critique of Judgement*. Reflective judgement is divided into aesthetic judgements of taste, based around the phenomenon of pleasure and displeasure, and teleological judgements with the phenomenon of finality. They share a 'common anthropological foundation' (1989: 302) which makes them appear prior to the distinction between understanding and intuition and therefore prior to the *a priori* synthesis of subsumptive judgements. The point here is that subsumptive judgement now appears to be predicated or contingent upon a prior judgement which somehow differentiates yet sustains the manifold. Such a judgement embodies the kind of unity that the categorical imperative claimed for itself, one where 'other' is its own universality. It remains to be seen if reflective judgement can gain a higher education regarding the subsumptive fate that befell the principle of practical reason.

For Caygill, in aligning reflective judgement with the differentiating activity of realisation and restriction in the manifold, Kant is already distinguishing between judgement as a third thing that mediates concept and intuition as a tool of the understanding, and judgement as a technic or an art which works intuitively and without the cognition of a set of pre-determined rules.[10] As Caygill notes, echoing Kant's own thoughts about the nature of enlightenment, 'schematism proceeds under the tutelage of the understanding, while reflective judgement legislates for itself through its encounters with individual things' (1989: 304). The implications of this imminent legislation over the mastery of a dominating transcendental are clearly identified by Caygill in Kant's own text. Reflective judgement 'legislates for itself' (1989: 305) and this act of legislation 'is itself reflection, being given by the judgement "to and from" itself' (1989: 305). The 'necessity' or law of this possibility Kant calls 'heautonomy'.

In reflective judgement, therefore, the representation of a representation can be said to be 'symbolic', or to proceed only by way of analogy where representations are continually compared to other representations, and where the only 'grounding' is the continual comparison. Kant's distinction of schematic from symbolic presentations (or hypotyposis) gives rise to the appearance of reflection as open-ended, achieving not a unification but only the eternal repetition of the infinite possibility that lies in analogy. Caygill summarises the difference between schematic and symbolic knowledge, and also subsumptive and reflective judgements in the following way.

> In the first case judgement arranges its materials instrumentally according to unification under a universal; in the other it proceeds artistically through analogy, or the discernment of a proportionate likeness which does not extinguish the differences of the particular in the uniformity of the universal (1989: 306).

Caygill, quoting Kant, also notes that analogy does not mean 'an imperfect similarity of two things but a perfect similarity of relations between two quite dissimilar things' (Caygill, 1995: 66; Kant, 1950: para. 58). It is the relation that is the judgement, or the unity here, and not the subsumptive understanding of nature by reason. The necessity of analogy, or the representation of representation, is suppressed in and by the latter, because subsumptive judgement does not recognise its own dependency upon a relation that makes its own judgement possible. In the relation of the relation of conditions of possibility of experience and of conditions of possibility of objects of experience, lies the prior necessity of the differentiation, or the relation of its own possibility and itself.

In this relation of the relation, then, representation is the condition of its own possibility which, of course, it must represent. But the principle by which it represents itself is posited 'as if' it were not a representation of a representation. It is posited 'as if' representation were the possibility of everything except itself. The necessity of its positing of itself 'as if' it were not itself[1] demands that analogy now be seen as the illusion of representation, or the illusion that is the dualism of the representation of representation. Analogy is represented by the latter 'as if' it were not its own truth. But this 'as if' is precisely its own truth. Within the dualism not only of concept and intuition, or necessity and freedom, but now also of representation and representation, analogy (as judgement-power) contains a truth which is determined as illusion and therein is lost to itself. In the loss, analogy represents itself as indeterminate contingency, 'as if' it is not the contingency of 'as if' represented to and as itself. This illusion not only determines the misrecognition of representation by itself, but, one could argue, it determines the categories themselves. As analogy, or contingency, is already the illusion of possibility (in itself) so possibility represents this illusion back to itself as the categories. They are, in this sense, the positing of analogy as proportionality. The truth of the categories awaits philosophy's higher education regarding the self-determinate truth of illusion as proportionality, or formation and finality. The extent to which this necessity upsets the mutual dependency of the representation of representation and of analogy as 'education', will be assessed in a moment.

Proportionality means, then, that some kind of work has taken place prior to representation, and in a sense *as* representation, but as yet we do not know what kind of work this is. It cannot be a subsumptive or determinant judgement for by definition proportionality is prior to the subsumption of imagination by understanding. This prior differentiation, if it works according to any principles, will not be those provided by the subsumptive understanding. Indeed, particularity now appears to have an 'irreducible contingency' (1989: 310).[12] This means, somehow, that it is particularity and not the universal which is unconditioned. But how can the contingent be universal and independent? Which law or accord does proportionality conform to in which its contingency is both dependent and yet a self-legislation? Or again, how is the representation of representation the truth of judgement?

6. FORMATION AND FINALITY

Caygill notes that human understanding, in conforming the manifold of its intuition to its own laws, 'cannot possibly achieve this without presupposing a different ratio to its own, a prior "harmony" or "accord" of "natural features with our faculty of conception," an accord which that faculty can only represent to itself as "contingent"' (1989: 311). From this, Kant is able to argue that our human understanding is full of illusion. It appears as if our understanding must move from transcendental universality to the subsumption of particulars. But it overlooks the fact that for there to be particulars in the first place the manifold of intuition, as representation, must already assume a conformity between parts and wholes such that differentiation is even possible. As such proportionality appears to be both the form of differentiation *per se* and the formation of actual difference. The manifold of intuition, prior to the transcendental condition of the possibility of objects of experience, entails a process of formation in which 'form is formative' (1989: 313). Kant argues that we can know illusion in the relation of understanding to judgement because we can know that our understanding is only one of other possible understandings. In Benjamin's terms, Kant is acknowledging that transcendental surfaces can be configured in other ways. Therefore for Benjamin, Kant and Caygill there is 'contingency in the constitution of our understanding,' (1952: 61, para. 77) which means not only that it is only one of many possible understandings, but also that our understanding of understanding may also change.

In this speculative condition of the transcendental categories, the configuration of the object—the colour of experience—is already within and without the surface which is also its own condition. Thus, 'the particular is not determined by the universal law of our (human) understanding. Though different things may agree in a common characteristic, the variety of forms in which they may be presented to our perception is contingent' (1952: 62, para. 77). The form of proportionality or differentiation and the formation of difference are, for Kant, one and the same activity and result. Caygill notes that 'formative activity consists in the assignment of differences and the configuration of a manifold. It inscribes finality in nature...' (1989: 313). Finality, then, is the 'law' of the irreducible contingency of formation upon itself. For Kant, 'the representation of a whole may contain the possibility of the form of that whole and of the nexus of the parts which that form involves' (1952: 64, para. 77). Faced with objects, however, our self-alienated understanding misses the law of contingency for it has 'forgotten' (1989: 313) that it is already dependent upon formation and its finality. But 'the unstateable accord between concept and intuition signifies a constant reminder to [it]' (1989: 313).

How are we reminded of formation and finality in nature? How do we come to 'know' the law of contingency that is the relation of nature and experience? Our self-alienated understanding has access to it only in the form of an objective finality which is already formed. This is the illegitimate ground of what Caygill calls 'the smothered accord' of formation and finality, and of the 'bad conscience of subsumption' (1989: 313). At this point neither Kant nor Caygill fall into the trap of saying either that this accord can be known or that it cannot. Both ride the ambivalence implicit in knowing illusion by finding another way in which the positive and negative implications of formation and finality in nature are available to us. Even though the harmony and accord of formation and finality is disowned by the understanding, nevertheless this accord 'can still make itself *felt*' (1989: 314) through pleasure and displeasure. We feel pleasure when we achieve an end. Thus, to feel pleasure or displeasure is to feel the presence of finality or conformity to the accord of nature.[13] Pleasure, now, replaces duty as the site of autonomy and self-legislation, but this time able to suspend the relation between universal and particular rather than overcome (or not overcome) it.

But is 'feeling' enough to provide for the relation of the relation? Feeling provides us with the indispensable yet contingent harmony of the configuration of the manifold, or differentiation by nature according to itself and as such is the beautiful. But feeling alone does not provide us with representation *itself* as an object. It does not in itself achieve philosophy. Feeling without its recognition in and as philosophical experience is like intuition without concepts. The latter is blind, the former is dumb. It is not simply ironic that the notion of experience which in Kant opposes the objective now becomes part of the objective truth of contingency. Kant's own formula for objective judgements—that the conditions of the possibility of experience in general are likewise conditions of the possibility of objects of experience—already contained the illusion of experience within it. *This* contingency is its own necessity, its own dualism, and its own differentiation. Thus it is a condition of its own possibility as experience that the contingent, which we now understand a feeling to be, be contingent not only as a representation, but as a representation of a representation. Without this truth the aesthetic and indeed the *Critique of Judgement* would not 'exist'. It is also the case that feeling without experience is formation or differentiation without finality, for it has no end, and if it has no end it does not have itself. Experience is a condition of the possibility of pleasure because formation and finality are the necessity that inheres in experience. If they cannot be known (or communicated) then this is not formation and finality and it is not the contingency of the representation of representation. It is not philosophy. Indeed, to refuse the 'need' for experience is not a reflective judgement at all. It is rather a return to the subsumptive assertion that 'feeling' is objective, precisely a domination of its difficult accord as formation *and* finality.

The recognition of illusion as the contingency of the possibility of experience become object to itself does not come from the understanding. How could it? Kant, and Caygill, argue that this experience, the experience that legislates itself under the conditions of its own possibility, is not 'a' judgement but rather the capacity for judgement, or judgement-power.[14] Judgement power is not the putting of a principle of the understanding into nature. On the contrary, it is realising, in the sense of formation and finality, the law of contingency as its own absolute law of self-determination. Nature's ordering of the manifold is in accord with the finality or end of nature, an activity of 'realisation and restriction' or of accord and differentiation. Our own apprehension of ordered differentiated objects is only a representation of that ordering, which is itself represented in judgement-power and as judgement-power. Understanding cannot dominate this representation for understanding is contingent upon it. But neither can representation be free from the understanding for it is not only known as contingency, it *is* contingency. Representation is always of itself. This is philosophy. And representation known as the representation of representation is philosophy's higher education about the absolute truth of thinking as contingency. In pleasure, finality and formation are known as an end. But it is an end without an end for it is finality without subsumption. This is the most important characteristic of reflective judgement, namely that as contingent upon natural accord it also itself conforms to the law of contingency for, in its own formation and finality as judgement-power, it too is an end without end. This principle it gives to itself, but is then forgotten by the self-alienated understanding. It is a pleasure which is itself grounded in judgement, although it is also a pleasure which we can no longer 'find' in ourselves, even though the most ordinary experience is impossible without it (1989: 314).

7. THE AESTHETIC AND THE TELEOLOGICAL

It is necessary now to explore how judgement-power conforms to the law of contingency, and how it is both natural and free, and both aesthetic and political. Finality, or self-legislated formation and end, can be accessed aesthetically and politically. Aesthetically its accord is present as the formative activity which affirms life, or itself. But, as finality or end are contained in this feeling, then the beautiful carries within itself the capacity and the compulsion for communication, or, we might say, for freedom. Thus the beautiful, as the pleasure of the accord of formation and finality, is substantial and as such it is a public and not a private experience. Part of its expression is the finality that it be expressed, i.e., that it conform to both unification and differentiation, that it be something that is already other. Implicit in this 'communicability', then, is the law of contingency, that in being true to itself, it cannot contain its own truth without also losing it, i.e., without losing finality to the conditions of its own possibility, or to proportionality. For the beautiful to be accord and differentiation, the feeling of proportionality must contain finality and exceed it. It is already other, and the other is not it. The excess appears in experience as the feeling of the sublime. The sublime is our cognition of beauty such that we can compare 'accords'. This raises us above nature but at the same time subjects us to the nature of the law of contingency. It is, says Kant, 'a negative pleasure' (1952: 91) and as such an educative relation of the beautiful to itself. In the sublime, although we appear masters over nature, in fact we become slaves of and as formation and finality, slaves who are the work that is end without end. Beauty and the sublime together are the whole of our experience or feeling of natural accord. It is an experience that moves between immediate pleasure at the harmony of differentiation in the imagination, mediated displeasure at its ability to 'know' beauty and to compare it, and the return to pleasure to know that this displeasure is itself the freedom and necessity which is the self-legislation of the law of contingency, or of finality. Here in the relation of beauty and the sublime is the relation of representations, or the accord of proportionality.

But contingency, or the natural accord of proportionality, also has its expression politically in what Kant calls teleological reflective judgements. Whilst aesthetic judgements compare beauty with the harmonious (although contingent) play of judgement-power, teleological judgements compare finality in the work of judgement with nature itself. Aesthetic judgements are formative, or educative of experience in recognising contingency as self-determination; teleological judgements are formative and educative in that they manifestly pursue this experience as their own end. The former are experienced in terms of pleasure and displeasure which together are the realisation and restriction, the formation and finality of life. Teleological judgements are our human efforts in the world to establish this freedom at the heart of the social and political order. In such judgements, proportionality is achieved for Kant through *culture*. Culture, as Caygill points out, is not contemplative, it is practical. But this is a dangerous distinction, for culture, like the sublime, is reflective and reflective here means the formation and finality of judgement-power, a representation which is already the relation of the relation between theory and practice. It would run counter to the insights already established by Kant, or within philosophy's higher education, to see aesthetic and teleological judgements as a division of theory and practice, or of theoretical philosophy and practical philosophy. The two types of reflective judgements are already working within the necessity of the conditions of possibility of the separation of theory and practice. Indeed, the division of reflective judgement into the aesthetic and the teleological is itself an analogy of its own law of contingency, of formation and finality, and as such true to itself in and as this learning. When analogy forgets that its truth is this learning, then the law of contingency fails again to re-cognise its misrecognition. The educational credentials of Kantian 'analogy' rely on its absolute universality. This has the most important implications for Caygill's question raised earlier about whether we should seek Kant's practical philosophy in the second *Critique*, or in the first and the third? In philosophy's higher education we re-learn the question, for we re-learn the conditions of the possibility of the question. The difference between what is and what ought to be is a representation of the accord of formation and finality. It is not a dualism that philosophy ought to solve. Nor is it a dualism that philosophy cannot understand. It is the dualism in which freedom is represented to itself.

Culture for Kant plays the same role in teleological judgements as the sublime plays in aesthetic judgements. Both are characterised by a resistance to, or a protest against, an undifferentiating power of necessity. Both 'register a relation,' (1989: 345) a relation in which comparison and analogy become possible, but only as a recognition of violence. In the relation, necessity provokes terror at its dominion over us, but the sublime re-minds us of our being more than the relation. This education is mirrored by culture which exceeds our domination by nature. As the sublime combines fear and joy, so culture aims to expose its own conceit (its own violence over necessity) and to work for 'a just proportion' (1989: 368) between concept and intuition. It is important again to note here that the sublime and culture are not theoretical concepts that state what is, nor practical concepts that state what ought to be. They are the relation of accord and differentiation representing itself. In philosophy's higher education, which is formative and teleological as this relation, the sublime and culture do not suppress their representation of contingency by being more or less than that contingency. They are the freedom of analogy, already other yet also not other.

Caygill, following Kant, distinguishes between the two ways in which life is a self-activity in and as the accord of proportionality. As was seen above, nature both realises and restricts, it forms its material as it differentiates it. In this way finality is formative and formation is also finality. The same distinction is now present in Kant's definition of culture, as the proportion 'between production, the selection and preparation of materials and the laws of political organisation' (1989: 375). Clearly what is at stake in culture for Kant, and for Caygill, is that analogy also be enabled to register this relation without subsuming finality under sovereign concepts, including those of unity. The 'as if' of culture has to fare better than the 'as if' of universal laws in the first two *Critiques*. It is significant that Kant turns to culture, with all its educational connotations, as the representation of the representation that is human experience.

He includes this educational aspect of judgement-power—the aspect in which the finality of nature works as a law of analogy or contingency and not a law of subsumption—in and as the accord that is expressed by beauty, culture, *summum bonum* and *servis communis*. Each has its own condition of possibility, not transcendentally, but as a store of learning, or as an accord of proportionality between production and political organisation. In each case, the judgement of beauty, culture, 'good life', and 'common sense' recognises the communicability of its experience as the necessity of any future experience. In each case, the proportionality of judgement-power (formation and finality, or production and organisation) is available as the unity and the manifold of what makes possible separation and construction. In judgements of beauty the necessity of unity and manifold as contingent is available in 'tradition;' in teleological judgements the unity and manifold is already present as a cultural representation; in reflective judgement as a whole the highest good is contingent upon the proportionality (or accord) in judgement-power of formation and finality, or production and political organisation, that is, that judgement-power is the highest good when what we can know and what we must do are one and the same finality. (We will explore further the nature of this 'bond' in a moment.) Finally, judgements of public reason, or the maxims of common human understanding are also reflective judgements, for they are contingent upon the unity and manifold whose formation and finality is communication. In short, tradition, culture and communication are the representations of representations which are the necessity and possibility of reflective judgement. They are the conformity to the law of contingency of formation and finality; they are the accord from which, and contingent upon which, analogy pursues its own end as an end without end. In this way is judgement-power alone the relation of nature and freedom, and of theoretical and practical philosophy, by being philosophy's higher education. The necessity of its conditions of possibility as experience and its conditions of possibility as an object of experience determines itself, and without introducing heteronomous principles or concepts which will prejudge any 'reconciliation' of dualism outside of the relation and law of contingency which it expresses. Finality is its own end, and as such an end without end.

8. ART OF JUDGEMENT

But can judgement-power, as philosophy's higher education regarding the necessity that conditions the conditions of the possibility of experience and of objects of experience, be called 'end without end'? There is a great deal at stake here, for much recent misrecognition of Kantian higher education asserts a philosophy of possibility and hope.[15] Caygill, setting hope against the dangers of a concept of finality as end which appears to close down the possibility of finality itself being re-formed, is cautious. He suggests that even education can become a sovereign unity over and against analogy and the representation of representation, and that a safeguard against the dogma of education is the eternally open *art* of judgement. In this art of judgement, of primary importance for Caygill is to maintain the infinite possibility that lies within the surfaces and configurations, or formations and finalities that constitute representation of representation. He suggests a view of formation as 'separation and construction' (1989: 377) but does not want to translate its 'result'—proportionality and/or finality—into the language of 'unity and manifold' (1989: 377). Further, he argues that 'the agreement of concept and intuition cannot be explained in terms of concept and intuition' (1989: 372). The formative power called life, which both forms and differentiates its material, 'is beyond the purview of judgement, and we may approximate to an understanding of it only through analogy' (1989: 376). The most we can achieve is to remain 'inventive' in our reflective judgements so that we do not allow the self-alienated understanding to dominate us with its hard, logical, brutal, violent yet ultimately illusory unificatory concepts. We should, instead, feel our way into our relationship with nature, hoping but never knowing for certain that our work will conform to the accord of proportionality. 'Reflective judgement,' concludes Caygill, 'is essentially procedural; it is not directed towards making a definitive judgement but is continually approximating to a fundamental accord or proportion' (1989: 379). And in this spirit Caygill notes that for Derrida in *The Truth of Painting*, even analogy and comparison can be seen as a violent conceptual subsumption of a 'nonconceptual field' (1989: 395).

In *Art of Judgement*, Caygill's conclusion regarding the transcendental in reflective judgement and the nature of the excess or 'beyond' of judgement is intriguing. There can be no beyond of judgement for us if beyond is taken to mean that we have left judgement behind. The third *Critique*, says Caygill, is Kant's acknowledgement that although he is 'bound' to judgement he can judge it according to itself. To do so is, for Caygill, to 'point beyond' judgement, (1989: 393) to 'transcend' (1989: 394) the limits of judgements, and to 'bear witness to a different relation or law' (1989: 394). But his method of achieving this is negative, achieved 'by saying what it is not, and cannot be' (1989: 394). Caygill ends by reminding us that Kant 'stands in the promise of a bond beyond judgement' (1989: 395) only by negating the claims which judgement made before it was subject to its own imminent critique. This critique is a 'de-legitimation of judgement, a questioning of the claims by which judgement-power has legitimated its prior occupations' (1989: 395).

However, Caygill does not leave us hanging merely with a promise borne of negativity. He tentatively suggests that we see the promise of a beyond and the negativity of judgement as a relation, as an accord, but not as a subsumptive accord. The relation, he says, 'is not a unification, but a binding or obligation' (1989: 394) which is both before judgement and after. It is a relation which cannot be written but it can be witnessed. This givenness of the relation he says earlier is transcendental because it is 'beyond the understanding' (1989: 315). It is therefore a relation of representations which makes itself felt as the aesthetic representation of finality (1952: para. vii). Thus the relation is the binding of pleasure and finality, a binding 'which exceeds our notion of unity,' (1989: 320) 'restores metaphysics to modernity' (1989: 320) and obliges us to act so as to realise the Good, the True and the Beautiful even in their 'unstateable proportion' (1989: 320).

Caygill's conclusion is a wonderfully intriguing and suggestive mix of transcendental, speculative, aesthetic and teleological notions. The usual Kantian dichotomies of necessity and freedom, and autonomy and heteronomy are reworked by Caygill around pleasure and finality, and formation and end. The result, both here and in *Colour of Experience*, is a philosophy of possibility. By ensuring the mutual dependence of concept and intuition, and of surfaces and configurations, as representations of representations, Caygill also ensures that this mutual dependence means the sovereignty of analogy and therefore of both instability and uncertainty and of hope and possibility. Caygill's philosophy of possibility expresses a nature which is fixed in its rules but infinite in its possibilities, even of transforming itself and its rules. This hope in infinite possibility and the art of judgement is symbolized in Caygill's decision not to end *Colour of Experience* with a full stop, preferring to express the finality of the text as an end without end.

Yet, beautiful though this representation of the art of judgement is as a climax in which the accord is both felt *and* lost, the actuality of finality as contingency is suppressed. As such, possibility and hope are fetishised and overcome the educational melancholy of the sublime which *again* must register a relation against this violence and as this violence.[16] When possibility and hope are registered as a relation, it is the 'beauty' of infinity that is itself lost, again, to finality, a loss which re-minds possibility and hope of their own necessity and their own contingency within reflective judgement. Possibility and hope cease to be 'analogy' when they become philosophies in their own right, 'as if' they and not the immanent relation of judgement-power are analogy *per se*. Ending without a full stop is beautiful, and speaks to differentiation and formation, but it is not teleological; it is formative, but not of finality; it is aesthetic but not cultural and political; it is felt, but it is not also a higher education regarding its self-determinative contingency. It is, therefore, not finality and is not a representation of representation, only a domination of representation. It is not law, and thus is not its own learning. All philosophies of hope and possibility fetishise contingency as excess rather than learn of excess as contingency. The lack of a full stop is a small point within the overall picture of Caygill's Kant, which is essentially one with philosophy's higher education. But it represents the representation of representation as a truth which, ultimately, is not its own. Yet, for it not to be its own, it must be risked and failed as its own. This relation registers itself so that the truth of learning returns excess to contingency and finality. The full stop is the beginning of higher education. The lack of a full stop is the refusal of that beginning. Here, for and against the full stop, Caygill's higher education must be fought for, over and against possibility and hope, but in and for the work he is and does...

NOTES

[1] Caygill's *Kant Dictionary* provides an interpretation of Kant that goes well beyond each of its particular definitions. The whole is greater than the sum of its parts.
[2] It is also the same as saying 'everything in morals which is true in theory must also be valid in practice' (1991: 72).
[3] even though the self is always turning up (Kant, 1990: 23). See also Kant (1991) p. 69.
[4] This is another way of repeating Hegel's criticism in the natural law essay that 'contradiction' in Kant's practical philosophy is only tautology. See Hegel, (1975), p. 78.
[5] Of course, if pleasure and displeasure are the same kind of self-relation as desire, then the *Critique of Judgement* will turn out only to be an aesthetic version of the *Critique of Practical Reason*!
[6] It reads:
'Perception is reading...
Only that appearing in the surface is readable
Surface that is configuration—absolute continuity' (1998: 3).
[7] The educative significance of the word 'and' here and elsewhere in acting as the relation or conjunction of dualisms will be explored in particular towards the end of chapter 6.
[8] although Caygill points out that both of these can be found in Benjamin's work at different times.
[9] In subsumptive judgements, as we saw above, intuitions serve to re-present the truth of the categories, but the categories, although blind without intuitions, nevertheless take for themselves the sovereignty of objectivity.
[10] To use a well-worn pedagogical dualism, (found, for example, in Aquinas (1998), p. 199,) where subsumptive judgement acts as the teacher who directly intervenes in the student's learning about the world, reflective judgement is characterised by a less directed, more open, more 'autonomous' and more intuitive enquiry into discovering how the world might be
[11] When I first wrote this sentence it was 'The necessity of its positing of itself 'as if' it were not 'as if' it were not 'as if' it were not...' and so on. It captures well the totality of illusion here, but not the higher education that is part of the whole of the repetition.
[12] But not quite an *absolute* contingency for Caygill, as we will see in a moment.

[13] And, to judge from much recent philosophising, the greatest pleasure of all is the subsumptive triumph of the aesthetic over the subsumptive

[14] As in Marx labour-power is not any particular piece of work, so judgement-power is not any particular subsumption.

[15] Hope is included by Kant as one of the three 'interests' of reason, alongside what is and what ought to be (1968: A805/B833). However, Kant is also clear that hope is returned to the present in the work of what is and what ought to be. This return of hope signifies reason's re-cognition of its misrecognition as other than its own self-interest. As such, hope is a higher form of reason's self-relation, but *not* the truth of reason's higher education in and for itself. As we will see with Kierkegaard below, the loss and return of hope to its truth in doubt (the *concept* of hope) is a pre-requisite for philosophy's higher education.

[16] I have not dwelt on it here, but in reading Kant on the sublime, I could not help but think that he was mischievously referring to orgasm. If so, the explosion of the sublime cannot be separated from the post-coital depression that registers the relation, and which is now the actuality of the hope and possibility that was the expectation engendered in foreplay.

REFERENCES

Aquinas, T. (1998) *Selected Writings*, London, Penguin.
Benjamin, W. (1996) *Selected Writings Volume 1 1913-1926*, Cambridge Mass., The
    Belknap Press of Harvard University.
Caygill, H. (1989) *Art of Judgement*, Oxford, Blackwell.
Caygill, H. (1995) *A Kant Dictionary*, Oxford, Blackwell.
Caygill, H. (1998) *Colour of Experience*, London, Routledge.
Hegel, G.W.F. (1975) *Natural Law: The Scientific Ways of Treating Natural Law, its Place in Moral
    Philosophy and its Relation to the Positive Sciences of Law*, Philadelphia, University of
    Pennsylvania Press, trans. T.M. Knox.
Kant, I. (1950) *Prolegomena to any Future Metaphysics*, Indianapolis, Bobbs Merrill.
Kant, I. (1952) *Critique of Judgement*, Oxford, Clarendon Press.
Kant, I. (1956) *Critique of Practical Reason*, New York, Macmillan.
Kant, I. (1968) *Critique of Pure Reason*, London, Macmillan.
Kant, I. (1990) *Foundations of the Metaphysics of Morals*, New York, Macmillan.
Kant, I. (1991) *Kant: Political Writings*, Cambridge, Cambridge University Press, ed. H. Reiss.

CHAPTER 2

HEGEL: MASTER AND SLAVE

1. THE CONVENTIONAL READING OF HEGEL

We reach here, if you like, the crucial distinction between the considerations I have been presenting to you and the Hegelian philosophy to which these considerations owe so much. It lies in the fact that Hegel's philosophy contains a moment by which that philosophy, despite having made the principle of determinate negation its vital nerve, passes over into affirmation and therefore into ideology: the belief that negation, by being pushed far enough and by reflecting itself, is one with positivity. That... is precisely and strictly the point at which I refuse to follow Hegel... for if I said that the negation of the negation is the positive, that idea would contain within itself a thesis of the philosophy of identity and could only be carried through if I had already assumed the unity of subject and object which is supposed to emerge at the end (Adorno, 2000: 144).

Hegel's response to this charge by Adorno might be as follows.

Should we not be concerned as to whether this fear of error is not just the error itself? Indeed, this fear takes something—a great deal in fact—for granted... To be specific it takes for granted certain ideas about cognition as an instrument and as a medium, and assumes that there is a difference between ourselves and this cognition. Above all, it presupposes that the Absolute stands on one side and cognition on the other, independent and separated from it ... or in other words, it presupposes that cognition which, since it is excluded from the Absolute is surely outside of the truth as well, is nevertheless true... (Hegel, 1977: 47).

The irony here is that whilst Hegel is chastised, not only by Adorno of course, for being an ideological philosopher, it is in fact Hegel's philosophizing that refuses to presuppose cognition of the Absolute.[1] It is Hegel who notes that judgements regarding the knowing and not knowing of the Absolute have already prejudged cognition as a reliable instrument by which to make such judgements. Why is cognition, the instrument, not also the object of an enquiry into the conditions of possibility by which the Absolute is presupposed as known or not known? It is Hegel, in fact, who labours with the phenomenological difficulty or aporia that the conditions of possibility of knowing the Absolute are a misrecognition of cognition by itself, and as such, composed of illusion. In turn, he refuses to presuppose this recognition of misrecognition as knowing or not-knowing, and explores instead how all 'knowing' appears only in the aporia of its conditions of possibility, or as what he calls actuality.

As such, Hegel's critique of all who attack him for presupposing the Absolute is that it is they who are presupposing that the negative *isn't* Absolute and that this is really the ideology of identity. Presupposing that the negative isn't Absolute is itself a philosophy of the thesis of the identity of subject and object. It is Hegel that does justice to the negative, showing that the presupposition of its own identity as non-identity must also collapse. What it collapses into—ultimately the learning individual— is now dealt with in the following chapter as the subject and substance of what we are calling philosophy's higher education.

2. THE HEGELIAN RELATION

The relation of master and slave is all Hegelian philosophy. Yet few writers explore the relation beyond its presentation in the *Phenomenology of Spirit*. The relation is the subject and substance of phenomenological experience, not only in the *Phenomenology of Spirit*, but also in the *Science of Logic*, and as the 'philosophy' or scientific thinking of right, history, nature, Spirit, religion and aesthetics.

Hegelian phenomenology does not bracket the world (Husserl) nor does it ontologise the world (Heidegger). Rather, Hegelian phenomenology is the culture of thought's relation to itself, a culture which contains misrecognition as its own movement and determination, or as philosophy's higher education. This culture, this education, is suppressed when relations between dualities, such as thought and being, theory and practice, subject and object etc., are stated without the accompanying difficulty that is determinative of their relation. The *Phenomenology of Spirit* traces the misrecognition of relation by itself through its various shapes in western history, up to the point at which relation becomes being-for-self, or achieves itself as a mind of its own. It is the central argument of this chapter that this relation in Hegel requires to be comprehended as 'education', and that the work by which relation gains a mind of its own is 'learning'. Further, that the master/slave relation is therefore the template of the culture of thinking, or is the structure of philosophy's higher education in Hegel. This will be explored below.

It is otiose to say that there are many examples of the master/slave relation in the *Phenomenology*, for the *Phenomenology* is nothing but the continual experience of misrecognition, an experience laid out for us who are observing this educational development. Indeed, there is nothing in the *Phenomenology* which is not misrecognition. Sense-certainty is a misrecognition of (natural) consciousness (1977: 64), perception of apprehension (1977: 71), objects of the understanding

(1977: 77), the person of substance, culture of Spirit, and freedom of the Absolute. That each coupling makes sense and can stand alone is evidence precisely of the misrecognition that defines them. Objects are understood, but equally are not; persons are substance but equally are not; and so on. We will return to the educational structure of such propositions later in this chapter.

If the key to Hegelian higher education is for relation to comprehend its own freedom, then this higher education is implicitly involved in re-cognising 'the object'. Relation is always a relation to an other and, within modern social relations, relation to an other is defined through ownership. As we will see in a moment, property is itself a misrecognition of freedom by freedom. Even though universal private property is the current form of this misrecognition, nevertheless the relation to the object has always defined freedom's own misrecognition of itself. As such, property in one form or another is always both the cause and the effect of our lack or freedom. The *non*-property based relation is part of our higher education regarding freedom but even this notion of freedom is substantial only within the property relation whose truth it is.

The relation to object is further complicated by the illusion that always accompanies it. The thinking that beholds the object appears to itself to be the natural or the given in the face of the contingent. For this natural consciousness the object is 'just an object for it' (1977: 79). But 'for us' (1977: 79) who can observe this presupposition of consciousness as 'natural', the relation of consciousness and object has 'developed through the movement of consciousness in such a way that consciousness is involved in that development' (1977: 79). There are two consciousnesses here. The one that performs the movement and development unseen by itself and the one which sees the significance of that work as determinative of what then 'naturally' appears. The latter is as it were the third party that observes the development of the relation between consciousness and object, or is philosophical consciousness. But of course they are the same consciousness, yet somehow self-differentiated in relation to the object. Philosophical consciousness is only the result of consciousness being in relation with the object. It is the realisation of itself as in relation. It is, thus, philosophical education.

Hegel points out that natural consciousness forgets its history and takes itself always at face value. Only philosophical consciousness, the for us of the relation of consciousness and object, sees the whole. There are two illusions here. The first is that the object is pure contingency. This is not to state that there is an object in itself that is independent of being known for, as Kant pointed out prior to Hegel, how could anything in itself be known that was not already mediated by the for us of experience? Rather, the illusion is that there is a consciousness in itself which is independent of its relation to objects. Again Kant had pointed this out stating famously 'that the conditions of the possibility of experience in general are likewise conditions of the possibility of the objects of experience...' (1968:

A158/B197). But Kant in the *Critique of Pure Reason*, and as seen above in chapter 1, then gives voice to the second illusion, namely that the possibility of knowing the first illusion enjoys a transcendental status. Such a promotion does not repeat but rather masks the illusion that the object (in this case, the conditions of possibility) was contingent upon and inessential to the essential, transcendental and unknowable *a priori*. Illusion here suppresses illusion by denying itself its own necessity and possibility becomes contingent upon a necessity that is independent of it. As such, the for us of experience, or illusion, is denied its own significance as that for which the relation to object is its own determination and formation as relation 'and' object. In Kant the illusion of the illusion, held as transcendental by a subsumptive judgement, is denied its educative import as formative and objective self-development, or as our experience of experience. The relation of illusion to illusion is denied its own contingent necessity. But in philosophy's higher education, illusion posits illusion, a self-negation which, known by us, is the formation of philosophical consciousness as relation and object. As such, illusion is affirmed in and as its own necessity and as true to itself.[2] For Hegel this is the law of contingency: 'what is necessary cannot be otherwise' (1969: 549). Posited illusion therefore is the Absolute, it is freedom and it is subjective substance. In the *Phenomenology of Spirit*, this education teaches of the relation of the relation as Spirit, and in the *Science of Logic*, Spirit is able to enjoy the freedom of learning as its own self-determination or teaching, or as its own formation and finality as education. As we will see in what follows, philosophy's higher education changes entirely our understanding of relation, and thereafter our relation to self, to others, to things and to property.

3. MASTER/SLAVE AS PHENOMENOLOGY

The developing comprehension of the relation between natural and philosophical consciousness is the phenomenology of Spirit. Natural consciousness has as many forms or beginnings as there is content in the *Phenomenology*. However, our higher education begins each time in our experience of 'nature' as posited. The master/slave relation is the template of this experience of positing. Therefore, philosophy's higher education is for us to see into the illusion of nature, into its prior determination and necessity, into the work of consciousness that natural consciousness has forgotten. As yet, we need not concern ourselves with the truth of the second illusion, the affirmation of illusion as formation and finality, for in the *Phenomenology* the second illusion is present only as suppressed by another form of 'natural' consciousness, be it 'morality', the person, stoicism, reason or whatever. As such, it is also present for us who are observing the dialectic of consciousness and self-consciousness, but we are only a third party to events. At the end of the *Phenomenology*, we as the third party will become complicit in events and find that what was being suppressed was the formation and finality of illusion as substantial and as subject. This recognition of illusion as the truth of the third party marks the end of philosophy's higher education for other, and becomes philosophy's higher education for us.

The higher education of the *Phenomenology*, then, consists in working backwards into the determination of each beginning. The first beginning is self-consciousness for this is the thinking force by which self is distinguished from other. But the condition of the possibility of objects of experience which self-consciousness takes itself to be is already an illusion *for us*, for this independence is therein an object and therefore also unessential or contingent. We can see that life in the form of an individual self-consciousness, or immediate 'I,' is a misrecognition of the relation of life and death. This relation is formative of the 'I,' but is forgotten by an 'I' which takes itself to be a natural beginning.[3] We see that the 'I' is life as 'not death'. But for life as 'I' that which is not itself is purely inessential and counts only as a thing, that is, as something without life. The misrecognition of death by life, and the illusory relation of 'I' to other is also therefore the foundation and the reproduction of all property based social relations including that of slavery. It is perhaps the most important aspect of philosophy's higher education in Hegel that the 'I' is already other, but the other, already, is not that 'I'.

We also see that the relation to death which the master suppresses returns to undermine him. As his own object (or, at this point in our education, as *our* object) he too shares with the slave a merely illusory being, a being that in itself is nothing. But when the master has become the slave, then the slave is not nothing, but is rather the truth of the master. Illusory being is now self-determined because what was merely posited is now posited by itself. Although in this experience the 'slave acquires a mind of his own' (1977: 119) we have to see this in two ways. For us, the observing third party, the slave is self-determined because he is life-less both in the work he performs on the thing for another, and he is life-less in himself. Since in the latter the slave counts only as a thing, then the work that the slave performs is work that shapes and forms himself. The slave and the thing enjoy a 'mutual' recognition that is denied to the master and the thing. However, our philosophical consciousness must wait awhile for this self-differentiation to be its own formation and finality. In the meantime, self-consciousness must undergo a series of misrecognitions of this 'mind of its own', misrecognitions which repeat in different ways, the relation of the essential and the inessential as object for consciousness. Until consciousness itself, or us the third party, are re-cognised to be that relation of the relation, (our higher education), self-consciousness will have the experience as other. This marks the beginning, now, of the education or the formation of self-consciousness to and in itself as Spirit. Each education will consist of another re-cognition of the relation between master and slave, and a further misrecognition of that re-cognition as other or object up to the education in which self recognises that it is already the other, even to itself.

The free self-consciousness that enjoyed itself as pure relation without object was Stoicism. Scepticism was the realisation of that indifference. We see that this thinking is 'the insight into this nature of the "different"' (1977: 124) but the experience of scepticism for self-consciousness is to have itself as different from the relation of difference. As such, it learns that it is 'a dual natured merely contradictory being' (1977: 126). It has the master/slave relation for itself, but not as itself. It manifests itself in the world as culture wherein the reconciliation of the contradictory relation lies elsewhere than on earth or within consciousness, and the latter is merely an interminable yearning for unification. Here the slave's mind of his own is lived out as 'the grave of its life,' (1977: 132) lifelessness without the truth of its illusory being.

But the seeds of greater transformation are present in the grave of life for self-consciousness. For us the unhappy consciousness is living out its own truth, but it 'merely finds itself desiring and working' (1977: 132) and living out the opposite of the reconciliation that it seeks. Here culture is self-alienated Spirit, where the external world is self-consciousness's own 'externalisation and separation of itself from its essence' (1977: 294). What characterises culture in Hegel is not externalisation *per se*, but the particular way in which self-consciousness and ethical substance work against each other in trying to reform each other. Attempts by one to reform the other are for us only repetitions of the pre-conditions of their separation. For consciousness, therefore, culture re-presents its interminable lack of foundation, or the aporia of reflective dualities. This is not the same culture seen above in Kant's *Critique of Judgement* for there the necessity of contingency was realised, whereas in the unhappy consciousness, necessity is precisely what is lost to the barbarism of force and violence.[4]

We can see that culture re-presents illusion as the relation between consciousness and the world, but for consciousness the world is 'an objective real world freely existing on its own account' (1977: 295). However, in the illusions that accompany this self-alienation are the moments again of the mater/slave relation, or the work wherein the illusion realises itself and gains its own substance, in this case, as reason.

The two moments of the unhappy consciousness play out their dialectical relationship such that the unchangeable surrenders its independence by becoming object to itself, and the changeable, already the work of illusion, sees surrender to be its own formation and finality or self-determination. For us, the slave gains a mind of his own, but for the mind in question this autonomy is now the single individual for whom all externality is itself, or is for itself as reason. But this 'I' can only assert itself alongside other such assertions. This is no longer the world of culture that is other, for the world is now part of the objectivity of the 'I'. Now otherness is in the form of all such 'I''s that face each other, equally immediately certain of themselves. For us, the third party, the differentiation of the notion into individuality is its truth. But for reason, here, differentiation is another misrecognition of the notion, this time as the formal equality of sovereign 'I's that characterises modern bourgeois social relations. 'Not until reason comes on the scene as a reflection from this opposite certainty does its affirmation about itself present itself not merely as a certainty and an assertion, but as truth; and not merely alongside other truths but as the sole truth' (1977: 141).

However, morality is the misrecognition of this reflective reason. Experienced as the judgement of this particular individuality, reason comes to know otherness within itself. Self-consciousness of this negation of universality takes many forms, all of which are variations of the law of the heart. Each law of the heart is an attempt to be true to the experience of the slave by the master, that is, to be true to his own downfall and his new life in contingency. But morality as such is not illusion in and for itself, it is illusion suppressed by being asserted, this time, as lying within. The law of the heart and the moral conscience are the self-assertion of the master as the slave. Such claims are always hypocritical for the master's claims to dependence are always a suppression of their own necessity. It is like the pious claim to being humble—the claim overpowers its truth.

Culture is not the only manifestation by which misrecognition and illusion are posited as substance. The second half of the *Phenomenology* chronicles these misrecognitions as the various forms of ethical life. For us, ethical life in whatever form it takes is always substance posited as other by a self-consciousness that fails to discover substance in the illusion of otherness and otherness in the substance of illusion. In Ancient Greece, custom re-presents a lack of illusion; in Rome, legal right is illusion personified through ownership; in feudal society, as mentioned above, law is absent to an essentially dualistic culture; now, in modern society, law is reason, masking and suppressing the work of illusion by granting rights of mastery to all. Philosophy's higher education, now, is to retrieve illusion in the master and to re-cognise that illusion as the self-determination of the Absolute. Put another way, now it lies within philosophy's higher education for us to realise the third party as our own re-formed relation to otherness, and therein to realise Spirit as self.

At the end of the *Phenomenology*, however, the slave does achieve a mind of its own. As in the master/slave relation, and as with the unhappy consciousness, moral self-consciousness surrenders its self-assurance and surrenders any claims to objectivity, and in doing so performs the truth of its own negativity. Conscience surrenders its inner objectivity and becomes what it always was, the negative of ethical life. This relation, now, of subject and substance is its own formation and finality, for it is its own third party, it is its own experience. However, the 'end' of the *Phenomenology* continues and is continuous. The *Phenomenology of Spirit* has been the 'appearance' of Spirit, or the different manifestations of the 'and' of the master and slave relationship.[5] It has been a journey of misrepresentation for us of the misrepresentation of consciousness by itself. For us, consciousness's own experiences are shaped by, reflective of, yet equally determinative of and prior to those misrepresentations. Now, for Absolute Spirit, this circular and contradictory state of affairs is revealed to be self-determinative. Now, at this end of the journey, Hegel notes three ways in which it continues. First the end of this education continues as science, where Spirit reflects into itself. Science in this sense is time and will continue to be time so long as the immanent self-differentiation of Spirit has the in itself over against the for itself. This self-opposition is the notion and it is the notion that 'is there' (1977: 487). Time is 'the destiny and the necessity of the Spirit that is not yet complete within itself...' (1977: 487). Further, 'until Spirit has completed itself *in itself*, until it has completed itself as World-Spirit, it cannot reach its consummation as self-conscious Spirit' (1977: 488).

The second and third ends of the education of the *Phenomenology* are the offspring of the notion that 'is there', or of time. Since the incompletion of Spirit is Spirit and is present as the notion, this self-opposition also has its 'moments', moments which constitute its 'supreme freedom and [the] assurance of its self-knowledge' (1977: 491). 'Nature' is the intuitive externalisation or limitation of time as space, and 'history' is the mediated externalisation or limitation of time as recollection. We will now explore the higher education of the first of these ends—science—in more detail.

4. MASTER/SLAVE AS PHILOSOPHY

In the *Science of Logic*, having become objective in and for itself as the notion, Spirit becomes self-reflective. Or, in the language of the master/slave relation, here Spirit gains a mind of its own, 'the reflection of substance or the process in which substance becomes self' (1977: 488). That this development should become 'systematised knowledge' (1969: 27) is, says Hegel, now our 'higher demand' (1969: 27). That it is a higher education in and of itself is revealed in the immanent way in which this unfolding and determinate systematised knowledge is a self-development. 'It can be only the nature of the content itself which spontaneously develops itself in a scientific method of knowing, since it is at the same time the reflection of the content itself which first posits and generates its determinate character' (1969: 27).

The higher education of the *Science of Logic* is therefore the relation of master and slave become subject and substance. It is here that Spirit learns about its self-determination in and as the education of itself; the education is the self-determination. Or, put differently, the higher education of the *Science of Logic* is the self known as and determined as philosophy (science). If, in advance of this education, you ask me to describe this philosophical self, I will say that it is where we learn to look with the eyes of illusion and not to suppress illusion either by claiming it or ignoring it. Such a self might be encapsulated by the contradictory notion of 'the child who knows'. Philosophers of all hews have sought to change the world; the point, however, is to understand the illusions that are constitutive even of the possibility of such a thought. The idea of change is itself changed within philosophy's higher education.

Such a higher education, philosophical and logical, necessarily contains illusions which oppose it. Illusion penetrates itself in two ways. First in suggesting that the labour of the notion is a purely ephemeral, intellectual and literally an academic pursuit with no 'relevance' or applicability to 'the real world'. What 'use' is such a higher education? Second, that logic provides categories as the means by which 'the serious business of life' (1969: 34) can be carried out. In the former they are granted 'the honour of being contemplated for their own sakes,' (1969: 34) in the latter 'they are degraded to the position where they serve in... [the] exchange of ideas' (1969: 34). For Hegel, philosophy's higher education is neither of these.

What is interesting for Hegel is that in the second case, where logical categories are used to understand objective relations, the truth of such thinking is made 'to depend entirely on the subject matter itself,' (1969: 35) with the categories of thinking 'not themselves credited with any active part in determining the content' (1969: 35). Thinking, says Hegel, here becomes subordinate, or slave. This philosophical view is the opposite view to that taken by abstract reason in the *Phenomenology* which saw all reality as dependent upon it for being known. But our philosophical higher education teaches us that the master (abstract reason) becomes slave as Spirit, and that Spirit comes to know itself as master and slave in its logical and philosophical self-determination. This means that thinking, taken as its own content, contains all of the relations that determine it as Spirit *and* the new relations that appear as its philosophical self-determination. Philosophy's higher education is therefore of Spirit, about Spirit, and this is not only a higher education called philosophy, it is the higher education of all that calls itself philosophy, for it is the higher education of thinking, by itself and about itself. It is, therefore, the higher education of 'relation', including, as we saw in chapter 1 above, where relation in reflective judgements is registered as the feeling 'and' cognition of formation and finality. The notion, for Hegel, is the universality of both of the illusions mentioned above. It alone is the relation that thought has to its objects which indicates within itself the misrecognition or 'figments of subjective thought' (1969: 36) that sees objects ultimately as unknowable in themselves. The notion is not merely 'an indifferent form attached to a content' (1969: 37). It is, universally, that which is always already any thought of an object at all, including in the *judgements* of reflective judgement.

In keeping with the master/slave relation of Spirit, the notion has a division within itself which is both its absolute truth and its actuality. On the one hand the notion's work is invisible to consciousness, a merely 'instinctive activity' (1969: 37) but, in its higher education about itself, it is 'the intelligent and free act... performed with an awareness of what is being done' (1969: 37). The task says Hegel, is 'to focus attention on this *logical* nature which animates the mind, moves and works in it' (1969: 37). What is at stake in this task is philosophy's higher education regarding its own nature as not only determinative but self-determinative.

> As impulses the categories are only instinctively active. At first they enter consciousness separately and so are variable and mutually confusing; consequently they afford to mind only a fragmentary and uncertain actuality; the loftier business of logic therefore is to clarify these categories and in them to raise mind to freedom and truth (1969: 37).

The notion is not only the truth of the contingency of all else, it is also the truth of contingency *per se* (or of the slave); it is the necessity of the possibility of contingency or the contingency of contingency being true to itself. We saw this above in regard to the slave, and to the unhappy consciousness. We have alluded to the way that the slave's mind of his own is the truth of illusion. What lies ahead for us now is to follow in the *Science of Logic* the way that illusion learns of itself from itself, an education that teaches us of dependence as freedom.

> The most important point for the nature of spirit is not only the relation of what it is in itself to what it is actually, but the relation of what it knows itself to be to what it actually is; because spirit is essentially consciousness, this self-knowing is a fundamental determination of its actuality (1969: 37).

For this reason, perhaps above all others, philosophy's higher education is not for the philosopher who seeks only and abstractly to argue a case. It is for 'students,' people who live by knowing the relation to be present everywhere, in all that we do, and knowing that this knowing is present in us and as us, or as the formation and finality that is learning. Philosophy's higher education is only something we can achieve in that it is something we already are. Its work, says Hegel, is the 'soul,' (1969: 37) and as such the soul is the master and slave, the work of self-relation, that is philosophy's higher education. Equally, as the truth of contingency it is not a higher education that offers the Absolute as complete and finished. On the contrary, it offers the Absolute as the truth of that incompleteness. Philosophy's higher education, in the notion, educates us about the truth and about our abstract expectations of what it 'ought' to look like.

The key difference then between the notion and all other figments of subjective thoughts is not that the latter contain illusion whereas the former does not, for all subjective thoughts at all the different stages of Spirit, contain illusion. The difference lies in the awareness of illusion as determinative and self-determinative. Spirit comprehends illusion as determinative throughout the

Science of Logic but the central unfolding of this higher educational process is found in the section on illusory being. The master/slave section in the *Phenomenology* and the section on illusory being in the *Science of Logic* both describe the educational structure of experience. What the master/slave relation outlines abstractly in terms of property and freedom, illusory being sets out in terms of the self-determination of the notion. In both, the work of illusion on itself re-forms its relation to the object or to other.

In comprehending illusory being we can re-educate ourselves with regard to concepts such as 'awareness', 'self-knowing' and enlightenment. Such ideas are often employed as if they were an overcoming of illusions, and as something achieved which has left behind prior distortions of the real picture.[6] But within the structure and necessity of illusory being, enlightenment is not applicable as a concept in this way, for what is learnt in and by illusory being is relation, not the overcoming of relation. For relation to be the result of learning it must also be the activity of learning. In knowing itself, it does relation. Such knowledge does not end relation for the knowledge precisely is the relation as relation. In this sense, philosophy's higher education educates us about the very meaning of education. Education, taken as providing knowledge merely as result, is another abstraction of possibility from its own necessity. In illusory being, as in the master/slave relation, education is true to its own conditions of possibility, suffering its contingency upon itself as formation and finality, or as the necessity (learning) that is its self-determination.

Hegel offers a foretaste of this education of illusion in the prefaces and introduction to the *Science of Logic*. Illusion is present in 'common sense' and in 'natural logic'. Thinking which takes itself to be free, in the sense that it is free to make up its own mind about things, remains unaware that 'it is in bondage' (1969: 38) to forms of thinking, or categories, that determine its unfreedom. Common sense is unaware that its own master/slave relation overpowers its naïve presuppositions of freedom. As with the master, so common sense takes itself to be independent. Yet its independence is dependent upon ways of thinking which it uses but does not determine for itself. In the realisation of the master's dependence upon the slave, the master is re-cognised to be the slave. This experience is a universal aspect of philosophy's higher education. It is the aspect often referred to as contingency or determinism, the realisation that the freedom of common sense thinking is illusory. But so often philosophy's higher education stops here and contingency and determinism become ends in themselves (its current form is 'post-foundationalism'[7]). The higher education that lies in store for common sense is to learn the truth of its contingency, or the truth of the slave. This it cannot do unless this higher education is the realisation of the notion. The beginning of this higher education, says Hegel, is the conflict that emerges within understanding. In other words, the experience of slavery for the understanding is present as a contradiction, or better, as an aporia, for its universal undermining of all mastery, including the mastery of even this experience, leaves it seemingly without import. For the understanding, nothing is learned in this conflict except that there is conflict. That illusion is still prevalent, or masterful, is evident in the way that the understanding presupposes that slavery is not truth. This prejudice is the illusion upon which post-foundational thinking is founded. In response to such illusory mastery Hegel says that insight into aporia is

> the great negative step towards the true Notion of reason. But the insight, when not thorough going, commits the mistake of thinking that it is reason which is in contradiction with itself; it does not recognise that the contradiction is precisely the rising of reason above the limitations of the understanding and resolving them (1969: 46).

When common sense sees the word 'resolve', it forgets that it is still 'in bondage to... unfree thinking' (1969: 38) and asserts, again, that this understanding is undermined by an internal instability. The realisation of philosophy's higher education is not a resolution (or an enlightenment, or an overcoming) as common sense abstractly understands it. This resolution is the notion, which includes the conflict within it as its own 'self-moving soul' (1969: 56). The notion is not *just* an abstract result—resolution, enlightenment, overcoming, whatever. The notion is a resolution of the understanding which does not know how to learn into one which does. Resolution here is its own education regarding itself, no longer merely a closure, but now the infinite closure of its abstract appearance as closure. This is an education, therefore, about the objectivity of what resolution, enlightenment, etc., mean as 'result'. Hegel complains

> I have been only too often and too vehemently attacked by opponents who were incapable of making the simple reflection that their opinions and objections contain categories which are presuppositions and which themselves need to be criticised before they are employed... (1969: 40-1).

However, this presentation of the notion in the prefaces and the introduction is, as Hegel himself acknowledges, just as abstract as the forms of reasoning he is aiming to educate. This is necessary, he says, because the introduction to the *Logic* must express the notion historically, that is, as developed. Such an introduction invites our abstract reason to note internal conflicts in what is being asserted and, therein, the 'self-moving soul' of the notion or of our philosophical education has already begun. But the education itself lies not in judgements about external objects, it lies solely in the judgement, and here Hegel uses the term as a logical category, of the notion by itself, or its self determination. It is in this self-determination that the notion is 'posited only under its own specifications' (1969: 61).

Our abstract consciousness has a further and still more powerful illusion to use to obscure the path of philosophy's higher education from itself. In the way that

the notion has been presented above, it appears that what is required for its recognition is that common sense be made aware of the contingency or determinate
nature of its thinking and therefore 'see through' the illusions of independence that
ground it. Such a view is one that has encouraged various critiques of the notion of
enlightenment, for such critiques merely point out the conflicts internal to any
view of 'overcoming', 'seeing through', 'enlightenment', etc. On the one hand
such critiques are trying to take the problem of illusion seriously and to prevent it
from being too easily comprehended. To overcome illusion is itself illusory. But,
and on the other hand, these critiques in taking illusion so seriously, miss the more
mischievous internal characteristics of illusion, that it also hides its own truth
within illusion, within itself. As such, unless we work with illusion to comprehend
its own re-presentation of itself, our critique of illusion will be without import and
significance, and precisely therefore the very triumph of illusion that the critique
aimed to 'overcome'.

How, then, in the *Science of Logic*, is illusion comprehended by illusion rather
than by a common sense notion of overcoming or a common sense (we might say
excessive) notion of not-overcoming? Hegel notes that in the division of the
notion, or in the self-determining judgement of its own necessity and possibility
(the *logos*), abstract thinking produces a twofold division. The notion is either
'unaware' in which case it is 'objective logic' or the notion in itself. Or, if the
notion is aware of itself then it is 'subjective logic' or the notion for itself. But the
duality of in itself and for itself is only another presupposition of what constitutes
knowing *per se*. Abstractly, 'awareness' means enlightenment and overcoming
such that the notion for itself has 'seen through' and left behind the implicitly
ignorant state of the notion that is unaware and merely in itself. But, even this
presupposition of 'knowing' manifests a conflict that renders it unstable. We can
neither 'know' nor 'not-know' that 'awareness' is overcoming. Is there here, then,
another form of enlightenment, or awareness, about knowing that is different from
merely abstract assertions of what is and what is not? Is there a higher education
to be gained from within the conflict, one that is not resolved by knowing what
constitutes an outcome or a result of the conflict, positively or negatively, in
advance?

This higher education constitutes the *Science of Logic*, and it is an advance
over the *Phenomenology of Spirit* in that in the latter the third party had observer
status only, but in the former the higher education is formative of that third party
such that its relation to otherness becomes its own self-determination, or finality.
The third party is now involved differently because the twofold division of the
notion is actually a threefold division. The notion is in itself and the notion is for
itself. But to be for itself it must also not be in itself. As with the slave, it remains
to be seen how the notion can gain a mind of its own when to be for itself, or
aware, or enlightened (or whatever) it must also of necessity not be in itself. How

can the dependent notion also be independent, free and self-determining? The truth of this relation is the third division of the notion, the sphere of 'mediation'.

Hegel notes that the objective and subjective logic are related in the sphere of their mediation by their difference. The notion is still external because it is an object for subjectivity, and as such is not, either, fully internal or subjective. 'This is the doctrine of essence which stands midway between the doctrine of being and that of the notion' (1969: 61). Essence prevents the presupposition of notions of enlightenment or knowing because it is precisely the sphere of the conflict that is presupposed as known or not-known. This conflict is present, or actual, as illusory being. We must now explore the workings of illusory being to see how the conflict of the understanding offers the higher education of philosophy, a higher education which changes our understanding of 'understanding' and thus our understanding of everything else including subjectivity and truth.

Subjectivity does not begin to think about itself. Subjectivity is already a result. But the nature of this result is hidden (from itself) by the illusion that it is reflection. Reflection appears to be the self-determining work of subjectivity wherein thought and ideas are 'grounded' in the thinking subject. It appears to be a critical activity for it appears to mediate the abstraction of a 'person'. This is the 'softness' of reflection that appears in education in a concept such as the reflective practitioner.[8] Reflection is taken to be a kind of self-relation wherein 'change' is brought about through the new understandings that are generated by its critical self-questioning. Reflection is taken to be synonymous with self-mediation, self-questioning and being self-critical. It is also the basis of notions of praxis for in the whole that is reflection, practice is not dominated by external theory, but rather thinking and doing constitute the whole of reflection.

Reflection so understood is the source and the perpetrator of the domination and suppression of philosophy's higher education. Yet also, it is the actuality of that higher education. Reflection is both misrecognition and the re-cognition of itself as misrecognition. For reasons that will now be explored, its re-cognition does not overcome the misrecognition. All philosophies of education, of praxis, of communicative action, of enlightenment, and which advocate 'becoming aware' as a form of understanding or Being, misrecognise the nature of misrecognition, and repeatedly mis-take reflection as the self-determination of subjectivity, whether that mistake is in a positive form (enlightenment) or a negative form (deconstruction).

The reason for reflection's continued and repeated misrecognition of itself as self-determination is that reflection *is* illusion. As stated above, subjectivity does not begin to think about itself, for it is already thought. The loss of the beginning, the knowledge of the beginning, appears as the beginning, but in fact is already itself determinate.

In the *Logic*, the constituent and self-determining components of Absolute Spirit unfold in and for themselves to reveal the Absolute Idea. The section on illusory being in the *Logic* is, in a sense, the whole of this process unfolding. In it, the negative that is Absolute gains a mind of its own, a mind that is the notion. If we comprehend the self-determining higher education of Absolute Spirit as illusory being, we also comprehend philosophy's higher education *per se* in Hegel.

Essence in relation to being is a relation of reflection. But in reflection, by definition, is illusion. Reflection is illusion because reflection is presupposition. Where reflection as presupposition dominates as illusion, there philosophy's higher education is suppressed. Essence presupposes itself to be sublated being. But, mistaking reflection for a beginning, essence now has being as its own object and therefore as the unessential in the relationship. Essence is therefore illusory being, for what is reflecting is nothing, and what it is reflecting upon (i.e. itself) is also nothing. Reflection *per se* is 'the movement of nothing to nothing, and so back to itself' (1969: 400). All that reflection amounts to is the presupposition of itself. It is the pure positing characteristic of all natural consciousness. But pure positing cannot survive its own insight, for the contradiction ensures the mediation of positing by itself. Here illusory being shines even more brightly. This reflection of reflection offers two results. Either this mediation undermines the independence of essence or reflection, in favour of an intersubjective relation between thinking and thought, or notion and object. Communicative action is an example of such a result. Or, the mediation undermines essence or reflection such that the very act of positing is itself deconstructed as another textual violence. These responses are still illusory being for both posit something other than illusion. Both responses, the positive overcoming of illusion or the unknowable (excessive) condition of its possibility, are 'essentially the presupposing of that from which [they are] the return' (1969: 401). But this is exactly what is suppressed when illusion is refused its own self-determination, or formation and finality, and made other to itself without also that relation being its own.

Such a suppression is what Hegel calls external reflection. In external reflection, illusory being is recognised as that which merely 'shines, or shows within itself' (1969: 391). Here, positing is 'related to itself as to its non-being' (1969: 403). It achieves for itself the relation of identity and difference, for it knows itself as its own object to be exactly the unessential that being was. But external reflection does not realise that relation of positing to positing as 'transition' (1969: 441) wherein 'the non-being of the finite is the being of the absolute' (1969: 443). External reflection is therefore the judgement *of* illusory being but not also judgement *as* illusory being. It is still a judgement that has illusion as other and is, still, a characteristically bourgeois judgement, enjoying its object but forming no educative relation to it.

5. THE EXPERIENCE OF REFLECTION

Illusory being, in realising a mind of its own and re-forming the relation to object, plays out its own master and slave relation, for it is Spirit's own experience of itself.

As in the master/slave relation, so in philosophy's higher education, the relation to death is formative. In the life and death struggle, nature is formed with death as other, or as the natural consciousness that enjoys its independent status as 'I' in relation to all that is not itself. Being, too, is determinate being in that it is not-nothing. It too has nothingness as other. Equally, determinate being enjoys its own self-relation for it is an awareness of itself, now, as other to that which is nothing. As such it is essence. In both of these examples, nature is misrecognised as life 'and' death wherein the 'and' is already the 'I'. Hereafter, necessity and freedom will be opposed until the 'and' is both the necessity of freedom and the freedom of necessity, or until they are the work and result of philosophy's higher education. Now, however, the 'and' of freedom and necessity constitutes illusory being.[9]

Essence or pure-being-for-self is the One, 'the independent consciousness whose essential nature is to be for itself' (1977: 115). The nothingness of mere being 'is the dependent consciousness whose essential nature is simply to live or to be for another' (1977: 115). To live for another is a living death for it is nothing in itself. It is 'in and for itself a nullity; it is only a non-essence, illusory being' (1969: 395). As such, essence 'is so only in relation to an other, in a specific reference' (1969: 395). This negates and undermines its claims to indifference. It is in fact dependent upon the other for its own relation to self. Positing as such cannot be both 'lord over the being of the thing and achieve absolute negation of it' (1977: 116). As such, 'the truth of the independent consciousness is accordingly the servile consciousness of the bondsman' (1977: 117). Now, just as lordship 'showed that its essential nature is the reverse of what it wants to be' (1977: 117) so we must see how the nullity and non-essence that is illusory being also turns 'into the opposite of what it immediately is' (1977: 117).

What does positing mean for the other whose existence is rendered as nothing, or as a mere thing? The illusory being that is other for essence is 'the nothingness which yet is' (1969: 397). As such it is the truth of the mediated essence whose relation to itself is now also a nothingness that yet is. Illusory being is now 'the negative nature of essence itself' (1969: 397). But this is only one side of the higher education of being and essence. If their education consisted only of this, then it would be merely the 'empty determination of the immediacy of negated determinate being' (1969: 396), or scepticism. That scepticism is so often taken to be higher education is not difficult to understand. It is by far the easier half of science, holding itself to be the only possible result of the negation of being. The irony is that this very conclusion is itself the most powerful form that is taken by illusory being because it is where reflection and illusion are one and the same. The other half of this one sided higher education still lies ahead, where reflection and illusion becomes self-determinate of and through their own work. But even in its scepticism, illusory being does experience 'its own essential nature' (1977: 117) even if, as yet, it does not recognise the significance of this experience. When illusory being is known as illusory, as a mere shining for others with no substance of its own, then 'its whole being has been seized with dread; for it has experienced the fear of death, the absolute Lord' (1977: 118). What for the lord, appeared as other, now, for the slave, is absolutely implicit. 'There is nothing present in it which could not be regarded as a vanishing moment' (1977: 114). But when illusion is scepticism, then the experience which offers fear of the lord as 'the beginning of wisdom' (1977: 117-118) becomes the possibility of everything, everything, that is, except truth. The former lies in the positing of scepticism that it is not positing. 'Scepticism permits the content of its illusory being to be given to it; whatever content it is supposed to have, for scepticism it is immediate' (1969: 396). This positing is the basis of all philosophies which eschew necessity for possibility, often in the guise of the 'hope' for and of infinite configuration.[10]

The fear of absolute vanishing cannot be posited for it negates positing. It is this experience where it 'has trembled in every fibre of its being, and everything solid and stable has been shaken to its foundations' (1977: 117) which is positing's own experience for it is here that independence comes face to face with its own status as a thing. When scepticism fights shy of its own negation, it is positing the property relation as universal and not merely over this or that object. Scepticism is the illusion of 'natural' property relation *par excellence*, for it is property relations made universal and immediate. Where the master dominates the slave, the property relation is transparent. But reason, and its bastard offspring, scepticism, turn illusory being into opaque universal social relations where formal equality and relativism are only two sides of the same coin, the coin being illusion posited as the law of all. Both are the positing of the nothingness of illusory being. Worse, scepticism is the misrecognition of service, turning this negative universality into self-satisfaction.

The higher education of being and essence consists not only in the 'nothingness that yet is' (or death). It also has another movement. The slave is not the 'dissolution of everything stable merely in principle; in his service he actually brings this about. Through his service he rids himself of attachment to natural existence in every single detail; and gets rid of it by working on it' (1977: 117).

Work has a different relation to the object than the mere desire and enjoyment of the master. The latter holds the object (including the slave) apart from the being-for-self of the One in order to enjoy it. But the enjoyment of this one-sided recognition is fleeting 'for it lacks the side of objectivity and permanence' (1977: 118). We have seen how this misrecognition undermines itself. The slave, on the other hand, realises a more permanent relation to the thing, for the slave and the thing can achieve a form of mutual recognition. Each sees in the 'independence' of the other their own 'independence'. But this relation is negative. The object is formed by the slave and crucially, the slave is the object that is formed. 'Consciousness, qua worker, comes to see in the independent being [of the object] its own independence' (1977: 118). In the negative relation of slave and object, both are equally themselves and the other.

For the slave this recognition has a twofold significance. In forming himself and the object he achieves two negative moments. First he sees himself reflected in the nothingness of the object, and second he knows that nothingness to be the absolute fear of his own absolute vanishing. This negative meeting is precisely where the slave 'becomes for himself, someone existing on his own account' (1977: 118). In work on the other he becomes himself. Death and service *are* as formative work. Or, we might say here, that formative work is formative in that it is self-educative. Death and service learn of themselves, are formed, in the formative work that is 'alienation,' or in the formative work wherein the thing is an externality which also is not other. 'Through this rediscovery of himself by himself, the bondsman realises that it is precisely in his work wherein he seemed to have only an alienated existence that he acquires a mind of his own' (1977: 118-119).

The experience of reflection, then, is the experience of Spirit as the relation that is the master 'and' slave. Essence has an independence that is merely posited. This positing is exposed when essence becomes its own object. As such it is illusory being to itself. This relation however is determinative for illusion is now known to be both the subject and object of reflection. Illusion here is self-determinative. For the first time, an object is of itself, or in Hegelian terms for the first time the in-itself that is for-itself is *also* and in addition for itself. This unification occurs as experience, for it can only happen in experience. To have the experience of illusory being in itself and for itself is the same thing as to do the work of positing and for that positing also to be its own knowledge of itself. The knowledge gained is not an object external to experience, it is the experience. Therefore we can say that from experience we gain only such knowledge that is experienced, or which happens. The knowledge which derives from philosophical experience is learning, for learning is both what experience is and what it is of.

Learning then is the work and the result of the experience of reflection. But who is this learning for? Already the question suggests a misrecognition, for if the experience of reflection, and of the master/slave relation, precisely re-educates us about the nature of notion and object, then perhaps the 'for whom' of the question is already included in the experience? This is, now, the final part of our examination of philosophy's higher education in Hegel, *who* is it for and what is its significance for them?

6. THE LEARNING INDIVIDUAL

In the *Phenomenology* we saw that relations between consciousness and object were an object for the observing third party. But in the realm of Spirit, the third party now re-cognises the object to be itself. The third party is true in that it is the relation of the relation of notion and object. It is the thinking of the object and it is the object in-itself. As such, the individuality of the third party appears as actuality, as the notion and as judgement. All three share the same triadic structure of formation and finality that constitute experience and learning, and constitute the 'I' of philosophy's higher education, the learning individual.

It is important to note in advance here that the learning individual of formation and finality will not appear familiar to our abstract consciousness. It is of course tempting to describe this individuality as 'new', for that gives our abstract thinking an object to fix on, something to aim at, and relieves this consciousness of the work of finding education within and as what it already is. The learning individual will be unfamiliar as a notion of subjectivity, but this is precisely because it is an individuality that has learned more about itself than when it still misrecognised and suppressed its prior relation to the object, or to the other.

Perhaps the strangest form and content that learning individuality takes is actuality, for here the relation that is subject and substance of that individuality is that between inner and outer. Actuality contains illusion. As such it requires to be differentiated from what we might call mere reality. Reality has illusion as other, either empirically where reason tests laws or reflectively for essence. As such reality is opposed to freedom for reality suppresses determination. Actuality on the other hand is freedom because actuality contains illusion as determination. This means that actuality is determinate. It is what freedom makes of itself, its mind of its own, under the prevailing conditions that pre-determine the shape of its misrecognition or its current social relations. What *is*, meaning what is known as internal and external, subjective and objective, is already actual, for our knowledge of what is is already posited. To comprehend actuality therefore requires us to see the way that illusion is necessity. The world appears as for us, but actually it is that relation that is not only for us, but already is us. We are already the relation of the relation but this, our higher education, is suppressed by the power of the illusion that objects can only be inessential. This illusion is what renders us less than significant as our own object. The learning individual knows that what is is not merely out there to be worked on but, in such work, is already a self-formation. This changes our relation to the world as to ourselves, for actually, we are already that relation. For Heidegger, actuality is reduced to a form of Dasein, or being there. But the authenticity of actuality does not belong to being, it belongs to illusory being. The difference between the two constitutes nothing less than the whole of philosophy's higher education. Only in illusory being is necessity true to itself as contingency, a truth that is contained in actuality but not, as we will see in the next chapter, ultimately in Dasein. Actuality is our first example of the 'I' of philosophy's higher education. It is the third that is already the duality of inner and outer. 'Individual and the actual are the same' (1975: 226).

That which determines itself according to its own necessity and of which actuality is its self-realisation, is the notion. We met the notion at the end of the *Phenomenology* when Spirit became object to itself as itself. In the *Logic*, this self-relation is worked through as the soul of that Spirit, developing itself according to its own 'inner' necessity. As actuality is the third to inner and outer, so the notion is the third to being and essence or to master and slave, or is the third for which experience is self-differentiation. In experience, the in and for itself is also for itself and is only the latter as the relation or differentiation that is the former. When it looks as if the third is an other and therefore nothing, then we have forgotten that the third is actually the experience of the relation, determined in it, and, as necessity, determinative of it. The third is our thinking of relation and it is that relation. It is object and subject, or self-determination. Its 'otherness' is only how contingency must appear to itself to be contingency in and for itself. The other is, if you like, reflection's own reflection, or the experience of the illusory being of illusory being. The name that Hegel gives to this self-determining, self-differentiating contingency is the notion. But, given what we have seen above, the notion is also the learning individuality. The notion is the comprehensive view of experience as self-education for it is in the nature of the notion to divide itself from itself in order that the division necessarily returns to that whose division it is. This is the way the notion is. It is itself through learning, or put another way, learning is the soul of the notion, its inner movement and becoming.

As such, there emerges for us now the notion as comprehensive higher education, wherein the illusions of reflection can be known in and as the inner necessity of the notion. It is not that this higher education asks us to think about different things, but it does demand that we think differently about things. Nor do we have to do anything to make or force the necessity of the notion. All that is required of us is that we become open to learning from experiences which, all too often we judge from a reflective standpoint rather than as the necessity of the notion. To judge experience reflectively requires only that we continue to posit the other of the essential I as unessential, even when the latter is the essential I itself. To learn speculatively on the other hand, is to see positing return into itself and to experience this relation as the necessity of that for which return is the whole. The experience here is not only of relation, it is also the relation relating to itself according to itself. This is comprehensive learning, where each relation of subject and object is experienced by itself and therein learns of the totality of the conditions of its own possibility. This is not to posit a mutual dependence between experience and object. On the contrary, this higher education sees their imbalance for what it is, a positing of independence and dependence which is itself the truth of contingency unfolding itself according to its own necessity. It is this necessity, or in experience where dependence is self-determined, that reflection and its dualities give way to the notion, a necessity present to and know by us as learning. There is no choice but to learn—that is the nature of the notion.

So, the learning individual is the actual and the notion. But also, the learning individual is judgement. Judgement contains the same illusions and dialectical movements of the notion found in reflection, except that this time instead of necessity being present in learning, it is present in the syllogism or the structure of the possibility of judgement as self. This means that judgement too is an experience, and it is still true to itself only as learning. As with actuality, so with judgement, the learner does not become merely the judge of illusions who has them in his court as objects, but rather the judge who has *this* relation as his own determination. Not judge over illusion but judge as illusion.

Again, understanding the learner as judgement requires us to comprehend the third party that is the notion. Judgements are such that a subject x is said to be the bearer of content y, which therefore is the grammatical predicate of the subject. The two are joined by the copula 'is'. Hence the proposition is an assertion, e.g., this man is my father.

Viewed empirically such a judgement asserts an objective fact about the subject. Here the subject and the predicate appear immune from any relation other than their own. The objectivity of the judgement lies in its exclusivity and independence.

Viewed reflectively such a judgement is an object for consciousness. As such, for the essential I the judgement is contingent and is only in itself for consciousness. The latter is taken to undermine the independence of the former. Thus, reflectively, judgement is only illusory being.

Viewed speculatively, the judgement that judgement is only illusory being becomes an object for itself, and according to itself is now also illusory being. But this judgement is now an object for the judgement of objects *per se*, and is therefore in itself and for itself. The truth of the judgement is present as our experience of judgement, or is present in and as our learning.

Viewed as the notion, the judgement contains all three moments as its own necessity. But these moments are no longer abstraction, dialectic and speculative for now, the necessity that is the notion is all of these moments all of the time. These three moments appear in three different ways according to the different stages of its own self-differentiation. In other words the notion is always its own positing, but from within the differences that are its self-return, not instead of them.

> The notion does not, as understanding supposes, stand still in its own immobility. It is rather an infinite form, of boundless activity... and thereby self differentiating. This disruption of the notion into the difference of its constituent functions—a disruption imposed by the native act of the notion—is the judgement (1975: 232).

The three posited self-differentiated constituents of the notion's own subjectivity are individual, universal and particular. The universal notion is pure self-relation, pure return. As such it is self-determinate, a positing of itself as *this* notion alongside other notions. The universal self-positing is therefore always this particular notion, always already this thought, distinguished from all other thoughts. The notion is already therefore divided into universal and particular just as reflection is always already divided into subject and object. Both re-present necessity as the loss of beginning or as division. In the notion, unlike in reflection, the particular is not 'other' to universality for their difference is only their self-relation. The actuality, as it were, of this self-differentiating self-relation is individuality, which is already present in the positing that is universality and particularity. Individuality is the relation of the relation, the third party, between universality and particular. It is, in fact, the notion known that it is known.

As in reflection, and as in the master/slave relation, illusion dominates judgement. Judgement appears to make a simple connection between two things, to affirm an identity between them. But such a formula contains (as we now know) all of the moments and movements that determine judgement as a form. To presuppose the form is the same presupposition that characterises the master and essence, both of whom, beginning with themselves, have an other as unessential or contingent 'thing'. Judgements taken at face value suppress the violence of this positing and 'naturally' accept that the predicate is only contingent upon the subject.

But judgement comprehended as the self-formation of totality plays out all of the same movements seen above regarding experience. A proposition of the whole (what is) by necessity must differentiate itself into universal and particular so that their relation, separate and together, is formative then of the truth of the relation, or is a judgement. A judgement therefore is always an experience. It cannot be stated without the relation being also an object for itself. A judgement, thus comprehended, is seen to be the notion's own positing which is already a positing of that positing. As such judgement is the actuality or the individuality of the notion, expressing its relation to and as otherness, but behind the ordinary reading that its grammatical structure encourages. The 'is' of a proposition contains illusion and is, as such, a mind of its own. In fact the truth of the judgement as notion is that it knows the 'is' to contain the lack of identity. The latter is precisely the necessity that is judgement, or the syllogism.

Individuality, then, in terms of actuality, the notion and judgement, has an educational significance. Each is formed in and as the experience wherein positing is the in and for itself of contingency, or of itself. Individuality is the truth of the lack of stability, the necessity, of positing *per se*. As such, we might say that individuality is formed in and as the experience of the truth of contingency where fear and work (or the illusory being of essence) become, for that whose experience this is, a mind of its own.

In this, then, the notion has universality as particular and individual; it has the particular as universal and individual; and it has the individual as particular and universal. It makes no sense to ask whether I am universal, particular or individual for I am already all of them in the question. Similarly it misses the point to ask now of my relation to others for externality is constitutive of my actuality, my individuality. The whole formative necessity of individuality is built around the way that I have become individual by knowing myself as other, and knowing the other to be the self-determination and the illusion of this individual. As the slave gains a mind of his own by recognising his work on the thing to be formative of his individuality, so my illusory being recognises its work on the other to be similarly formative. Without the work on the other, which shapes both the other and the worker, there is negation but no freedom. It is the relation to other that determines itself as individuality.

This is a very important part of philosophy's higher education in Hegel. The relation between the individual and the other is educational and significant, but it is not abstract or merely 'mutual'. The other, now, is known to be my illusory being, but by a 'me' which learns of illusion as formative. Presumptions of mutuality suppress the relation in which 'I' 'am' 'other' because the other is not me. This contradiction can only be 'overcome' through the suppression of the learning individual, that is, through the domination of the other as equally the same as me or different from me. Bourgeois relations maintain this domination. Moreover, the misrecognition implicit in the usage of the term 'mutual recognition' in so much work about Hegel, makes it perhaps impossible for the term to carry its educational significance. Mutual recognition has become so much 'the result' that 'ought' to be achieved, that it is unlikely that it can retrieve its spiritual and contradictory philosophical structure against its posited and abstract identity. Where mutual recognition has come to mean knowing the other to be a person in his own right, the learning individual understands that 'I' am already only myself because I am also already the relation of otherness to itself. This nothingness which is something is precisely my self-determination in and by illusion, and is what constitutes philosophy's higher education. This is the re-forming of social relations in philosophy's higher education, rather than the mere repetition of the dualism self and other and ingenious ways by which they 'ought' to recognise each other. In the work of learning, the other enjoys no closer relation to me than this, that its illusory being is necessarily also my own. Differentiated individuals

> immediately are, but further, this sundering is reflection as such, the illusory being of one in the other; thus they stand in essential relation. Further, the individuals are not merely *inertly* present in relation to one another; such plurality belongs to being; the individuality, in positing itself as determinate, posits itself not in an external difference but in the difference of the notion (1969: 622).

NOTES

[1] I have kept the upper case for the Absolute and Spirit in this chapter. Other terms are reduced to lower case except in quotations from translations.

[2] As we saw above in the first chapter, contingency in Kant's education is suppressed until it is recognised as the immanent and aporetic necessity of formation and finality within judgement-power.

[3] To say in Hegel that the 'I' has forgotten itself as relation is the same as saying, in Nietzsche, that remembering ties us to an historical continuum. Forgetting the life and death relation is remembering the historical 'I'. We will explore the latter below in chapter 5.

[4] This is not to say that Kant did not foresee the cultural activity of reflective judgement having as its end the preparation for war, and literally turning formation and finality into formation *for* finality! See *Kants Political Writings*, (1991).

[5] This 'and' is constitutive of all the dualisms and all of the relations of philosophy's higher education that are explored in this book. 'And' is discussed below in chapter 6. But in Hegelian terms, we can say that 'and' is where the Idea is present as illusion, where philosophy lies suppressed by property relations, and where this suppression is self-determinative as the 'I'.

[6] As Plato's cave is also so often (mis)understood. The following critique of abstract notions of enlightenment and overcoming can also apply to such interpretations of the cave. See also Tubbs, (2003).

[7] See also the essay 'The End of Culture' below.

[8] For example, in the work of Donald Schön. It has spawned a plethora of MA's in education which ground teachers as researchers in this illusion called the reflective practitioner. See Tubbs (2000).

[9] See footnote 4, above.

[10] And therefore ultimately characterises Caygill's aporetic philosophy, outlined above in chapter 1.

REFERENCES

Adorno, T.W. (2000) *Metaphysics: concepts and problems*, Cambridge, Polity Press.
Hegel, G.W.F. (1969) *Science of Logic*, London, George Allen and Unwin, trans. A.V. Miller.
Hegel, G.W.F. (1975) *Hegel's Logic*, Oxford, Clarendon Press, trans. W.Wallace.
Hegel, G.W.F. (1977) *Phenomenology of Spirit*, Oxford, Oxford University Press, trans. A.V. Miller.
Kant, (1991) *Kant's Political Writings*, Cambridge, Cambridge University Press.
Tubbs (2000), 'From Reflective Practitioner to Comprehensive Teacher,' in *Educational Action Research*, vol. 8, no. 1.
Tubbs, N. (2003) 'Return of the Teacher', *Educational Theory and Philosophy*, 37:1.

CHAPTER 3

HEIDEGGER: BEING AND TIME

Heidegger's phenomenology offers a version of philosophy's higher education that appears to have all the qualities of the notion with none of its metaphysical presuppositions. This makes Heidegger not only Hegel's greatest adversary but also a particular challenge to philosophy's higher education as we are presenting it. Heideggerian philosophy can offer all of the negative aspects of higher education, struggle, service, self-sacrifice, loss, movement, a spiritual recognition of the contingent truth of the individual and, above all, a phenomenological journey into the being and essence of 'the question'. It does so seemingly by exposing both the intellectual prejudices of 'conceptual' thinking and of dialectical or circular thinking. Both, he says, fail to acknowledge the priority of Dasein[1] that is the condition of their possibility. From this critique Heidegger is able to offer a philosophy of higher education that, whilst holding onto the spiritual significance of learning, discards the illegitimate presupposition of 'logic' and frees learning to be genuinely itself. Heideggerian learning claims the universality of authentic relation as Being, rendering all other claims for universality, authenticity and relation, including that of dialectical and speculative relation, as a suppression of that fundamental relation of Being.

Being, for Heidegger, is not a self-relation in the sense in which it has thus far been part of philosophy's higher education. The relation of Being is not a 'self', it is Being and Time. Ultimately, as we will see, this is the crucial difference between Heideggerian phenomenology and philosophy's higher education. Both have difficult notions of the 'self' but the differences between the two versions reveal the violence implicit in an education that usurps its own law. To try and understand this difference we will explore not only the phenomenology of *Being and Time* but also the philosophy of education, particularly the question of learning that Heidegger offers both in 1933 and in 1951-2. It is in the realm of education that the implications for learning of the assimilation of metaphysics into the nothing of Dasein become apparent. But let us be clear here. A great deal is at stake in this comparison. Philosophy's higher education as we are exploring it will collapse if it cannot prove itself to commend the absolute for a self-negating consciousness against the immediate claims of Being as already the conditions of all possibility. This is the crux of the clash in particular between Hegel and Heidegger—'what calls for learning?'—or, the same, how is necessity?[2] If Being is all, then necessity belongs to Being as its own possibility. But if Being is only

49

the misrecognition of itself as possibility, then necessity lies in the misrecognition. To the victor go the spoils of philosophy's higher education.

The structure of our discussion is as follows. First, to examine what Heidegger says of learning in 1951, then to relate that to the discussion of the nothing in 1929, which will, in turn, take us back to *Being and Time*. I then argue that the claims of *Being and Time*, related now to 'the question' and to 'what calls for learning', reveal their import in the philosophy of higher education that Heidegger offers from 1933-4. In particular, the whole of Heideggerian philosophy is epitomised within the teacher/student relation and within the claims for the Being of the teacher. I argue that not only for Heideggerian higher education but for Heideggerian Being and phenomenology as a whole, the necessity of philosophy's higher education becomes the desperate yearning for a God, or for the self-negation in relation to the other that Being eschews throughout Heidegger's writing.

1. THINKING, LEARNING, BEING.

At a time when recruitment and retainment of teachers in England is proving so difficult, let us imagine for a moment a Heideggerian campaign to meet this challenge. It would be a campaign that conjoined the career and a 'calling'. It would offer a vision of teaching that embodied service to others, service to society as a whole, and service to truthful being. In addition it would find the truth of the teacher to consist in humility, anxiety and difficulty, but also in courage, resoluteness and anticipation always of the way in which learning, for the teacher as for the student, is an end in itself, or the very being of Being. We will quote Heidegger at length here to gain an impression of how inspiring his vision of the work of the teacher is.

> Teaching is more difficult than learning. We know that; but we rarely think about it. And why is teaching more difficult than learning? Not because the teacher must have a larger store of information and have it always ready. Teaching is more difficult than learning because what teaching calls for is this: to let learn. Indeed, the proper teacher lets nothing else be learned than – learning. His conduct therefore often produces the impression that we really learn nothing from him, if by 'learning' we now automatically understand merely the procurement of useful information. The teacher is ahead of his apprentices in this alone, that he still has far more to learn than they— he has to learn to let them learn. The teacher must be capable of being more teachable than the apprentices. The teacher is far less sure of his material than those who learn are of theirs. If the relation between the teacher and learners is genuine, therefore, there is never a place in it for the authority of the know-it-all or the authoritative sway of the official. It still is an exalted matter, then, to become a teacher—which is something else entirely than becoming a famous professor (1993: 379-80).

What a beautiful passage, resonant with philosophy's higher education as we are presenting it throughout this book. It defines teaching as learning, teacher as learner, and knows their conjunction to be difficult, and the difficulty, precisely, to be the learning. It shows how the purpose of education and therefore of the teacher is not to fill students with knowledge, but to let them learn and, most importantly, to let them learn learning itself. It highlights the necessary humility of the teacher, for the success of his teaching will not seem to reflect on him at all. But this humility is part of being the teacher who knows himself to be a learner— for he knows that he will learn of his pupils' success as their leaving him. In this, the teacher must above all be teachable and this teachability alone must be his only authority.[3]

Is this, then, not our learning individual seen in the previous chapter? There seems to be no important distinction between the educational relationship of the master and slave seen above, and Heidegger's teachable teacher. In both, the identity falls to the movement that is learning. In both, there is some kind of negative recognition that one only does education authentically when one is fully 'done' by education. In both, there seems to be a shared perspective that the teacher who learns must understand himself negatively. As Hegel might commend education as a spiritual struggle, so Heidegger says that learning and education are our being drawn into the draft or current that is produced by the withdrawal of that which would end our learning, that is, any kind of abstract certainties and identities.

Surely both Heidegger and Hegel could be employed in the same campaign to regenerate the call to teaching, finding in it the most fundamental truths for both practitioners and their students? They are defining teaching as the most authentic expression of the enhancement of life against all the forces (different though they are for Heidegger and Hegel) that seek to suppress or misrepresent the significance of life itself. No wonder then that the campaign might appeal to young warriors prepared to stand and work 'in the storm' (Wolin, 1993: 39) of modern and post-modern anxieties and dilemmas.

In the same essay that Heidegger extols the virtue of learning and of the teacher, he explores how this notion of learning is connected to thinking and how, together, they open for us an understanding of learning and thinking as 'calling'. This too would be an important notion to use in the campaign for teachers as it might retrieve the idea of teaching as a vocation. He makes the phenomenological case that thinking and learning are a calling in the sense that they set something in motion, they call something to happen and that what they call to happen are themselves. To know thinking as this self-possibility (not Heidegger's phrase) is already to have learned learning to be the calling, and to have learned learning is to know thinking itself as the calling. The calling to become a teacher in this sense then would be none other than thinking of thought as Being. Equally, the calling by a teacher to his pupils—'learn from me'—is not in this sense a command over against the pupil, or any kind of heteronomous domination. It is rather, 'an anticipatory reaching out for something that is reached by our call, through our calling' (Krell, 1993: 386). The call of the teacher is not just to his own thinking being, it is to the anticipation of the thinking being of others. What prevents his dominating them is that what the teacher calls, or points towards, withdraws from him. As he is drawn towards that which withdraws so this is his learning about that which he has called to learn. The withdrawal of the student is the learning, the education, of the teacher. (We will see later in this chapter how the withdrawal of the student represents the positing of illusory being in Heidegger.)

The same phenomenology applies to thinking as to learning. Heidegger argues that when we ask what it is that is called thinking, we are already part of the possibility not so much of the answer, but of the possibility that is already the question. As we will see in a moment, the nature of the 'of' here is what is at stake between Hegel and Heidegger. Heidegger says,

> It is we ourselves to whom the question 'what is called thinking—what calls for thinking?' is addressed directly. We ourselves are in the text and texture of the question. The question 'what calls on us to think?' has already drawn us into the issue in question. We ourselves are, in the strict sense of the word, put in question by the question. The question 'what calls on us to think?' strikes us directly, as a lightning bolt. Asked in this way, the question 'what calls for thinking?' does more than merely struggle with an object, in the manner of a scientific problem (Krell, 1993: 385).

Thus thinking is already learning and learning is already thinking. Heidegger argues here that thinking is thought provoking, not only, as it were, in being thinking but, as learning, also being what is thought about. The questions 'what is called thinking' and 'what is called learning' are here the one question, viz. what is the possibility that is already the question? Most thinking he infers proceeds without us ever being able to think, for we do it 'without thinking'. It is this negative aspect of thinking which is really most thought provoking for it provokes thinking to do itself, that is, *with* thinking, or with a certain awareness and learning about what is happening. Such provocation, says Heidegger, requires a kind of leap from not thinking properly into the question wherein the possibility of thinking lies. This leap is towards that which, even in the question, withdraws. As Heidegger also says of the question 'what is the nothing', 'our very first approach to this question has something unusual about it' (Krell, 1993:96). This is because to ask of thinking, or learning, or of the nothing is to ask of that which in the asking has withdrawn, has turned away, and to which, now, we can only point. With the nothing, by asking of something, 'the question deprives itself of its own object' (Krell, 1993: 96). As such, says Heidegger, 'every answer to this question is also impossible from the start. For it necessarily assumes the form: the nothing 'is' this or that. With regard to the nothing, question and answer alike are inherently absurd' (Krell, 1993: 97). Similarly, with thinking or learning, the withdrawal of thinking from its own question is the being of thinking, but not in any way that the 'reigning and never-challenged doctrine of "logic"' (Krell, 1993: 97) can make sense of. In learning thinking, and in thinking learning we need, says Heidegger, 'to brush the intellect aside' (Krell, 1993: 97) such that our leap 'takes us abruptly to a place where everything is different... [and] what the leap takes us to will confound us' (Krell, 1993: 377). Our leap therefore is out of science (logic) and into thinking so that we may learn the possibility of the Being of 'thinking'.

So, how is the leap also the possibility of thinking? It is so, says Heidegger, because

> What withdraws may even concern and claim man more essentially than anything present that strikes and touches him. Being struck by actuality is what we like to regard as constitutive of the actuality of the actual. However, in being struck by what is actual, man may be debarred precisely from what concerns and touches him— touches him in the surely mysterious way of escaping him by its withdrawal. The event of withdrawal could be what is most present throughout the present, and so inherently exceed the actuality of everything actual (Krell, 1993: 374).

Written in 1951-2, there is nothing here to contradict the longer phenomenological exploration undertaken in 1927 in *Being and Time*, and we will return to that treatise in a moment. Heidegger goes on to describe the 'relation' between our question and what withdraws as a being drawn into the current or draught produced by the withdrawal. Man, pointing or drawn toward that which falls away, where pointing is being drawn into the draft, or being called, is a sign towards something, but is a sign 'without interpretation' (Krell, 1993: 375). This open-endedness of questioning and learning makes Heidegger's phenomenology attractive to those who wish to combat the seemingly closed and totalizing narrative of the logos. It is the 'without interpretation' which now brings us back to Heidegger's notion of learning, for that which withdraws can only be learned about truly as its possibility, or as Being. It cannot be finally interpreted because 'arrival' is only a prejudice of the intellect. As the cabinetmaker learns from the wood what slumbers within it, so the teacher must learn about learning from his non-arrival and his lack of interpretation, or closure, of the student. In the question in which thinking is, nothing else is presupposed as known—not teacher, nor student.

So far so good? But when we examine this educational philosophy in practice the phenomenological sleight of hand that it conceals becomes clearer. We will postpone this discussion however. Thus far we have worked back from 1951-2 to 1929. In the following section we will take this model of thinking and learning to *Being and Time* itself to see how all of these ideas of thinking, learning, calling, withdrawal and the leap have their origin in this seminal phenomenological work.

Only then will we return to 1933, to Heidegger's pronouncements on education and to their necessary distinction from philosophy's higher education and its learning individual.

2. WHAT IS THE QUESTION?

Heidegger asserts the educational credentials of Dasein at the beginning of his great work *Being and Time*. Dasein says Heidegger, is the entity that exists as its own question, or which has itself as its own issue. To ask about the meaning of this question 'demands that we look that question in the face' (1992: 23) and recognise that the question is already a particular comportment of Being towards itself as an entity. There is no abstract beginning from which to carry out such an enquiry. The enquiry itself is already the being of Being, or 'is'. As such, and this is what is at stake in the whole of *Being and Time,* Being is already its own conceptual crisis, it is its own difference from itself. *In Identity and Difference* (published in 1957) Heidegger asserts that this 'ontological difference' is 'different' from Hegel's in that whereas Hegel's absolute reconciles being and Being, 'for us, formulated in a preliminary fashion, the matter of thinking is the difference *as* difference' (Heidegger, 1969: 47). It is this claim of identity by Heidegger that ultimately leads to the erasure of difference altogether, which as we will see below has disastrous consequences for the teacher of Dasein and for Heideggerian higher education.

   Being and Time takes up the challenge of thinking the ontological difference as a mode of Being. This is its phenomenological form, a thinking *of* the Being of enquiry *as* the Being which is enquiry. For Heidegger this is not a circular argument because he is not presupposing Being in his enquiry. On the contrary his enquiry (as *Being and Time* will show) 'belongs to the essential constitution (*Verfassung*) of Dasein itself' (1992: 28). Presupposition is replaced here by the way that Dasein is its own possibility, and which becomes available as a concept for the first time. One of Heidegger's most powerful insights, taken up in and as the significance of hermeneutics in social theory, is that a question, any question, is already a kind of understanding, already conditioned by and upon a pre-emptively understood horizon of meaning. Heidegger says, 'in the question of the meaning of Being there is no "circular reasoning" but rather a remarkable "relatedness backward or forward" where what we are asking about (Being) bears to the inquiry itself as a mode of Being of an entity' (1992: 28). In the difference of Being being itself 'something like a priority of Dasein has announced itself' (1992: 28).

   The first phenomenological discovery for Dasein in investigating itself, then, is its difference from entities which are merely 'present-at-hand'. Whilst the latter are 'in' the world as things and in a sense sit alongside each other on the surface of the world, Dasein's 'Being-in-the-world' is its own existence in which it resides not on the surface of an external world but 'at home', or in Being being itself. To be, for Dasein, is already to be in-the-world, a world which is already that mode of Being as an entity. But, at first, being-in-the-world is misrecognised by a Dasein which does not know that its enquiry is already the Being of the world as an entity. Instead, Dasein takes the world at face value and takes its experience of the world to be as a relationship between subject and object (1992: 85). This 'inappropriate interpretation... becomes the "evident" point of departure for problems of epistemology or the "metaphysics of knowledge"' (1992: 86). In such ways of thinking says Heidegger, 'the question of the kind of Being which belongs to this knowing subject is left entirely unasked' (1992: 87). This question, Dasein's own issue, belongs to the Dasein for whom Being-in-the-world is necessary *a priori* (1992: 79), a Dasein which lives not on the world alongside other things, but in and alongside the Being of the world itself. Unlike the metaphysics of knowledge or epistemology, when Dasein says 'I am', it is not a subjective statement in relation to an external world, it is a statement in which Being resides and 'comports itself understandingly towards that Being' (1992: 78).

Because Dasein is Being-in-the-world, the world itself is always pre-understood. What this means is that Being in the world is necessarily already the work of Being-in-the-world. But the two are easily mistaken. Heidegger argues that tools and equipment in the world appear 'ready to hand' but are the result of a prior involvement in which the use (or the 'towards which') of the equipment has been previously assigned. But Dasein's involvement, unlike equipment (and, as Heidegger sees it, epistemology and metaphysics of knowledge) is not some kind of hidden relation. On the contrary, Dasein's involvement is its own Being, its own issue. 'To Dasein's Being an understanding of Being belongs. Any understanding has its Being in an act of understanding' (1992: 118). This involvement of Dasein is not an involvement of Being with itself in relation to an external world. This involvement is the involvement, the being of Being, when it is already Being-in-the-world. This 'relational totality,' (1992: 120) says Heidegger, is the significance of Being-in-the-world as Dasein's 'own act of understanding' (1992: 120). Dasein's Being is that it 'has always submitted itself already to a "world" which it encounters, and this submission belongs essentially to its Being' (1992: 121). Dasein therefore is not an entity which exists in 'world-space'. The 'place' in which Dasein is, is the space which is 'involvement,' a space which Heidegger describes as Being-alongside. It lies in the very nature of Dasein as involvement always to have entities close by or 'de-severed' (1992: 139). The 'where' of the other entities is made possible by the involvement which is already the space which is Dasein or Being-in-the-world. 'Space is rather "in" the world in so far as space has been disclosed by that Being-in-the-world which is constitutive for

Dasein' (1992: 146). Or again, Dasein's 'primordial spatiality' (1992: 155-6) is existential not categorial.

The seductiveness of Dasein as the act of understanding which is its own involvement and issue is its character as 'care'. Because Dasein's Being is Being-in-the-world it is also a Being-with-others. Here others does not mean entities, things or equipment which Dasein distinguishes from itself. Rather, others for Heidegger are 'those from whom, for the most part, one does not distinguish oneself' (1992: 154). It is another constitutive characteristic of Dasein that one is 'with' others existentially not categorially. As such, this involvement with others is not 'humanistic' in the sense of a relation between individual subjects. The involvement is Being. Being-with-others is Dasein's Being at home with itself. The relation to others is something Being gives to itself, by itself, as itself. When the significance of Being as the home of the issue of Being is forgotten, or when involvement is misunderstood as between subjects, then Dasein is homeless. Humanism in its metaphysical form says Heidegger has come to express this homelessness not only by not posing the question 'concerning the truth of Being' but also by obstructing the question 'insofar as metaphysics persists in the oblivion of Being (Krell, 1993: 247). What is needed says Heidegger in his 'Letter on Humanism' is to 'redefine the meaning of the word' (Krell, 1993: 248) so that it 'contradicts all previous humanism' (Krell, 1993: 248). The concept of 'care' in *Being and Time* is just such a contradiction of the view that the essence of the 'human' lies in 'a merely terrestrial being' (Krell, 1993: 249). The involvement which is Dasein must be interpreted says Heidegger not as the concern for one subject by another but as the mode of Being in which they are already 'close by'. Dasein, which is Being-in-the-world and is already Dasein alongside others, 'must be interpreted in terms of the phenomenon of care, for as "care" the Being of Dasein in general is to be defined' (1992: 157). Dasein 'performs' its B(b)eing care when it is thrown away from itself. In this being thrown or falling away from itself Dasein 'does' or is Being. There is in care an authenticity of Dasein for what is thrown and what does the throwing are the same one constitution called care. This is the being of involvement which, as seen above, is Being-in-the-world or the pre-emptive understanding which lies beneath all other understandings.

There is here an educational significance to 'care'. As Dasein is that whose Being is its own question and whose issue is its own Being, so we can say that Dasein is care in that its Being is its (being) concern. To care is, for Dasein, the same as to enquire or learn. It is Being called thinking and learning. The space which is the question is the Being of care or the Being which is concern. As a questioning, 'learning Being Dasein' is fundamentally a caring Being where care is its own self-educating nature.

In its 'throwness' or 'falling away from itself' the Being of Dasein can find itself as a state of mind which 'understands' itself as its own possibility. This is a step up from the Dasein which is thrown into the public or average world of the 'they' as Heidegger puts it. In this 'everyday Being-among-one-another' where Dasein has neither found itself nor yet lost itself, is a way of Being which is 'of inauthenticity and failure to stand by one's self' (1992: 166). Everyone, says Heidegger, is the other and 'no one is himself' (1992: 165). What lies ahead for authentic Dasein is a 'clearing away of concealments and obscurities' (1992: 167) which prevent Dasein from submitting to its own throwness. Such a clearing away produces a space, a 'here', in which Dasein is also 'the clearing' (*Lichtung*) (1992: 171) or in which 'Dasein is its disclosedness' (1992: 171). Heidegger sees this clearing as available to Dasein as a state of mind. A 'mood' is the B(b)eing of how one 'is' and is the 'place' in which that Dasein finds itself at that moment. A state of mind is the 'throwness' of Dasein in which it is disclosed, or in which it is the 'there' of Dasein, a there or disclosure in which 'it finds itself' (1992: 174). 'Falling,' says Heidegger, 'is a definite existential characteristic of Dasein itself' (1992: 220). As such 'in a state of mind Dasein is always brought before itself and has always found itself, not in the sense of coming across itself by perceiving itself, but in the sense of finding itself in the mood that it has' (1992: 174). Any experiences which follow rely on the 'there' of the state of mind in which Dasein is disclosed as throwness. All such experience, all openness to the world, is already circumspective, that is, constitutive of the care which is already the Being-in-the-world. But when Dasein misses this, its own throwness, and surrenders to the world instead of to itself, then 'Dasein evades its very self' (1992: 178). What it evades is precisely the understanding which is already a constituent of its throwness or Being-in-the-world. Being 'there' is already to be understanding. Thus understanding in this sense is Dasein's own possibility, or, in Heidegger's terms, 'its ownmost potentiality for being' (1992: 183). It is therefore only in being thrown or in falling away from itself that Dasein is 'delivered over to the possibility of… finding itself again in its possibilities' (1992: 184), a possibility called understanding in which Dasein's projection says to itself 'Become what you are' (1992: 186). This possibility is not a 'point called the "self,"' (1992: 187) it is the full disclosedness of Dasein being the mode of Being which is understanding, a disclosedness which Heidegger later describes as the truth and the untruth of the thrown Dasein which 'is "in the truth"' (1992: 263).

However, this Being understanding is always likely to misrecognise its ownmost Being as Dasein and become an understanding of everything which lies alongside it ready-at-hand, instead of becoming what it is, or being its own possibility. As a collector of the knowledge of entities which it encounters, like Plato's cave dwellers, or as a raconteur of 'idle talk' in the capacity of the public 'they', Dasein is always losing sight of itself and becoming alienated from itself as its own possibility. In a wonderful insight Heidegger notes that this alienating tranquillity which closes Dasein off from its authenticity and possibility is not an alienation from certainty but from uncertainty, from the throwness of a Dasein which loses itself. The alienation of this tranquillity is that it closes Dasein off from 'the possibility of genuinely foundering' (1992: 222). It is, however, as we will see below, precisely this insight into 'genuinely' foundering which is suppressed when care comes to be interpreted as temporality. What is characterised as 'turbulence' (1992: 223) in terms of space becomes, in part two of *Being and Time*, the 'resolute anticipation' and 'anxiety' of (Being as) Time.

3. WHEN IS THE QUESTION?

If part one of *Being and Time* discloses that the 'whole' of Dasein is an existential 'Being-there' in which understanding and throwness are Dasein's ownmost 'space', part two tries to reveal the 'when' of Dasein. When is this space called Being-there? When, that is, is care its own possibility? Or again, if Dasein is constituted as its own issue, when is this learning and thinking? When is the question?

At the end of part one of *Being and Time* Heidegger makes some dramatic admissions about the nature of Dasein. In its disclosedness, where it is closest to itself as thrown from itself, lies truth as a mode of Being. But this possibility of Dasein performs a dual function. Disclosure also covers up, in that Being-in-the-world is hidden under Being and the world. So its truth and its untruth coexist as the 'truth' that Dasein, by the very fact that there is something rather than nothing[4], must presuppose. This truth, says Heidegger, is 'the ontological condition for the possibility that assertions can be either true or false' (1992: 269). That 'there is' (il y a/ es gibt) anything at all presupposes a self-disclosing Dasein and as such 'all truth is relative to Dasein's Being' (1992: 270). Finally, therefore, even though truth is an ontological (not metaphysical) condition of uncovering, it has a transcendental status for Heidegger in that '"in itself" it is quite incomprehensible why entities are to be uncovered and why truth and Dasein must be' (1992: 271).

The intention behind part two, announced very early in *Being and Time,* is to show that temporality is 'the meaning of the Being of that entity which we call "Dasein"' (1992: 38). What Heidegger then proceeds to argue is that the being-there of Dasein is not only the space which is its own possibility, but that possibility is also the Being-there of Time. Dasein is both 'in' time as time is ordinarily understood and it is temporality *per se*. As such, Dasein has 'historicality' as its own determinate character. It is in itself the unity of past, present and future, a unity which includes their inauthentic appearance apart from each other.

The temporality of care discloses itself in relation to death although for Heidegger this is not a 'relation'. When Dasein faces death, then possibility is face to face with itself. This is because in facing death possibility is its own issue. The possibility of no-possibility is as pure an issue as Dasein can be for itself. Anxiety is that state of mind of this Dasein. With anxiety 'there is' the Dasein which has been thrown towards its end or towards death, a throwness which is its own possibility. To be possibility it must also face itself as impossibility. This is the 'ownmost' being of care and it is the kind of Being of Dasein 'in which Dasein, *as Dasein*, can be a *whole*' (1992: 303). Heidegger calls this 'throwness towards itself' *anticipation*. Anticipation is determinative of the 'there is' of care's own possibility. Anticipation of death, or throwness towards its own end, is, says Heidegger, 'what first makes this possibility possible, and sets it free as possibility' (1992: 307). This possibility of possibility Heidegger calls 'authentic existence' (1992: 307) in that 'Dasein discloses itself to itself' and in which 'its very Being is the issue' (1992: 307).

The relation between Dasein and death is not therefore a relation between two different entities, it is the 'relational totality' (1992: 120) or the 'significance' (1992: 120) of possibility. It is possibility's own possibility. There are no relations external to the house of Being for all anticipation is in the home of Being. The problem with this, as we will see below, is that this immediate total relation of non-relation, the family of Being, asserts itself over all experiences which represent Being as other than itself.[5]

Anticipation, then, discloses Dasein in its totality. This totality discloses Dasein to be constituted by guilt. It is guilty because as possibility it is 'nothing'. Indeed, it is doubly nothing. It is guilty in the interpretation of its own Being that possibility is a not-yet, a nothing, and it is guilty that it is also the basis of that possibility. Throwness is not only the nullity of possibility; it is the null basis of that possibility or nullity. 'Care itself, in its very essence, is permeated with nullity though and through... This means that Dasein as such is guilty' (1992: 331). But there is an 'ontological source' (1992: 332) of this nullity which according to Heidegger lays undiscovered. Conscience calls this Being-guilty back from its falleness, back to itself as the totality which is care or back to itself as its own issue. This call amounts to a challenge to Dasein to stand firm in the anxiety of anticipation so that it does not flee this throwness but remains resolute in its difficulty. In other words, the call of conscience to itself by a Dasein whose possibility is nullity is a call to *anticipatory resoluteness*. In being resolutely anticipatory Dasein does not flee the difficulty of its being a nullity, it faces up to itself by continuing to anticipate, continuing to be thrown towards its end. In so doing, resoluteness says Heidegger 'appropriates untruth authentically' (1992: 345) because it discloses the Being-in of every situation. He notes therefore that the call of conscience calls us into the situation by calling us back from it to a resolute anticipation. Falleness into the world and the call back from the world are both equiprimordial characteristics of a resolute care, or authentic care.

Anticipatory resoluteness is not only authentic Being-there in terms of space. The 'where' of possibility or care corresponds to the 'when' in that anticipatory resoluteness is also temporality. Resoluteness, in the disclosure of Dasein, reveals its nullity 'as something constant' (1992; 353). When anticipation is resolute this is the constancy of possibility or the disclosure of possibility as possibility. As Heidegger says, 'when Dasein is resolute it takes over authentically in its existence the fact that it is the null basis of its own nullity' (1992: 354). Put another way, anticipatory resoluteness becomes, constantly, its own guilt which it then 'holds open' so that the Being-there of every situation can be disclosed. But how can resolute anticipation be said to be 'constant'? Heidegger begins to answer this question by suggesting that authentic resoluteness 'resolves to keep repeating itself' (1992: 355). Such a repetition means that Dasein will repeatedly heed the call back to its own throwness and that the constancy of this heeding is precisely the constancy of anticipatory resoluteness. Such a constancy is the certainty of constant possibility where 'anticipation brings Dasein face to face with a possibility which is constantly certain' (1992: 356). The significance of this constant possibility, or, as we might say, of the certain possibility of possibility, is that it produces 'an unshakeable joy' (1992: 358) at its authentic totality.

Constancy of possibility is imbued with temporality. Care is ahead-of-itself in that it is thrown forwards towards itself. In this sense care is futural. Also, care in being thrown is already fallen, an 'already' in which care is essentially not futural but a having-been. Finally, care is Being alongside or present in its encounters with entities in the world. Just as spatially this Being 'ahead-of-itself—Being-already-in (a world) as Being alongside' (1992: 364) is the disclosure of the 'space' which is the totality of possibility so, also, it is the temporality of the same totality. Past, present and future for Heidegger are inauthentic conceptions of ordinary time which fallen Dasein seizes upon. But for the Dasein which is called back and which is constant anticipatory resoluteness, those 'moments' collapse into the constancy of temporal possibility (1992: 37). Heidegger states

> The character of 'having been' arises from the future and in such a way that the future which 'has been' (or better which is in the process of having been) releases itself from the Present. This phenomenon has the unity of a future which makes present in the process of having been; we designate it as 'temporality' (1992: 374).

It is as temporality that Dasein's authenticity is revealed as care for care is the totality of the already-having-been (past) of anticipation (future) which is Being alongside (present). Ordinary conceptions of time have their origin in this primordial temporality. Not just past, present and future, but immanent, transcendent, subjective and objective time (1992: 374) are all modes of the Being of temporality. Our ordinary conceptions of time are, in this sense, the Being of temporality as Time.

In a way, the past and future modes of care have already been explicated by Heidegger. The past is the mode of Being which finds itself as that which has already been thrown. Here Dasein's possibility is its own possibility as a result of what has already happened. The future is the same as this past. It is the truth of this possibility as its own potential. Replacing past and future and trying to avoid misrecognising care as constituted by ordinary time, Heidegger argues that 'the primordial unity of the structure of care' (1992: 375), its Being-in-the-world, is disclosed in its character of being 'before' and 'already' (1992: 376). The possibility which is Dasein as care is both already itself and before itself. These are the same, for to be already itself is to be its possibility, and to be before itself is also to be its possibility. *When*, then, are they the same?

To answer this question Heidegger turns to the question of constancy. 'When is' the constancy of possibility, or 'when is' the certain possibility of possibility? Two answers suggest themselves. First, the question 'when is constancy possible' can be answered by removing the question mark. Thus 'when' *is* the constancy of possibility, or, to say the same thing, Time is temporality and temporality is Time. This first suggested answer is akin to the idea mentioned above that resolute anticipation resolves to repeat itself, for here it could be said that Time is the constant repetition of temporality as its own 'constancy' of possibility. But here repetition or resoluteness can mean two very different things. It could, on the one hand, mean the repetition of a will-to-power which, in Time, is always opposing itself. Here, *ressentiment* against what has been and what must be again is a moment of *ressentiment* which, whilst inevitable, equally inevitably must collapse. Nietzsche says 'yes' to himself as a 'No-sayer', or temporally, the will-to-power is always eternal return. But Nietzsche's yes-saying to all such moments of *ressentiment* has a subjective significance and actuality that is suppressed in Heidegger's yes-saying. The time of Nietzsche is never 'now' for 'now' is the overcoming of will-to-power that must itself be overcome. This is Zarathustra.[6] But Heidegger's 'now' eschews its own overcoming.

The second answer for Heidegger has resolute Dasein as the constancy of already and before, or as 'there' 'in the "moment of vision" (*Augenblick*) as regards the situation that has been disclosed' (1992: 376). This moment of vision is a unity of the ecstatic moments of future, past and present in and as temporality. In other words, temporality, or authentic care, is not an entity; it is the Being of Time 'outside of' itself. 'Temporality is the primordial "outside-of-itself" in and for itself' (1992: 377). Or, we might say, Dasein as the authentic totality of care, is the unity of past, present and future, or is the total Being of Time. The title of Heidegger's treatise now moves. No longer are we dealing with Being *and* Time. Now, in the unification of the moment of vision, Being *is* Time and Time *is* Being.

Or, to put it another way, when the 'and' of Being and Time is lost to the unity of Being Time, then the law of learning and the learning of law that is the necessity of the difficult relation is suppressed, and indeed, usurped.[7] Whilst Zarathustra has a book IV in which this unity is again re-cognised as misrecognition, Heidegger remains on the mountain dancing and singing to the ring of rings.

The Dasein that understands the Being-there, the Being in Time and the Time in Being of every situation, gains for a 'moment' a 'mastery over the everyday' (1992: 422). This mastery gains for itself an understanding of the authentic future (1992: 388) as already contained in its own history. This Dasein is already its future and will be its past. It is, in the moment of vision, the unification of possibility with itself. Heidegger calls this resoluteness a repetition (1992: 388) and in one sense it is. This ecstatic unification repeats possibility, and asserts its constancy. It repeats the assertion that the truth of potentiality, of possibility, is the presence of the past and future in *this* Dasein. But such a repetition is assertion precisely because it is freed from the one condition that has, all along, been the condition of its own constant possibility. This ecstatic understanding of Being Time, or Being-possibility, is not subject to itself as its own law, its own necessity, and is now free, for example, to align itself with or identify itself as the authentic possibility or constancy of a people, a race, a nation, or any collective form of Being that it chooses. 'Now' it can assert itself as the Being of history. Disastrously for Dasein, in becoming the constancy of possibility it is no longer even its own potential. 'Now' possibility is no longer the educational significance of learning as care. 'Now' possibility is at an end which is not its own, or is (very) care-less.

We might be tempted to say here that Dasein as its ownmost authentic possibility can be separated from the movement of its unification, or from the moment of *ressentiment* against life itself. If Being were temporality wherein the now is also overcome, would this Being be care-ful? The answer to this question is also 'no'. It is to this no that Zarathustra teaches us to say yes. No to the now and no to the overcoming of the now are both, for the yes-sayer, the eternal return of will-to-power. Dasein, from the very beginning, has no way of opposing itself in the way that will to power, dialectic and experience do. Whilst the latter are 'self' as this opposition, Dasein, even as the question, is already structured in such a way that it cannot say no to itself. Dasein as such is amoral. It is not beyond good and evil; it just isn't good and evil. And, unable to say no, its yes is not its own, or is not yes to itself as good 'and' evil.

The implication here, I hope, is clear. Part I of *Being and Time* needs part II because the structure of care in part I is without the actual significance or actuality of throwness. This actuality is the anticipatory resoluteness of Dasein or its constancy. The constancy of this anticipation is Being as Time. But the separation of Being from Time in parts I and II has its own significance. Far from 'brushing the intellect aside', part I abstracts possibility or the 'already' from its own lived necessity and then, intellectually, has to try and re-insert this actuality in part II as Time. Part II is Heidegger's version of actuality, but it is an actuality freed from the domination of contingency, or necessity, that it claims as its own. Here Heidegger has to claim that Being *is* Time in order to retrieve a lived significance for care. We should not be surprised therefore that this lived significance or actuality for Heidegger is destiny. It was indeed the 'fate' of care, separated from time in part I, to have to reassert itself 'in the world' in part II. But such a separation from the world can only be repaired by a forced reconciliation. For Heidegger that forced reconciliation is the actuality of Dasein as destiny or as the disclosure of anticipation towards death as a collective mood, the anxiety (or spirit) of a people or a community. The constancy of care is not individual; it is in the historical community. 'Dasein's fateful destiny in and with its "generation" goes to make up the full authentic historizing of Dasein' (1992: 436). Lacking the mediation of actuality in part I, Dasein is free violently to overlook the world as object for-us and to assimilate it into the non-mediated relational totality that is the phenomenology of care. Has there been a more violent assertion of lived significance in western philosophy than Dasein's assertion of care as the collective constancy of the community?

4. PROPERTY OF DASEIN

Rose's recent critique of Heidegger (1984) focuses not on Dasein but on the Event (*Das Ereignis*). She finds in the latter that which we have described above regarding the former, that it contains the assertion of Being Time or of being the happening which is present as (someone's) history. As Dasein in *Being and Time* is the being-there of past, present and future in the moment of vision which has those ecstasies as its own, so, in the Event, man and Being are delivered over to their shared identity. At the heart of Rose's critique of Heidegger is the way in which he imports property relations into his fundamental concepts and tries to mask their work or representation by assertions of a special kind of binding. *Contra* Husserl, Heidegger posits a concept of Time where its separation into outer (flow) and inner (measurement) has not occurred. That separation is itself based on a prior division for Heidegger, one of events as completed and incomplete. Events are incomplete in their duration in time, they are imperfect. Events are completed in their change of place in time, i.e., what has happened is 'now' finished. For Rose, as for Hegel and Nietzsche, when we 'have' an event, or when we 'perfect what is present' (1984: 56) what we are actually doing is 'putting it in the past, attributing properties to it, and then re-presenting it as an image, as a presence in space' (1984: 56). But Heidegger seeks to circumscribe events as having properties by events as 'being history'.

This circumscription, says Rose, is achieved in *das Ereignis* even though its translation as the Event *of* appropriation undoes what Heidegger seeks to claim for the Event. Heidegger's Event, argues Rose, posits itself as both duration and perfection, as continuous and completed. As such, complete within itself as Being Time it 'connotes identity without representation, property without having, and completion without reflection of a point in time' (1984: 58). The result is that the political significance of time as property is lost to a phantasmagoria of Dasein in which, just as in the phantasmagoria of commodity fetishism, it is the distortion of relation or property which sustains the illusion. Even more fundamentally for Rose, the courtroom where reason tries its own authority is never opened by Heidegger whose Event, lacking the actuality or concept of itself as illusion, defies the legal nature of its claims. As a result, says Rose, Heidegger has, unknown to himself, claimed for the Event the properties of the 'Event of events' (1984: 78) wherein Being is triadic, an eternity whose presence is past, present and future, and which redeems the latter in the former by being present. But Heidegger's Event is not triadic. He offers us the Event as 'I am I' but not the relationship between God and man, that is, the law. 'Heidegger seems to have given us Yahweh without Torah: the event seems to include advent and redemption, presence and owning, but not the giving of the law on Mount Sinai, and its repeated disowning' (1984: 80).

Rose concludes that Heidegger proffers 'a law without legalism', or a framing of law as event which is not actually lived by us, not our law. Heidegger's philosophy becomes, therefore, 'a characterless, empty infinity,' (1984: 82) one which offers no dispute, no representation of the relations of the representations of presence and owning (intuition and concept), no recognition of misrecognition, no judgement of judgement and no spiritual struggle. As such it is a suppression of philosophy's higher education. Rose's interpretation of the Event, however, is within this higher education. The Event is that which 'gathers people together into each other's presence over something (sic) which concerns them' (1984: 63). This gathering, the Event, is already a litigious space, and is the reconstruction or representation of its own possibility and necessity, its own 'time'. The concern of Dasein, which is law without legalism, becomes in Rose's interpretation of the Event, the concern with things, which is both the event of legal dispute and the event of law. Similarly, the 'time' of Dasein which in Heidegger is its own Being, in Rose becomes the time of law, and the time of law is antinomical precisely because it cannot be and is not appropriated. The question of appropriation is the time of law, not of authentic Being. What Heidegger has refused which Rose is retrieving here is Dasein's own utmost possibility as its own necessity. The question of the time of law for Rose is the time of the court proceedings, a time which does not 'have' its own 'perfect' beginning and end except as it is represented in the dispute over precisely the nature of such a possession. 'This antinomical history of the subject is the Event which has led an unknown judge to open proceedings in the critical court: it explains why... everyone's status is so confused, and why [such] a court... cannot reach a conclusion or complete its proceedings' (1984: 65). Rose describes her speculative interpretation of the legal event of the law as a 'self-perficient nihilism' (1984: 69) which represents itself, and thus is its own event of law in law, or, which is to say the same thing, is its own event or moment of time in time. For both of these, law and time, the Event represents the disowning of that 'which is to be owned' (1984: 69). Nietzsche's will to power still lives 'in the opposition between will and representation' (1984: 71) says Rose. This self-perficient nihilism

> becomes a new moralism: it concerns a conscience which, consciously willing what it previously disowned as its willing, overcomes and absolves what was a bad conscience in willing; but this good conscience still lives in the opposition between will and representation, between denying and affirming values (1984: 71).

But Heidegger's nihilism 'perfects time not the will' (1984: 77) and as such is propertyless, literally nothing, nihilism. She concludes that

> Heidegger takes us so far away from the antinomy of law, of theoretical and practical reason, of knowledge and ethics, that this 'place' in which we are de-posited is irrelevant to a life which is lived, understood and transformed in and through that antinomy (1984: 83).

5. BRUSHING THE INTELLECT ASIDE

Our critique of Heidegger thus far is that his phenomenology suppresses the social and political relation of the object, and as such, philosophy itself. Variously this accounts for Heidegger's assertion that Being is not a self-relation, is not a category of the intellect, is not a categorial 'other', and is not a property of the *logos*. Similarly from this suppression comes the claim in Heidegger's phenomenology that Dasein is its own possibility as the throwness of care and of temporality where the 'of' is not proprietorial but rather an ontological bonding that has priority over other perceived or intellectually constructed relations. This critique now leads us to see how Heidegger's educational philosophy can encompass both the teacher whose own being is 'to let learn' (Krell, 1993: 380) and the Rector for whom this learning teaches that 'the Führer alone is the present and future German reality and its law' (Wolin, 1993:47). It also enables us to discuss the difference between Heidegger's higher education and philosophy's higher education.

Heidegger's speeches made between 1933-4 together with the lecture notes and other sources show how his philosophical and educational thinking are explicitly the one perspective, resolutely anticipating its own historical Dasein. The seduction of resolute Dasein as a version of philosophy's higher education is that authentic Being demands self-sacrifice in so many ways. It requires 'what is called thinking' in order to overcome or sacrifice the mis-thinking that is the humanistic self. It requires thinking and learning to be recognised as the work of Being, and it requires service to the community through the learning and education that is the question. His speeches of 1933-4 invoke a spiritual mission, a call to conscience back from the falleness of the 'They' to the authentic mode of Being Time. He calls for individuals to devote themselves to working in the service of Being Time, be it military, labour or educational. Above all it calls for such work to seek to disclose 'the essence of all things' (Wolin, 1993: 33).

In specifically educational terms, Heidegger calls for knowledge to be made subservient to the thinking and learning, the Being, which is disclosed in the question. Such an education he admits will require 'new teachers' (Farias, 1989:146) whose questioning will be 'a marching ahead, sounding the future' (Farias, 1989: 147). This questioning will be radical in that 'questions are posed in opposition to those who hold the power' (Farias, 1989: 147). Questioning he says is not

> to serve those who have grown tired and their complacent yearning for comfortable answers. We know: the courage to question. To experience the abysses of existence and to endure the abysses of existence is in itself already a *higher* answer than any of the all-too-cheap answers afforded by artificial systems of thought (Wolin, 1993: 51).

And again, 'questioning will itself become the highest form of knowledge,' (Wolin 1993:33) a will to essence that will 'guarantee our *Volk* greatness' (Wolin, 1993: 34) and create a 'truly spiritual world' (Wolin, 1993: 33) that will release the powers and the forces which are 'rooted in the soil and blood of a *Volk*' (Wolin, 1993: 34).

On the one hand this will to essence is a will to 'the most constant and most uncompromising and harshest self-examination,' (Wolin, 1993: 29) requiring the courage of questioning that will put us 'in the midst of the uncertainty of the totality of being' (Wolin, 1993: 33), and 'in the most acute danger' (Wolin, 1993: 35-6), and which can only be embodied as Being in risk, struggle and work. To do so, is to 'will ourselves' (Wolin, 1993: 38) and for the *Volk* to 'fulfil its historical mission' (Wolin, 1993: 38). But, and on the other hand, these new teachers are imbued with more than anxiety, risk and uncertainty. They have as their own Being the certainty of the historical fulfilment that their teaching will now serve. They share the certainty of the fate that lies ahead for their students, that they will 'become a historical being in the state' (Farias, 1989: 145).

It is here, then, in Heidegger's educational philosophy that the implications seen above of the relationship between parts I and II of *Being and Time* now become very clear. Dasein, as care, is abstracted from actuality in part I and then equally abstractly is claimed as its own historical authenticity in part II. As such, it becomes now an absolute education which is 'of' contingency in that the latter is known, but not 'of' contingency such that the latter is allowed to be its *own* self-relating necessity. This absolute 'non-relation' of possibility and necessity permeates everything in Heidegger's educational philosophy from the teacher/student relationship to the content of Dasein's historicality as education. In this absolute non-relation Being is absolute and, having no master, is *all* master. Thus, in Heideggerian higher education, 'knowledge means: to be *master* of the situation into which we are placed' (Wolin, 1993: 58). This knowledge is the basis of new studies, new teachers and new students who together will 'consolidate this knowledge of the people in virtue of which they will become a historical being in the state' (Farias, 1989: 145). 'The struggle that is beginning is the struggle for the new Teacher and the new Führer of the university,' (Farias, 1989: 139) those for whom the moment of vision is their re-education regarding historical Dasein as Being and Time. It is the true comradeship found in the moment of vision that 'educates the Führers' (Farias, 1989: 145). Indeed, 'the Führer alone is the present and future German reality and its law' (Wolin, 1993: 47). In this 'jargon of authenticity' Heidegger summarizes his educational philosophy as 'learn to know ever more deeply: from now on every single thing demands decision, and every action responsibility' (Wolin, 1993: 47). He advocates this education as 'a spiritual will to serve,' (Wolin, 1993: 149) sacrificing the self for a genuine understanding of Being as this destiny, here and now, in the *Volk* and in the National Socialist revolution which will engender 'the total transformation of our German existence (Dasein)' (Wolin, 1993: 46).

Heidegger's association with National Socialism is well rehearsed. Its significance for our purposes lies in the way that the educational substance of Dasein is a deformed version of the actuality of the learning individual. This deformation lies in Heidegger's turning the absolute in education into a 'totally' finite historicality, a totality of Being and Time that can be its ownmost authentic possibility only by suppressing the otherness of the eternal that lies within the illusion of the 'and', or by suppressing philosophy's higher education *per se*.

Interestingly in this regard, Heidegger is more careful with the educational nature of Dasein in some of his later comments. In his letter of 1945, trying to explain some of his actions and views whilst Rector of the University of Freiburg (1933-4), he argued that his joining the National Socialist Party was to 'deepen and transform' (Wolin, 1993: 61) a number of its essential elements, thereby contributing 'to overcoming Europe's disarray and the crisis of the Western spirit' (Wolin, 1993: 62). This was to be undertaken from within the University, 'the locus of spiritual legislation' (Wolin, 1993: 62). But this vocation to re-educate students regarding 'the world of spirit' (Wolin, 1993: 66) says Heidegger, could not be reconciled with 'the political will of those in power' (Wolin, 1993: 63) and he resigned the Rectorship in 1934.

Even if it is true that by 1934 Heidegger had come to realise that the mastery of possibility by the German *Volk* was going to be deformed by the National Socialists, nevertheless Heidegger in this period retained the mastery of 'the moment of vision' outlined in *Being and Time* as the centrepiece of his ontological higher education. With or without the Party, this mastery found form in the *Führerprinzip*, and in the dissemblance of his concepts of labour, military and knowledge 'service'. It is this mastery that underpins his pedagogical claims that in the withdrawal of the student from the teacher, the teacher learns from the student, and which therefore is the intellectual defence for the study camp at Todnauberg. As 'the question deprives itself of its own object' (Krell, 1993: 96) in Heideggerian phenomenology, so it follows that the authentic learning of the teacher deprives itself of a student—an other—to dominate. Yet the withdrawal of the student is precisely the suppression of genuine leaning. Without the object of learning, without the slave for whom learning is negation, and without the student who can gain a mind of his own in his struggle with the teacher, then the master has no recognition of that which, as master, he is the misrecognition. It is exactly this assertion of the withdrawal of the student by the teacher that is the basis of Heidegger's claim that true education 'means allowing oneself to be beset by the unknown and then [become] master of it in comprehending knowing' (Wolin, 1993: 45).

When Hegel says in his letter of 1812 that knowledge or science is 'a treasure of hard-won, ready-prepared, formed content... [and that] the teacher possesses this treasure; he pre-thinks it [whilst] the pupils rethink it,' (Hegel, 1984: 280) this looks like an unpalatable domination of the autonomy and creativity of the slave by the master. One could then turn to Heidegger's comments to find a pedagogical relationship in which the truth of the student remains 'without interpretation' (Krell, 1993: 375). But this example of their differences on pedagogy is an exemplar of the differences between Heideggerian and Hegelian higher education as a whole. The actuality of Hegel's teacher means that he is already in relation to the student as other, and in relation to himself as student. The teacher is other, but the other is not the teacher. It is precisely because he cannot think for or on behalf of the student that his mastery is negated and collapses. It is in this negation and collapse that the student and the teacher gain (and gains) a mind of their (and his) own. This is the humility and necessary vulnerability of 'pre-thinking', for pre-thinking is only the re-cognition of the teacher's own necessary negation.

But Heidegger's teacher has only the pretence of learning from the student. He is protected from humility and vulnerability by positing the student as withdrawn but not other. Because the student for Heidegger is 'without interpretation' the student is denied an identity of his own in relation to the teacher. For the illusory being of the teacher, the student is posited as nothing in himself, which in turn frees the teacher from any responsibility towards the student. The latter is not even seemingly the property of the master because withdrawal in Heidegger denies property relation, or other, *per se*.[8] It is the very openness of the posited identity of the student in Heidegger that allows for his complete domination in and by the Being of the question. Only in negation, in the relation of abstract domination between teacher and student, is the student's identity as learning respected and recognised. Only in negation *is* the student, and therefore only in the negation of the teacher *is* learning. What Heidegger's phenomenology offers is a phenomenology without the actual relation to and necessary domination of the other. On the surface this openness looks to avoid categorial imperialism. But this is mere dissemblance. As the educational philosophy of 1933-4 shows, without the actuality of its social and political relation to other, and without its dialectical and speculative negative significance, phenomenology is nothing more than mastery and domination of the question posing as its essence. Heidegger in fact protects the learner from the social and political significance of his contingency in and of the question by claiming Dasein to be that contingency. In the higher education offered elsewhere in this book the lack of protection from contingency, its universality, particularity and singularity, is the actual necessity of contingency as education and freedom. Where the *is* of Heidegger is merely posited Being, the educational *is* of philosophy's higher education is the contradiction of actual being and essence, or is (B)being *known*.

Later, in 1966, Heidegger refers to another reason for his support of the Nazis. Much of his later work was concerned with the way in which technology posed a threat to authentic Being. By technology Heidegger did not mean particular forms of technology. He was interested in the essence of technology as a way of thinking which, although currently dominant, was contrary to the truth of Being that *Being and Time* had disclosed. Whilst philosophical work was carried out by Dasein in its own home, viz. Being, technology characterised a form of work which attacked that home from without. Technology extracts from Being and stores that work elsewhere. So dominant is the work of extraction that Heidegger came to believe philosophy to be dead. In place of philosophical knowledge, where knowledge means 'to be master of the situation into which we are placed,' (Wolin, 1993: 58) a new knowledge had gained mastery, one which framed all questioning and thus all Being from without. Even more significant, this framing concealed itself to the extent that Being did not see that extraction as its own alienation. Technology frames Dasein not only to be uncanny (*unheimlich*) but to be the work and source of its own alienation. Dasein is framed not to care, not to be resolute in the anticipation which is Being Time, but to challenge from without that work, facts and things be given up or yielded. Questioning, enframed by technology, has become exposure, and falleness is now that technological demand.

Technology for Heidegger is an alienation of the education that is Dasein's own education, but it is no more or less of an alienation than Heidegger himself achieved for Dasein at the end of *Being and Time*. Just as the superior power of being the Being and Time of all possibility suppresses the necessity of Dasein's own negation and actuality in relation to other, so, technology for Heidegger robs Dasein of its own philosophical and educational work, its ownmost Being. If Dasein in these circumstances cannot be resolutely itself, says Heidegger, then 'only a god can save us' (Wolin, 1993: 107). But this applies as much to the Dasein that is under attack from technology as to the Dasein that is granted finite mastery as all historicality at the end of *Being and Time*. Philosophy, and philosophy's higher education, 'is at an end' (Wolin, 1993: 107) not only in 1966 but in 1927.

6. MIND THE GAP

Heidegger's educational odyssey through Being is traduced into a fetishism of authenticity as all possibility. This fetishism casts authentic, caring Dasein as Hegel's illusory being where that which is other is nothing. Just as illusory being is the source of scepticism (Hegel, 1969: 396) so Heidegger's phenomenology claims to be 'without interpretation' of that to which it is called. Yet in *Being and Time* this scepticism becomes the certainty of its unhappy consciousness. When scepticism achieves a mind of its own in this way the slave is eradicated and the 'Being' that is this scepticism takes that positing as authentic. It is ironic, perhaps fateful is better, that the critique in *Being and Time* of totalizing intellectual and dialectical philosophy is performed in a book of 'natural law' where otherness in general is overcome by a positing 'naturalised' and therefore illusory essence. The natural law of Dasein is that it *is* otherness. This is different from the higher education of philosophy in which otherness has an identity true to itself, that is, as 'other' than itself. Here the in and for itself of the slave does not become just the master, nor does the master become just the slave in 'having' the slave as his own. The safeguard that necessity provides against the positing of natural law is that it must act as itself and has already done so. This is the actuality of otherness. As such, otherness is the master 'and' the slave in a way different from how Dasein is Being 'and' Time.

Being 'and' Time in Heidegger resolves the necessity that inheres in the relation. In his phenomenological exposition of the innermost, Heidegger has offered us a testament to life lived as Being, no longer having the ontological difference as an object for the enquiring but ultimately presupposing mind, but this time having the difference as what *is* Being. He does not work outside of the difference or the gap that is care. Instead he discloses its full Being and invites us to know ourselves as care and to work to be resolute in our anticipation. In doing so, we will *be* the gap, or authentic care, which can see through the subject and the public world, and which *is* by struggling to hold to true Being, to live inside the Being of an issue *as* that issue. To live as that issue is to live with the anxiety of a call to conscience which calls us back to the anticipatory resoluteness of what the gap is. It is a call to *be* the gap.[9]

Yet, as we have seen, Heidegger's presentation of the gap as an issue runs counter to the notion of philosophical higher education presented in this book. The ontological difference is no difference at all. Heidegger's new teacher closes the gap that was its own beginning, the question of the ontological difference between being and Being. In closing the gap the new teacher is the end of education not as *telos* or necessary self-mediation but as closure, for now the question is no longer its own necessity. Now the question is authentic as care, but as such, it is careless with the question, for to be care-full would be to know that the gap is *not* Dasein. When the negative is turned into identity by denying the negative an identity, as in Dasein, and when that Being is all historicality, then the universality, the very necessity of the question against itself, is suppressed. Being is essence or illusory being even and especially when Being vehemently defends itself against such a claim. Being in Heidegger is illusory being *par excellence*. It has all otherness as other, that is, it claims for itself the status of pure contingency, the Being of contingent Being, a self-contingency. In doing so, it is all possibility; indeed it is the possibility of possibility being itself. Necessity is asserted as Being by Heidegger, but this is not its actuality. This is the suppression of otherness that finds its voice in National Socialism. Unless necessity is 'other,' not only for us but of us, then necessity is usurped by that which denies its own determination by necessity.[10] If necessity is not for us then we are not of necessity, and if we are not of necessity, we are free to be any and all possibility.

Of course, Heidegger defends himself against carelessness or indifference towards the other. In *The Basic Problems of Phenomenology* (1988), for example, he argues that our being with others is the basic way Dasein has of being alive and that, moreover, our being in a world with others is exactly the truth of Dasein. Our social relations, our being-in-the-world, have Dasein as their foundation. For Heidegger, this relation of determination by an other becomes a self-relation that claims to be the being of other and of self. But the claim is already the illusion of modern social relations. The master/slave relation that Dasein likes to claim for itself (by not claiming it), and which underpins its claims to service, is one that is not itself determined by its relation to other. It is because other is only other to Dasein, and not also self as other, that Dasein can claim to be Time, and authentic Being. This is self-care; care not to allow the property relations that Dasein repeats to infect the purity of its Being. Dasein in this sense is the most insidious form of bourgeois theorising for it abstracts itself from property relations to the thing, and turns these relations into relations of Being. This far surpasses the naturalization of property relations that Marx criticised. Dasein turns property relations into a law of explicitly natural being. Its most powerful deception is to mask its 'naturalizing' of Being behind a form of phenomenology that appears to be a critique of nature. Yet Heidegger's form of phenomenology does not even have nature as nothing, surpassing the illusion of essence that characterises illusory being. By denying our relation to the thing as determinative of Being, the thing plays no part in our authenticity. And when this happens, we have no relation to the thing at all. And without this relation, we are all masters, we are pure Being, we are authentic contingency, 'we' have no other... and we are no longer learning.

NOTES

[1] In this chapter I have kept upper case for the notions of Being, Time and Dasein.
[2] I am taking Hegel as representative of philosophy's higher education in this chapter.
[3] I have written about the concept of 'teachability' in Tubbs (2003).
[4] See Heidegger (1987).
[5] And, as we will also see in a later section, suppresses the illusory being of property relations.
[6] This is explored more fully below in chapter 5.
[7] This 'and' is referred to again in the final section of this chapter and below in chapter 6.
[8] Of course as it denies 'other' as part of any external relation of its own, so it is free to label as 'other' all who are not part of its totality.
[9] See also Tubbs, 2000.
[10] Denial has become a major theme in criticism of Heidegger, particularly in relation to the death camps. See, for example, Lang (1996).

REFERENCES

Farias, V. (1989) *Heidegger and Nazism*, Philadelphia, Temple University Press.
Hegel, G.W.F. (1969) *Science of Logic*, London, George Allen and Unwin.
Hegel, G.W.F. (1984) *Hegel: The Letters*, Bloomington, Indiana University Press, trans, C. Butler and C. Seiler.
Heidegger, M. (1969) *Identity and Difference*, New York, Harper Torchbooks.
Heidegger, M. (1987) *Introduction to Metaphysics*, Newhaven, Yale University Press.
Heidegger, M. (1988) *The Basic Problems of Phenomenology*, Bloomington, Indiana University Press.
Heidegger, M. (1992) *Being and Time*, Oxford, Blackwell.
Krell, D.F. (1993) *Basic Writings: Martin Heidegger*, London: Routledge.
Lang, B. (1996) *Heidegger's Silence*, London, Athlone Press.
Rose, G. (1984) *Dialectic of Nihilism*, Oxford, Blackwell.

Tubbs, N. (2000) 'Mind The Gap; The Philosophy of Gillian Rose', *Thesis Eleven*, No. 60.
Tubbs, N. (2003) 'The Concept of Teachability,' *Educational Theory, vol. 53, no. 1.*
Wolin, R. (1993) *The Heidegger Controversy*, Cambridge MA, The MIT Press.

CHAPTER 4

KIERKEGAARD: RECOLLECTION AND REPETITION

If Heidegger is the unironic and therefore dissembling representative of philosophy's higher education as the moment of history, then Kierkegaard is the genius who, like Nietzsche, reveals philosophy's higher education as the history of the moment. But as anyone who has tried to read Kierkegaard will know, his work presents the student with considerable difficulties. To begin with, it is hard to see how Kierkegaard's project can be understood without an accompanying knowledge of Hegel. As we will see below, Kierkegaard is perhaps the most rigorous and consistent example of philosophy's higher education in the tradition. He is the living actuality of the 'self' who is the learning individual. Yet to introduce, for example, undergraduate students to Kierkegaard as an example of this actuality is very difficult. The amount that he wrote even between 1841-44 covers some 15 books, with *Stages on Life's Way* and the seminal *Concluding Unscientific Postscript* published in 1846. In addition, we are unsettled in trying to assign authorship to these works for they are written through some eight pseudonyms as well as under his own name. We are equally unsettled by strategic irony, not least the systematic denial that his work is systematic. Further, the breadth of his insights are as daunting as the lengths of his works, covering opera, Shakespeare, the Bible, religion, theology, philosophy but also the 'everyday' phenomena of education, love, death, friendship and explicitly marriage.

1. TO MARRY OR NOT TO MARRY?

How then to begin our chapter on Kierkegaard? In *Stages on Life's Way*, Constantin Constantius arranges a dinner party for himself and four others. The subject they are to discuss is erotic love, and the first to speaker is someone we know only as 'the young man'. The defining characteristic of this young man is that he 'thinks' love but has no particular relationship through which to practise that love. Yet this does not disqualify him from speaking. On the contrary, 'that he had had no love affair, was *also* a love affair' (1988: 32, my emphasis) because 'in his thought he could be said to have a relationship to the whole sex and not to individuals' (1988: 33). Here is Kierkegaard in a nutshell. He is a man who thinks too much, apparently to the detriment of his lived life. He thinks so much about love that, as we learn in *Either/Or*, he thinks himself out of his engagement to

Regine and thinks both of them out of marriage. He thinks so much, and writes this thinking, that it determines his whole existence.

> I go for a brief walk in the morning. Then I come home and sit in my room without interruption until about three o' clock. My eyes can barely see. Then with my walking stick in hand I sneak off to the restaurant, but am so weak that I believe that if somebody were to call out my name, I would keel over and die. Then I go home and begin again (1988: viii).

The young man at the dinner party explains his life. 'To me,' he says, 'the thought is and remains the primary point' (1988: 33). But in thinking about love he has come face to face with a seemingly irresolvable contradiction. The point is well made by Judge William later in *Stages*. He notes that falling in love is immediate, it is spontaneous. But marriage requires a decision or a resolution to love in the future. How can one plan for or resolve to remain spontaneously in love 'till death us do part?' 'How can this immediacy (falling in love) find its equivalent in an immediacy reached through reflection?' (1988: 123).

The young man's answer is clear. 'I refuse to be unfaithful to my thought... which I dare not abandon in order to cling to a wife, since to me it is my eternal nature and... even more valuable than a wife' (1988: 46).

The themes that characterise, even determine Kierkegaard's life and writing are present here. First is his commitment to thinking and second his commitment to remaining faithful to thinking despite the difficulties, contradictions and even impossibilities that it produces. In this way Kierkegaard lives a life of doubt. But, like Hegel's pathway of doubt (1977: 49) this is not a commitment to doubt or scepticism as dogma. On the contrary, and again like Hegel, it is the resolve 'not to give oneself over to the thoughts of others, upon mere authority, but to examine everything for oneself and follow only one's own conviction... and accept only one's own deed as what is true' (1977: 50).

Closest to Hegel as a pseudonym is Johannes Climacus.[1] Johannes was 'in love—with thought or more accurately with thinking' (1985: 118). Like his namesake John Climacus and his ladder of divine ascent,[2] his joy is to climb, step by step, to higher thoughts. Even more joyful was to make the same movement, up and down, down and up, to try and ensure that the movement and the result were perfect to each other and complete. 'His soul was anxious lest one single coherent thought slip out, for then the whole thing would collapse' (1985: 119), but he learned early on that in thinking co-exist joy *and* anxiety. His father embodied a Socratic spirit, listening to the arguments of his guests before 'in an instant, everything was turned upside down; the explicable was made inexplicable, the certain doubtful, the opposite was made obvious' (1985: 122).

Whilst for Johannes Climacus his 'whole life was thinking,' (1985: 123) nevertheless even as a university student it had not occurred to him to want to be a philosopher. Whilst the latter sought the answers, Johannes was in love only with the process. Indeed, as his reading proceeded, he began to learn that the results that philosophers offered were often rife with dissembling. Titles did not fulfil their promise and lacked the 'rigorous dialectical movement' (1985: 130) that he loved. In addition, he noticed how alert he was at the beginning of lectures, but 'how dejected at the end, since he perceived that not a single word had been said... although it gave the appearance of saying something' (1985: 165).

So, Johannes was forced to abandon the philosophers and the teachers and resort to the necessity of his own thinking. In particular, he set to trying to understand the thesis *de omnibus dubitandum*, everything must be doubted. It is not hard to understand why he was drawn to this thesis. Not only did he hear it stated often, but it also embodied his father's dialectical rigour and it struck at the significance and the process of Johannes's own thinking. Indeed, it embodied his critique, stated above, of philosophy lectures and books. They may well state that everything must be doubted, but in fact they doubted only those aspects that they chose to doubt. Where their doubt was selective and arbitrary, Johannes's doubt was universal in that it doubted all such arbitrary doubting. He was doubting everything but finding nowhere that his universal difficulty was shared. His doubting of the philosophers, then, became its own doubt about itself. Most significantly, it was said that philosophy must begin with doubt, yet for Johannes, such a beginning was an impossibility for it expressed a tautology. How does one begin to doubt? In an insight that is central to understanding Kierkegaardian thinking and education, he notes that if one doubts, then it must be because doubt has already existed.

> He thought through the thesis again and again, tried to forget what he had thought in order to begin again, but, lo and behold, he always arrived at the same point. Yet he could not abandon the thesis; it seemed as if a mysterious power held him to it, as if something were whispering to him: something is hiding behind this misunderstanding (1985: 139).

Johannes Climacus and the young man at the dinner party in fact share the same problem, one that defines Kierkegaard's life and philosophy. Thought, or thinking, undermines, negates and contradicts all immediacies, all beginnings, and all origins. For the young man, thinking contradicted an immediate promise of love; for Johannes, thinking opposed any beginning to doubt or to philosophy. What Johannes and the young man have experienced here is what Hegel put succinctly in the *Science of Logic*. 'There is nothing, nothing in heaven or in nature or mind or anywhere else which does not equally contain both immediacy and mediation' (1969: 68). Indeed, as Hegel says in the shorter *Logic*, 'thinking is always the negation of what we have immediately before us' (1975: 17). How, then, for the young man, could marriage not be the knowing of love in a way which destroyed love? And how for Johannes Climacus could philosophy know eternal truth without annihilating the moment in which and for who it is true? 'If he were to have an opinion about the implications of the thesis under discussion, it would be this—that it was an impossibility' (1985: 143).

Before we look at the ways in which Kierkegaard learns of these impossibilities as philosophy's higher education, it is instructive to look at some of the ways in which he tried to be faithful in his writing and in his life to these difficulties. What his thinking and doubting have produced is a set of dualisms which, whilst always appearing with the other, nevertheless also negate each other. How is someone to live like this? For each of the impossibilities Kierkegaard personifies both sides of the dualisms in his pseudonyms. Let us explore marriage a little further as an example.

At the dinner party in *Stages* the young man's doubts about marriage are shared by the host, Constantin Constantius, who argues that the impossibility of the relation between man and woman, or the 'misrelation,' is in fact 'a jest' (1988: 48). Victor Eremita sees the erotic to be annihilated by ideality, and the fashion designer sees immediacy 'reflected' more in woman's obsession with clothes than is possible in marriage. But these negative positions towards the impossibility of reflection and love are countered by Johannes the seducer who argues that the seducer can eat of the fruit of the difficulty but 'they are never trapped' (1988: 75). The eternal can be present, he argues, in the seduction, but only aesthetically. If the reflection of love is resolved in marriage then this 'ethical' reconciliation annuls the deception that is knowingly entered into. When reflection is deception, then love can be known and enjoyed without being chained to the temporal. But when the deception is no longer present, or is destroyed in and by marriage, there reflection has annihilated the erotic.

At the end of the dinner party the guests stumble across the thoughts of Judge William who extols the ethical and religious virtues of marriage. His argument is that marriage is divine because it translates its immediate enthusiasm into a lived actuality. It is, he says, where 'reflection is discharged into faith' (1988: 162). This faith is 'a new immediacy,' (1988: 162) one that is never available to the necessarily unhappy bachelor whose resolution to remain true to reflection may be signed in heaven, but is never 'countersigned in temporality' (1988: 112).

We will see below how Kierkegaard assesses these two impossible positions[3]—to marry or not marry. But the duality is rehearsed earlier in his two volume *Either/Or*. The two sides of the impossibility are embodied by the writers of two sets of papers whose authorship the editor assigns the epithets 'A' and 'B'. A is the aesthetic seducer, the man who, being true to what reflection and doubt have taught him, knows that the immediacy of love cannot be reconciled with the resolve of marriage. Therefore he warns against the illusion of uniting the opposites in any form of temporal relationship be it marriage or friendship. Such illusory middles or reconciliations are 'superfluous third[s]' (1987a: 295). Instead, what reflection has taught A is that any actuality is not negative enough and requires therefore to be negated. This life can be lived, but only as a life of suspension and forgetting, a life that can be lived poetically or aesthetically. The erotic does have an infinity, but 'a poetic infinity' (1987a: 297). What A means by this is that the infinity of the erotic can only be maintained if it is suspended, that is, it will only be true to its own immediacy if it is refused its time. Its infinity, as reflection teaches, is negative, and therefore 'when two people fall in love with each other and sense that they are destined for each other, it is a question of having the courage to break it off, for by continuing there is only everything to lose, nothing to gain' (1987a: 298).

This is a paradox he says, but only for the feelings, 'not for the understanding' (1987a: 298). The seducer understands that the immediacy of love can only be sustained if it is suspended and lived as the negative of its earthly form. If his beloved does not understand this, then the seducer must teach this negative truth to her. At first in his manoeuvres she 'has no inkling of the law' (1987a: 341) by which he is working. She does not realise that he works not purely in the immediacy of love but for 'the interesting' (1987a: 351). He sees it as his task to bring the beloved into conflict with herself so that she too may come to understand the joy of infinite possibility in the affair, rather than the crushing of immediacy by the resolution of engagement and marriage. So, at first she will fear his intellect because it constitutes 'the negation of her entire womanly existence' (1987a: 362). But this negation is precisely the seducer's *telos*. So, when eventually the beloved agrees to an engagement, then the work of the seducer must immediately reverse itself. 'To poetize oneself into a girl is an art; to poetize oneself out of her is a masterstroke' (1987a: 368). So, from the seducer's diary, we learn this art and masterstroke.

> What I have to do now is, on the one hand, to organize everything so that the engagement is broken in such a way that I thereby secure a more beautiful and significant relationship to [her]... When I have brought her to the point where she has learned what it is to love... then the engagement will break like a defective mold and she will belong to me (1987a: 376).

This, we might say, constitutes the seducer's version of philosophy's higher education. He is the teacher of the negative because he has 'grasped the nature and the point of love' (1987a: 368) to be true only negatively, that is, as infinite possibility. To be true to his understanding of love he has first to deceive in order that she may 'discover the infinite' (1987a: 391) for herself and make her own leap into its negative truths.

> What she must learn is to make all the motions of infinity... to confuse poetry and actuality, truth and fiction, to frolic in infinity. Then when she is familiar with this tumult, I shall add the erotic; then she will be what I want and desire. Then my duties will be over... (1987a: 392).

Now the beloved's passion is also dialectical. Not, notes the seducer, in quite the same way as a man is dialectical, for where he leaps, she glides (1987a: 392) across the abyss or the separation of immediacy and mediation, 'more beautiful, more soulful than ever' (1987a: 392). But nevertheless he has corrupted her innocence and, at the same time, her innocent faith in marriage, and has enabled her to see for herself the greater beauty that love has in its negative, dialectical form. Once she sees this, she will herself want to break the engagement, destroying 'an imperfect human form in order to hurry onto something that is superior to the ordinarily human' (1987a: 428).

At the end of the diary, the educational complexities of the relation between lover and beloved are made explicit. As we might expect, the art of dialectical love is not merely to know about how love is dialectical, it is also to know how the 'art' of that love is itself dialectical. The seducer does not admit to being judged by the ordinarily human. On the contrary, 'in this relation there is profound irony' (1987a: 431). What is gained in the relation is the substance of woman, a substance that man has only reflected on and worked for. As the teacher he has asked a question, but the answer has been hers and he now, in order to be true to the new freedom that she has discovered, must again be released by her to infinite possibility. 'The engagement is broken, but she herself breaks it in order to soar to a higher sphere' (1987a: 438).

We will return to the ironies of the teacher/student relation that works in and for the negative a little later. But it is worth noting at this point how much the seducer's diary reflects the events of Kierkegaard's own life. He is a lover, as Lowrie says, 'unable to take a single step without reflection' (1944: 137) and unable to marry the woman he loves. The more she loved him, the more he hated himself for letting her believe that he was a man capable of marriage. He had tried to warn her, for example of his melancholy, of his inner difficulties, but he had not done well enough to ensure that she would leave him. 'Essentially I live in a spirit world. I was engaged to her for a year, and still she did not really know me... I was too heavy for her, and she was too light for me...' (1944: 140). Having failed in a sense to produce the masterstroke that would poetize himself out of the girl, he reasoned that 'to get out of the situation as a scoundrel... was the only thing there was to be done in order to work her loose...' (1944: 142).[4] Later Regine married Fritz Schlegel.[5] Kierkegaard of course never married.

If the aesthete serves the infinite possibility of immediacy by never marrying, Judge William serves the infinite necessity of finite and temporal mediation by extolling the virtues of marriage. He does this as B in *Either/Or II* and in his reflections on marriage in *Stages*. His judgements of the aesthete are clear. The latter seeks first to corrupt and then to preserve this corruption, searching for its perfect expression. He seduces into unhappiness and refuses any resolution of unhappiness in the ordinary actuality of life. He seduces in the name of an eternal possibility that must never be realised, and holds that true love can only be expressed by its denial. He revels in the sadness and despair of his particularity and in the impossibility of (positive) union with the universal. On the other hand, for the Judge, marriage is the exact antithesis of the fate that has befallen marriage in the reflective age. Against the claims of the aesthete that he is true to the contradiction of reflection, the Judge has a different interpretation of the relation between thinking and the immediacy of love. Love, he argues, can be contained in marriage if that marriage expresses its unity spontaneously in religion. It is futile to hope that the 'first love' can recur eternally, but how then can the Judge claim that its immediacy can still be present in marriage? His answer is that 'what the first love lacks... is the second aesthetic ideal, the historical. It does not have the law of motion in itself,' (1987b: 96) whereas 'marital love manifests itself as historical by being a process of assimilation; it tries its hand at what is experienced and refers what it has experienced to itself' (1987b: 97). It is this inner history of the experience of love that is genuinely aesthetic, rather than the merely abstract aesthetic of the seducer. Only in the former—the ethical—is the aesthetic fully and explicitly 'lived' (1987b: 137).

In his later reflections on marriage Judge William adds that it is not in the aesthetic but in marriage that 'the first effervescent passion of falling in love... can be sustained' (1988: 95). This is because the negative resolution of the aesthete, by being continually in suspense, can never actually be tested against its own truth. Precisely the reason that the aesthete chooses suspension[6]—to remain true to the difficulty or impossibility of maintaining love by conquering resolution—becomes for the Judge a way of never being true to itself at all. Whereas in marriage faith means no reassurance is required, in the aesthetic the lack of faith means no reassurance is possible.

The Judge concludes that marriage—the ethical choice—is 'a synthesis of falling in love and resolution' (1988: 109). This is because marriage is divine but also temporal. When given this religious significance, marriage is no longer 'immediacy's angel of death' (1988: 157). On the contrary it is resolution added to falling in love in such a way that it produces 'a new immediacy' (1988: 162) where reflection 'is discharged into faith' (1988: 162). Marriage becomes an expression of the immediacy of God, an immediacy that the aesthete could never enjoy or achieve because for him, immediacy is always impossible except by refusing its countenance in earthly, everyday, ordinary actuality.

2. CONTRADICTION OF IDEALITY AND REALITY

We have concentrated so far on using marriage as an example—a very important one—of the collision between ideality and reality that is produced in and by thinking. The philosopher, Johannes Climacus, is able to abstract from the example of marriage to the 'logic' of this collision for thinking in general. Having decided no longer to follow the philosophers who, like the aesthete, fail to refer what is experienced to itself, Johannes has resolved to follow the path of doubt by himself. In thinking about the thinking of anything he learns now that there is a question of truth that accompanies all philosophizing, all thinking. In thinking about anything, marriage, whatever, the structure of that thinking seems predetermined to ensure that the object of contemplation is annihilated in its immediacy. When this failure to know the object in itself is taken as the object of the enquiry, then truth itself is immanently under investigation. So, says Johannes,

> How does the question of truth arise? By way of untruth, because the moment I ask about truth, I have already asked about untruth. In the question of truth, consciousness is brought into relation with something else, and what makes this relation possible is untruth (1985: 167).

As reflection cannot remain in the immediacy of love, so consciousness cannot remain in immediacy for then 'there would be no consciousness at all' (1985: 167). Echoing Hegel, Johannes notes that immediacy is always cancelled by mediation and that as such, mediation can only presuppose immediacy. So, he asks, what is immediacy? Immediacy is 'reality' (1985: 167), whilst mediacy is the expression of reality. In their relation is always a contradiction, for what is expressed is never its expression. 'The moment I make a statement about reality, contradiction is present, for what I say is ideality' (1985: 168).

Clearly the young philosopher is covering the well trodden path of how the object in itself can be known as an object for us, or how the dialectic of immediacy and mediation plays itself out as our higher education. Johannes Climacus expounds the logic of this education, but in each of his works between 1843-46 Kierkegaard is trying to express this nature of the dialectic.

In *Fear and Trembling* the dialectic is presented dramatically through the story of Abraham. To the non-dialectical, understanding the story of Abraham on Mount Moriah, ready and willing to sacrifice—no, to kill—his own son is a story of madness and murder. The parishioner who, on hearing the preacher's sermon about Abraham, goes home wanting 'to do just as Abraham did' (1983: 28) becomes 'a despicable man, [the] scum of society' (1983: 28) and will probably be 'executed or sent to the madhouse' (1983: 29). The remarkable thing about Abraham is that 'what he does is great and when another man does the same thing it is a sin' (1983: 30). But to the dialectical understanding Abraham represents the truth of the contradiction that has to be lived between immediacy and mediation. It is only when the anxiety of this paradox is included in the story that Abraham appears as he really is. The dilemma for Abraham is stark. As 'a devout and God-fearing man' (1983: 31) Abraham is chosen by God to be put to the test. 'Take now thy son, thine only son Isaac, whom thou lovest and get thee into the land of Moriah; and offer him there for a burnt offering upon one of the mountains...' (Genesis, 22:2).

How are we to understand Abraham's actions in this situation? They can only be understood as the same paradox seen above regarding marriage. Reflection upon the spiritual task makes it impossible to unite the contradictory forces. The moment the task is set, it exists as untruth. The relation to God is already, now, that untruth. If Abraham resigns himself to the loss of his son then he becomes 'the knight of infinite resignation'. As with the aesthetic resignation that marriage cannot express eternal love, so, here, he who is being spiritually tested recognises that the earthly and the temporal—the ethical—cannot express the eternal. The only way to be true to this impossibility is to negate any form of possibility that it takes. Thus, as the seducer must ensure the engagement is broken off, so the knight of infinite resignation must lose his love (in reality) in order to keep her for ever (in ideality). Where in marriage the seducer has an aesthetic resignation, Abraham must have a religious resignation wherein the very denial of earthly fulfilment reconciles him 'once more in the eternal consciousness of its validity in eternal form that no actuality can take away from him' (1983: 43-4). Thus the knight makes 'impossibility possible by expressing it spiritually, but he expresses it spiritually by renouncing it' (1983: 44).

This is one way in which the knight is true to his being tested, for he is true to his understanding of the contradiction between thought and its object. But as we saw above with marriage, there is a second way of being true to the contradiction. The knight of faith 'does exactly the same as the other knight did: he infinitely renounces the love that is the substance of his life, he is reconciled in pain' (1983: 46). But, in addition to this infinite resignation, this knight makes one further movement. Despite the absolute resignation of the loss, nevertheless, and absurdly, he still believes that by remaining true to the impossibility and sacrificing his love, he will gain his love. This leap of faith, or the absurd, does not 'lie within the proper domain of the understanding. It is not identical with the improbable, the unexpected, the unforeseen' (1983: 46). The understanding continues to see faith as impossibility but the knight of faith realizes, just as clearly, that he can 'be saved only by the absurd, and this he grasps by faith' (1983: 47). Thus, in contrast to infinite resignation, but building upon it, 'faith is no aesthetic emotion but something higher; it is not the spontaneous inclination of the heart but the paradox of existence' (1983: 47).

It is tempting to think that this leap of faith, then, is the kind of higher education that is the subject of this book. Abraham, being infinitely resigned to losing his son, nevertheless absurdly and by faith alone, believes that by sacrificing his son he will *not* lose him. But the relationship expressed here in *Fear and Trembling* between faith and the paradox of existence is not at all clear. It is not clear, for example, how the movement from paradox to faith is made. The author of *Fear and Trembling*, Johannes de Silentio, admits to us that 'I cannot make the movement of faith, I cannot shut my eyes and plunge confidently into the absurd; it is for me an impossibility' (1983: 34). His reason is that his attempts to believe in faith—to have faith in faith—suffer the same fate as all relationships between thought and object: they express only the impossibility. Thus to 'choose' faith is as impossible an expression of the eternal as any other. De Silentio's problem becomes that 'he who loves God without faith reflects upon himself' (1983: 37) and enjoys the pain of absence. 'He who loves God in faith reflects upon God,' (1983: 37) and enjoys the absence of pain. Thus, says de Silentio, 'every time I want to make this movement [the leap of faith] I almost faint' (1983: 48). 'By my own strength I cannot get the least little thing that belongs to finitude, for I continually use my strength in resigning everything' (1983: 49). Thus he concludes, I 'can describe the movements of faith, but I cannot make them' (1983: 37). If this is a higher education, then for de Silentio it is not one in which we necessarily make the leap of faith to faith. On the contrary, if it is a higher education for de Silentio it is to know the contradiction of reality and ideality, of the aesthetic and the ethical, now in a further dualism, as infinite resignation and faith. But this is more of the same.[7]

From *The Concept of Dread* we might say that this kind of learning is quantitative but not qualitative. Here, Kierkegaard explores the impossibility of another immediacy, that of sin. If sin is immediate, just as if faith is immediate, then each is 'deprived of what legitimately belongs to it: its historical presupposition' (1967: 10). This historical presupposition is what we have seen above to be the difficult relation between reality and ideality. In terms of sin, this relation is the difficulty between 'Adam's first sin and the first sin of every man' (1967: 27). If Adam sins as a consequence of original sin, that is, immediately, then every man, every generation after him, sins as a condition of that immediacy. As the thought or reflection upon love require a resolution that separates them from the immediacy of love, so the sin of each of us is known (reflected upon) as a condition of the way that Adam, precisely, did not know sin. As marriage cannot be the immediacy of love, so our sin cannot be the 'same' as Adam's. 'If that were so, then Adam would really be outside the race, and the race did not begin with him but had a beginning outside itself...' (1967: 27). Man is separated from Adam *by* Adam. The understanding can know this difficult relation in two ways. Abstractly and undialectically, it can see a merely quantitative relation such that 'once is nothing much, but that many times is something' (1967: 27). But a continuous quantitative progression cannot make the leap, as it were, to a new quality of sin as ideality. 'More' immediacy is not the qualitative transition to the significance of sin for the race as its condition of possibility. For that qualitative leap from innocence to sin to be possible there must be something present other than 'more' of Adam. There must be something in sin that ties us to Adam in such a way that, as religion ties immediacy to reflection, so we are both more of the one sin and different from the one sin.

The second way of understanding how sin came to be in the world is dialectically. Here, the author of *The Concept of Dread*, Vigilius Haufniensis,[8] says that the 'account in Genesis is the only dialectically consistent account' because it understands that 'sin came into the world by a sin' (1967: 29). 'The difficulty for the understanding is precisely the triumph of the explanation, its profound consistency in representing that sin presupposes itself, that it so came into the world that by the fact that it is, it is presupposed' (1967: 29). But this poetic myth rather explains away the very difficulty whose immediacy it sets out to express by not explaining it at all. We have seen this absurdity above in terms of the leap of faith. If sin has entered the world by sin then logically 'sin has preceded it' (1967: 30). This contradiction 'is the only dialectically consistent statement which is able to do justice' (1967: 30) to both the immediacy and the mediation of the origin and the actuality of sin in the world. But 'logic' does not understand the contradiction either. In logic what is immediate is annulled by the mediacy that is reflection. This is why logic cannot synthesize its opposites. As seen above, the synthesis requires the leap of faith that logic cannot make. Only when logic itself is sacrificed will the immediacy that is impossible be gained. In *Fear and Trembling* the leap of faith in the absurd which returns to Abraham that which he is infinitely resigned to losing, and is the 'new immediacy' that Judge William talked about, is now the concept of 'dread', the relation between innocence and guilt that is the 'new immediacy' of sin in the world.

In terms of impossibility, 'the annulment of immediacy is therefore an immanent movement within immediacy... by which mediacy presupposes immediacy' (1967: 33-4). Thus innocence is not lost, it endures as a new immediacy; it is 'a quality, it is a state which can very well endure' (1967: 34). Innocence therefore 'is a something' (1967: 34). So how is this new immediacy related to itself? How is it both the origin and the qualitative leap into the sin of each man? (We could also ask how, as marriage, the new immediacy is both the spontaneity of erotic love and its ethical resolution?) Haufniensis' answer is that this new immediacy, we might say the religion that is implicit in all men and in each man, is 'dread'. Dread is a suspension of impossibility, that is, in suspension *is* the relation of innocence and sin. Dread is not a fear of something. On the contrary, it is the apprehension of nothing, but as this feeling it is the presence of innocence as something and it is the possibility of innocence as sin. In Adam, dread is present as the 'possibility of being able' (1967: 40) but 'what it is he is able to do, of that he has no conception' (1967: 40).

3. PASSION OF LEARNING

We will not continue our discussion of dread here. Our point has been only to show how dread is another example of the difficulty that reality and ideality make unavoidable. But as Johannes de Silentio cannot make the leap of faith into the absurd that states that something can be both immediate and mediate, so, he might criticise the concept of dread on the same grounds. Hasn't Haufniensis as a watchman merely described the relation of sin to innocence by positing that the two are 'united in a third factor?' (1967: 39). He has not told us how we might achieve this new immediacy. As de Silentio *is able to say*, 'in learning to go through the motions of swimming, one can be suspended from the ceiling in a harness and then presumably describe the movements, but one is not swimming' (1983: 37-8). Of course, dread, like all of Kierkegaard's absurd new immediacies, is pregnant with philosophy's higher education. But before exploring how this is so there is one last example of the impossibility of immediacy and mediation I should like briefly to describe. This returns us to the *Philosophical Fragments* of Johannes Climacus, that is, to the man in love with dialectical thinking and who is training himself 'to be able to dance lightly in the service of thought' (1985: 7).

The question that Johannes addresses in *Philosophical Fragments* is 'can the truth be learned?' (1985: 9). Taking his cue from Socrates that 'all learning and seeking are but recollecting,' (1985: 9) he reveals the underlying structure of this idea. If what I learn or recollect was already in me then the teacher cannot sustain himself as the historical occasion or moment of decisiveness of this learning. On the contrary, my recollection marks the assimilation of the teacher's work into eternity. This is the poetic or aesthetic immediacy where finite time or the real world do not disturb the beauty of the eternal discovery.

> The temporal point of departure is a nothing, because in the same moment I discover that I have known the truth from eternity without knowing it, in the same instant that moment is hidden in the eternal, assimilated into it... (1985: 13).

Such assimilation into the eternity of the ironic and Socratic not-knowing is described aesthetically in *The Concept of Irony* as where the teacher satisfies his thirst (momentarily!) for the 'annihilating enthusiasm of negativity' (1989: 175).

If this assimilation of the teacher's decisiveness is not the case then it must be that 'the eternal, previously nonexistent, came into existence in that moment' (1985: 13). For this to be true the occasion must be the mediation of eternity, but such a moment is unable to establish anything but a negative relation to the eternity that recollection reveals. In this relation, again, of immediacy and mediation, lies the question of whether truth can be learned. It appears that if the truth is learned (in the moment) then it is never learned as (eternal) truth and if the truth not learned (in the moment) it is never learned at all. Johannes states that if the moment is to acquire 'decisive significance,' (1985: 13) i.e., if it is to be *educational*, then, *contra* recollection, it must mean that the seeker, up to that point, must not have had the truth. Recollection and moment, like eternity and the temporal, and immediacy and mediation, cannot co-exist.

> In *the moment*, a person becomes aware that he was born, for his previous state, to which he is not to appeal, was indeed one of 'not to be'. In *the moment*, he becomes

aware of the rebirth, for his previous state was in deed one of 'not to be'. If his previous state had been one of 'to be,' then under no circumstances would the moment have acquired decisive significance for him... Whereas the Greek pathos focuses on recollection, the pathos of our project focuses on the moment... (1985: 21).

And yet, as we have seen, in marriage, in doubt, in faith and in sin, somehow they do co-exist. Johannes is left to ask 'is what has been elaborated here thinkable?' (1985: 20). As a man in the service of thinking, like the young man at the dinner party, Johannes is faced again with contradiction. How can the immediacy of the eternal in recollection find its equivalent in the decisive movement of mediation by the teacher when there is a fundamentally 'unequal' (1985: 25) relation between the eternal and its significant moment or occasion? How can the knight of infinite resignation regarding the ubiquity of reflection and negation reconcile his learning with the leap of faith required to find equality in the inequality? 'This, as you see, is my project' (1985: 21) says Johannes.

The remainder of *Philosophical Fragments* looks at different ways in which this impossible relation is manifested. We must explore one aspect of this in detail.[9] Section III deals with the fundamental paradox of thinking and learning about the truth, that is that it wants 'to discover something that thought itself cannot think' (1985: 37). But Johannes reminds us that 'one must not think ill of the paradox, for the paradox is the passion of thought, and the thinker without the paradox is like the lover without passion' (1985: 37). As every passion wills its own downfall, so, too, does the passion of thinking.

That with which thought collides is 'the unknown' (1985: 39) or 'the god' (1985: 39). The paradox, as above regarding faith and sin, is that the unknown is always present through 'its historical presupposition' (1967: 10). Here, as for Meno, (Plato, 1956) if the unknown does not exist then it would be impossible to demonstrate it, and if it does exist, any demonstration would already 'presuppose it not as doubtful... but as decided' (1985: 39). As Hegel reminds us, 'to seek to know before we know, is as absurd as the wise resolution of Scholasticus not to venture into the water until he had learned to swim' (1975: 14). Thus Johannes similarly concludes 'the whole process of demonstration continually becomes ... an expanded concluding development of what I conclude from having presupposed that the object of investigation exists' (1985: 40). However, the unknown does have an historical point of departure, and this is 'the difficulty' (1985: 41 fn), for the difficulty, say Johannes, is already the 'concept' (1985: 40)—thus, this god is 'not a name but a concept' (1985: 41). This presupposition is very different from presupposing that the object of investigation exists or does not exist. This is a leap into the absurd because precisely in letting go 'of the demonstration, the existence is there' (1985: 43).

But now Johannes goes further that we have seen him go thus far. Now he is prepared to expound upon the missing equality between immediacy and mediation. Now he is prepared to conceptualise, to know, the 'absolute relation' (1985: 41) between God and his works, or between reflection and its object. But he does not 'name' (1985: 49) this relation in the same way that the understanding knows or does not know the unknown. He names this relation by way of philosophy's higher education. Faith, we find out, is not something we choose, it is something we learn. The leap of faith, therefore, that Johannes de Silentio could not take, Johannes Climacus cannot take either. But what the latter learns that the former never did is that faith is the condition of understanding, and is learning. Understanding is not the condition of faith except in willing its own downfall.

Johannes' exposition of this learning (or faith) is difficult. In summary[10] he says that 'the paradoxical passion of the understanding' (1985: 44) is that it wills its own downfall by seeking to know the unknown. Saying merely that it is unknown will not do 'since just saying that involves a relation' (1985: 44). This 'frontier' (1985: 44) is the 'passion's torment' (1985: 44) as well as its 'incentive' (1985: 44). The understanding cannot even know the unknown as 'the absolutely different' (1985: 44) because the understanding cannot 'absolutely negate itself' (1985: 45) and therefore it 'thinks as above itself only the sublimity that it thinks by itself' (1985: 45). We have seen this relation of the sublime above, in Kant. For Johannes this cognitive wonder[11] 'cannot be grasped securely' (1985: 45) for in each attempt 'the understanding ultimately goes astray' (1985: 46), that is, the difference is known only in terms of 'likeness' (as for Kant where proportionality is always analogy). Bluntly, the immediacy of the unknown, or God, in being known, is not known.

But, and here Johannes advances his understanding of the nature of the paradox, if difference is sin, and difference is our own fault, then difference has a duplexity which is the absolute relation of immediacy and mediation. Just as the understanding wills its own downfall in its passion (as the seducer wills the end of the engagement) so too, the paradox itself also 'wills this downfall of the understanding' (1985: 47). How? By being the consciousness of sin wherein the difference is known. Why? To understand the understanding of this single individual. The two, understanding and the paradox, 'have a mutual understanding' (1985: 47) that the annihilation of each is their equality. But this is not open to the understanding unless it is released from itself in and through its passion, and it is not open to the paradox unless it is released from itself.[12] The release therefore is education which, as the collision of the paradox and the understanding, is its own formation and finality. This is the only time that it is legitimate to talk of mutuality, that is, when we are referring to the absolute (negation of mutuality) that is education.[13] All other posited mutuality[14] suppresses the collision, suppresses God's work as teacher, and therein suppresses our higher education about 'the higher'.

Johannes states 'if the paradox and the understanding meet in the mutual understanding of their difference, then the encounter is a happy one... happy in the passion to which we have as yet given no name' (1985: 49). 'The difference was precisely this—that the understanding surrendered itself and the paradox gave itself' (1985: 54) just as in Hegel the slave surrenders himself and in the work paradox (i.e. sacrifice and negation) 'acquires a mind of his own' (1977: 119). If the understanding should take offence at its suffering, that is just the moment again and we are returned to the passion and difficulty of that moment (again) as of decisive or educational significance. Its taking offence means that it has missed the point. 'Everything it says about the paradox it has learned from the paradox' (1985: 53). To take offence is to say that *this* understanding is *not* understanding, which is precisely the posited mutuality referred to above. Says the paradox to this offence, 'it is just as you say, and the amazing thing is that you think it is an objection' (1985: 52). The paradox says exactly the same to those who take offence at the 'negation of the negation' in Hegel, arguing that its 'synthesis' is forced and only another illegitimate presupposition of identity. To refuse the significance of the negation as a decisive moment of educational significance is to assert that the paradox has originated in the understanding. This may be quantitative education—there are so many ways of being a clever philosopher—but it suppresses the qualitative leap from the immediacy of infinite resignation to the mediacy of learning that makes immediacy 'mine' and makes it 'me', the single individual. The uncertainty has to learn to take its downfall personally. As Kierkegaard said in his PhD thesis,[15] 'if our generation has any task at all, it must be to translate the achievement of scientific scholarship into personal life, to appropriate it personally' (1989: 328), or to 'know thyself' within and as philosophy's higher education.

This is exactly what Kierkegaard does in his various authorships. He lives the whole of the relation between understanding and the paradox by giving each constituent of the whole a voice. The 'young man' thinks so much that he cannot live normally; Judge William's faith in marriage is so total that one has to doubt his lack of doubt; Johannes de Silentio knows Abraham as a man of faith but cannot speak that faith; the aesthete refuses the credibility of faith and speaks his infinite resignation in the suspension of the ethical; the philosopher Johannes Climacus knows infinite resignation in and as doubt but finds in doubt a passion that can come to its own truth in and through its own paradox and impossibility. By the end of *Philosophical Fragments* Johannes has named this passion; it is faith. But, as we will see in a moment, it is not a faith that the understanding can choose or reject, for faith is the condition of understanding, and all that understanding has to do is to learn this through the passion that is (already) and will become its downfall, or through philosophy's higher education. And Kierkegaard is all of these, for they are the paradox and understanding in him, as him. As he says, as Johannes Climacus, 'all I have is my life which I promptly stake every time a difficulty appears' (1985: 8).

4. INTEREST IN LEARNING

We have in chapter 1 above seen how Kant saw the educational nature of this difficult relation to be the higher education of reflective judgement which came to know the absolute relation of formation and finality. Also we saw that for Hegel the necessity of positing comprehends its own necessity as the notion and therein as the absolute. Finally we saw that Heidegger turned the difficulty of the relation to the object into a merely unmediated self-relation with disastrous consequences for the philosophy of learning that it then espoused. Now we return to Johannes Climacus who, like Kant and Hegel, works out the structure, the logic or the 'system' that expresses itself in and through the contradiction.

Johannes extends his insight into the contradiction between ideality and reality. He notes that this contradiction is the coming into existence of consciousness and is its nature. As for Hegel, so for Johannes, whilst categories of reflection are always 'dichotomous' (1985: 169) because they make possible the relation or the dualism, the categories of consciousness are 'trichotomous' (1985: 169). This is because only in the latter is doubt possible as the relation to, or of, the relation.

> Consciousness is mind, and it is remarkable that when one is divided in the world of mind, there are three, never two... If there were nothing but dichotomies, doubt would not exist, for the possibility of doubt resides precisely in the third, which places the two in relation each other (1985: 169).

Reflection produces doubt only in the sense that doubt presupposes reflection, i.e., doubt is already the (consciousness of) the dualism, but equally doubt is nothing without the dualism. In Kantian terms—trichotomous and not dichotomous, as we saw in chapter 1—the conditions of the possibility of doubt are likewise the conditions of the possibility of doubt as its own object. And this is why doubt is philosophy's *higher* education. It is a 'higher expression' (1985: 170) and a higher form than reflection. Reflection is disinterested, it is 'objective thinking,' (1985: 170) and, *contra* the interest and telos of philosophy's higher education, 'objective indifference can... learn nothing at all' (1968: 51).[16] But consciousness is both 'between' the reflective relation (concept and intuition, for us and in itself) and is the 'interest' in that relation. The immanent and absolute nature of this 'interest' we have yet to explore.

Kierkegaard first describes the higher nature of this interest in his PhD thesis, published as *The Concept of Irony* in 1841. In this work philosophy's higher education marks an advance on merely Socratic doubt. The latter asks questions 'without any interest in the answer except to suck out the apparent content by means of the question and thereby to leave an emptiness behind,' (1989: 36) what Kierkegaard later calls Socrates' 'dialectical vacuum pump' (1989: 178). In contrast, the question with an interest in the answer is a speculative question, and it is this type of question that is therefore interested in and open to 'the deeper and more significant' (1989: 36) nature of what is learned. This higher education over the irony of Socrates Kierkegaard calls 'subjectivity raised to the second power, a subjectivity's subjectivity' (1989: 242). It contains exactly the paradox of learning—the paradox that *is* learning—seen above in *Philosophical Fragments*, that 'inasmuch as subjectivity was unauthorized it could obtain its rights only by being annulled' (1989: 242).

The *Concluding Unscientific Postscript* also explores the triadic logic of subjectivity's subjectivity. Here Kierkegaard (again as Climacus) describes 'interest' or 'absolute interest' as existence. He distinguishes the real from ideality or the thinking of the real in the same way as he (Johannes) did above. The possibility of reality appears dialectical, but it is the illusory being of existence or reflection which overlooks the possibility of *this* possibility, i.e., the conditions of the possibility of possibility itself. In fact, the relation of the possibility of reality or existence 'is the dialectical moment in a trilogy' (1968: 279). The third aspect of the possibility of reality or existence is that the existing individual is already 'himself in the dialectical moment' (1968: 279) or, put another way, the pure thinking philosopher 'forgets' (1968: 284) that he is already existing.[17] Thus in the triadic relation of existence pre-existing itself, our relation to reality and to thinking return us to the paradox that what we see as the result of our thinking is in fact already presupposed or posited in and as our thinking.[18]

But the question remains, why or how is 'interest' a higher education and an absolute education in the way that reflection or mediation or irony are not? We saw that in *Philosophical Fragments* Johannes Climacus was prepared to name this higher education as faith. But faith carries much of the Judge's ethical baggage with it, and we may well find ourselves resembling de Silentio as the man unable to make such a religious leap. If we are to understand faith in its comprehensive sense, that is, not as the Judge expounds it, but educationally, as 'infinitely interested passion,' (1968: 32) we have to explore Kierkegaard's own rewriting of Socratic higher education as philosophy's higher education, or as *repetition*.

5. RECOLLECTION AND REPETITION

These two concepts together constitute Kierkegaardian higher education. Doubt for Johannes Climacus is repetition.[19] Consciousness, he says, emerges through the collision of reality and identity, but also presupposes it. This contradiction, the very relation of consciousness, is 'repetition' (1985: 171). 'As soon as the question of repetition arises, the collision is present, for only a repetition of what has been before is conceivable' (1985: 171). Repetition, then, is precisely not reflection for repetition realises reflection. But, and it is vital we keep stressing this, repetition is not itself purely reflective because it is both dependent upon the reflective collision and it presupposes that reflective collision. As the latter it is the only way the collision is conceivable, that is, as its repetition, but as its repetition it is also dependent upon (and as) the relation. I am sure that if you are reading the book from start to finish you are already ahead of me now. The relation of independence through dependence is exactly the necessity we are calling philosophy's higher education everywhere we meet it, in Kant, in Hegel, now in Kierkegaard and in Nietzsche and Rosenzweig yet to come. If so, you, now, are my repetition, but in your learning, and our education.

If we now combine the concept of repetition with the analysis of the paradox taken from *Philosophical Fragments* we will see exactly how repetition is interest or is an absolute relation or 'absolute equality' (1985:47). The paradox revealed that not only was sin 'our own fault' but that only in sin is the unknown conceived or truly (known as) unknown. Now, we can see that our doubt is only the repetition of the collision between the unknown (reality) and its being unknown (ideality). Thus, doubt is the repetition of the unknown, or is our higher education regarding the absolute equality of difference and likeness (formation and finality, master and slave). Johannes Climacus states 'thus the paradox... has the duplexity by which it manifests itself as the absolute—negatively, by bringing into prominence the absolute difference of sin, and, positively, by wanting to annul this absolute difference in the absolute equality' (1985: 47). And when reflection is offended at the talk of repetition as equality it is precisely because it has suppressed again what it has learned.

But what of recollection? In *Philosophical Fragments* Johannes argues that recollection is the ancient form of repetition, lacking as it were, subjectivity's subjectivity. Above we noted that recollection, viewed Socratically, does not have the significance of an historical point of departure. Thus Socrates is midwife but not teacher. But recollection as the higher education of the duplexity of consciousness, or as doubt, becomes a moment 'in time [that] must have [a] decisive significance' (1985: 13) for it is when the previously unknown and nonexistent eternal 'came into existence' (1985: 13). The decisive significance of this historical point of departure, where recollection is higher education, is repetition, or is subjectivity's subjectivity, or again is doubt. And I repeat these are not reflective categories for they exist in and as the historical point of departure and not merely as Socratic irony.

Constantin Constantius can argue that 'repetition is a crucial expression for what "recollection" was to the Greeks' (1983: 131) because now a modern philosophy with its new form of irony understands that 'all life is a repetition' (1983: 131) and that as such repetition is 'an expression for immanence' (1968:

235). Not only is repetition a higher education of recollection, but this education in itself forms Kierkegaard's version of the philosophy of history. In subjectivity's subjectivity 'a contradiction appears, by means of which the world process takes place' (1989: 260).[20] Constantin Constantius argues, 'repetition and recollection are the same movement, except in opposite directions, for what is recollected has been, is repeated backward, whereas genuine repetition is recollected forward' (1983: 131). As for philosophy's higher education, then, recollection is the relation between ideality and reality but repetition is the decisive educational significance of that relation, not just as moment, but as the paradox of the moment. Just as doubt is the only way the dualism can be known but is itself dependent upon the dualism for doubt itself being known, so repetition is how recollection is known, but recollection is also the knowing of repetition.

Throughout our examination of Kierkegaard's work we have seen over and over again how this triadic structure underpins all of his most difficult relations. The key question for philosophy's higher education, whether it be in terms of subjectivity, sin, love, doubt, faith (or the soul, below) is how can something be possessed (recollected) yet also gained, or given, at the same time? The answer is now apparent. What is already possessed can be gained only in the decisive educational significance of its being lost, and gained such that what is gained is what was already possessed. Gaining, or receiving, is learning that possession, loss and gain are the absolute relation of repetition and recollection. If you like, we can say as a definition of philosophy's higher education that repetition is the actuality of the education of recollection. It is when we know that our learning is both backwards as a recollection of what was and forwards as a repetition of that recollection. If this repetition is only of the same (something we will explore in the next chapter) then nothing is learned and nothing can be said. But it is too late for such an abstract and dogmatic assertion about the nature of 'nothing'. Our higher education is already present in the very question that has the movement (of nothing) as its object. To see repetition as either of the same or of the different is to return to reflective dualities and to miss the significance of the historical point of departure. It is to suppress the nothing. What is repeated is repeated differently, but the different is only the knowing of what is repeated as the same. In the contradiction is our higher education and, further, in their mutual 'equality' that relation is an absolute (and absolutely unequal) mutuality. 'The dialectic of repetition is easy, for that which is repeated has been—otherwise it could not be repeated—but the very fact that it has been makes the repetition into something new' (1983: 149). Further, and echoing Hegel, 'when one says that life is a repetition, one says: actuality, which has been, now comes into existence' (1983: 149). Thus although philosophy arrives on the scene 'after' actuality, it is of course there 'before', and eternally.

Of equal significance for some current philosophy is Constantin Constantius' critique of 'hope'. Hope is for the 'new garment' (1983: 132), something new to wear, whilst recollection is something we have outgrown. In a sense hope is a *ressentiment* against this outgrowth. In a truly Nietzschean sense, repetition 'is an indestructible garment that fits closely and tenderly,' (1983: 132) one whose necessity or interest is precisely the absolute nature of the higher educational relation. Thus whilst one can in bad faith hope against that necessity and feign disinterest, 'it takes courage to will repetition' (1983: 132). To will repetition is to learn of interest, and necessity, and contingency upon the historical point of departure, as becoming what we are, what we have been, and of course will be (already) again.

6. UPBUILDING HIGHER EDUCATION

We have now achieved sufficient distance from the different characterisations of Kierkegaard to have our work present not reflectively but speculatively. We could recollect, reflectively, on parts of Kierkegaard's authorship but that would be to suppress the repetition of that work, i.e. to suppress its significance for us regarding its significance for him. If we lack the will for repetition then we lose the man who has risked losing himself that we may be his repetition, and our education. But, in having Kierkegaard now as repetition we can be his 'reader,' 'that favourably disposed person whom I with joy and gratitude call my refuge, who by making my thoughts his own does more for me than I do for him' (1990: 53).

What then does this repetition of recollection look like, feel like and mean to the man Soren Kierkegaard? Or, in our terms, what do we learn from philosophy's higher education? For this, we turn to the upbuilding discourses that Kierkegaard published under his own name, for these are the repetition of the recollection that is Kierkegaard. Indeed, in terms of upbuilding, we can now add further educational significance to the repetition of recollection. The epithet 'know thyself' which was on the oracle at Delphi characterises the ancient Socratic higher education of recollection. 'Know thyself' for Socrates, as for Nietzsche, meant 'become what you are'. The educational process by which this was to occur for Socrates as for Plato was recollection. As Socrates showed Meno that 'his soul has been for ever in a state of knowledge' (1956: 153) and requires him only to recollect what is already there, so, for Plato, education does not 'implant' (1992: 204) knowledge in the soul, it turns the soul towards itself. But repetition is the modern form of this upbuilding education. To 'know thyself' now includes the repetition of recollection, or the actuality of the self who knows subjectivity's subjectivity. Or, again, 'know thyself' now means know thyself in the absolute relation of doubt and reflection. This is no longer merely a dialectical reflection of negation. Now the higher education is that there is a relation of the relation, and that this relation, as interest and necessity, is absolute. Know thyself, as repetition, is a triadic relation in which the 'self' is known to itself through the understanding which annihilates it and as the paradox in which the downfall of the understanding is both presupposed and yet that upon which the paradox itself is contingent. Know thyself now involves a different understanding of the same contingency that always was. Now, as repetition, know thyself means learn of thyself as already (and always having been) in the absolute relation of sin to the immediate or the eternal. There is no escaping the 'religious' significance of the new education that is repetition as 'know thyself'.

So, to learn from Kierkegaard what know thyself as repetition means for him, we will turn to what on the surface are the overtly religious *Upbuilding Discourses*. But before we explore some of the ways that repetition appears in Kierkegaard's higher education, we must signal a caution, indeed, an inaccuracy, in seeing these discourses as 'religious'. They are religious, but they are also aesthetic and philosophical, the three great manifestations of absolute spirit. If the *Discourses* are not seen as both the result and the interest of philosophy's higher education as it has been explored above in Kierkegaard's work, then we are not his reader. The *Discourses* are now the whole of the relation between immediacy and mediation understood as repetition. That is the whole reason that they are upbuilding, the repetition *is* a learning, and learning *is* repetition. As such, this higher education cannot be assigned to one side of the relation or the other. It is aesthetic because it knows that recollection cannot survive the temporal and can only be enjoyed in negative (eternal) suspension. It is religious because it also knows that the knight of infinite resignation must take one further leap and believe in the impossibility that he defends. But the relation of the impossible and the absurd is only actual as the learning that the collision both creates and has always been. As upbuilding, this is philosophy's higher education of the relation between the aesthetic and the religious, where both are present, where both are equally impossible, and where that impossibility is equally impossible as the contradiction, the education, that knows it. Here, what is upbuilding is precisely the trichotomous relation referred to above; 'when one is divided in the world of mind [and here the one is truth as infinite resignation and faith] there are three, never two' (1985: 169). As such the *Upbuilding Discourses* are what philosophy's higher education looks like, understood now as aesthetic, religious and actual as the learning of this single individual.

At this point, I know from experience, that some say, ah, well, such an education is solipsistic, concerned only with the self. Such a criticism has missed the whole significance of philosophy's higher education. This self for whom the aesthetic, the religious and the philosophical are upbuilding is *not* himself. He has long since vanished into its separate characteristics, is long since annihilated as something that can understand or be understood. Indeed, it is this loss that in the work of upbuilding is being repeated as not-the-self. Others will still ask, where, then, is the relation to the other? I refer them back to the discussion of the object in chapter 2. But for Kierkegaard, the 'other' is precisely what has arisen in the historical point of departure, not only as the generations and the individuals within them, but also, for them, the departure itself. Otherness is the whole of the relation that now learns of and from itself. Any 'other' kind of otherness is only again, a recollection, a 'new immediacy' or a 'new ethics', that lacks the decisive significance of its own otherness. As Kierkegaard says in the *Postscript*, faith 'accentuates the existence of the other person, not one's own significance' (1968: 514).

There are many examples of philosophy's higher education in the *Upbuilding Discourses*, and I will briefly explore just a few of them here. Each however, can now be seen as an example of the higher education that is the repetition of recollection.

Faith is the key to understanding the *Upbuilding Discourses* as higher education. For the 'cheerful disposition that has not yet tasted life's adversities... [and] has not been formed by the dubious wisdom of experience,' (1990: 19-20) the expectancy of faith is victory in all the struggles that lie ahead in the future. Equally, for 'the troubled person' (1990: 20) the expectancy of faith is that the future will 'at least grant him the peace to be quietly occupied with his pain' (1990: 20). However, neither of these reflective positions comprehends the repetition of faith. As recollection 'faith has never existed in the world precisely because it has always existed' (1983: 55). Thus, the expectancy of faith in the future, in victory in any of its forms, is not the repetition of faith. 'The reason we so often go astray,' says Kierkegaard, 'is that we seek assurance of our expectancy instead of faith's assurance that we have faith' (1990: 27). The repetition of faith, or faith as repetition, means that faith is not 'the spontaneous inclination of the heart but the paradox of existence' (1983: 47). It has two tasks, 'to take care in every moment to discover the improbable, the paradox; and then to hold it fast with the passion of inwardness' (1968: 209). Faith is 'no aesthetic emotion,' (1983: 47) it is a choice. But it is not a choice of 'something particular,' (1990: 27) it is to choose the eternal. The eternal is chosen not only *as* repetition but by the very impossibility of choosing that lies within (and is) repetition. When the eternal is chosen it means that one chooses the necessity of repetition as oneself.

> This self that he chooses in this way is infinitely concrete, for it is he himself, and yet it is absolutely different from his former self, for he has chosen it absolutely. This self has not existed before, because it came into existence through the choice, and yet it has existed, for it was indeed 'himself' (1987b: 215).

Note here, that repetition is not self-creation, it is self-choosing. Self-creation would be a reflective category that did not understand the decisive significance of requiring 'faith's assurance that we have faith' (1990: 27). As Johannes de Silentio noted above, as recollection faith has never existed in the world because it has always existed. But as repetition, the movement of recollection forwards, faith must learn of itself as dependency upon what has been whilst at the same time (sic) being the condition of the possibility of that dependency. To see the relation of dependency and pre-condition or of recollection and repetition as creative is to assume that the self gives the gift to himself. But as we will see in a moment, doubt is not a gift that we can give to ourselves, it is a condition (and a pre-condition) that we have to choose as ourselves. When faith seeks assurance of itself it repeats itself as the absurd and repeats only the annihilation of faith. 'For the movement of faith must continually be made by virtue of the absurd, but yet in such a way, please note, that one does not lose the finite but gains it whole and intact' (1983: 37). Such is the necessity that relates infinite resignation and faith.

To understand faith in this way opens up an understanding of one of Kierkegaard's most difficult concepts as philosophy's higher education. We saw earlier that the suspension of the ethical[21] is the action of the aesthete who eats of the fruit but is never trapped by it. Kierkegaard suspends the ethical when he ensures that the engagement is broken so that she may 'discover the infinite' (1987a: 391). Here, the suspension of the ethical asserts the individual as less than the universal. But the *teleological* suspension of the ethical that concerns Johannes de Silentio is different again, for it includes within it the telos that such assertions of being less than the universal are also assertions of being more than the universal. Thus, the suspension of the ethical is teleological when, in full awareness of the absurdity of this contradiction, the single individual nevertheless places himself higher than the universal in order to include within the universal the negation of his assertion and of himself. This suspends the ethical teleologically because, although it is his ethical duty 'to annul his singularity in order to become the universal,' (1983: 54) he knows that he can only be annulled and become the universal in and through the necessity (the teleology) of the paradox. The teleology of the suspension is that the annihilation of the universal is the becoming of the universal, and the downfall of the understanding is its own 'equality' with this universal. To suspend the ethical teleologically is to hold apart in contradiction that which is a 'unity' in contradiction. Faith, then, absurdly is 'this paradox that the single individual is higher than the universal' (1983: 55). Here faith can exist because it has never been in existence, until now, and in which moment it again becomes the loss of faith and its repetition of itself as its own passion. A teleological suspension of the ethical is not a mediation in the same way as an ordinary suspension of the ethical, for the former has undermined the understanding teleologically in a way that the latter has not. The teleological suspension of the ethical is not a choice of something particular, for example, for the eternity of love and against its reduction to finitude in marriage. It is, rather, to choose the universality of the paradox, or to choose the conditions of the possibility of choosing. It is to choose the self that must choose that it has already chosen.[22] 'An existing individual... has always a telos' (1968: 278) for he is always a repetition forwards of what he has already (not) been. To know this telos as self is to choose the *necessity* of repetition as oneself. For Johannes de Silentio such a self cannot speak, for to speak is to mediate between the universal and the particular and, as such, is to place oneself higher than the teleological suspension. Therefore he reasons that in the paradox which he cannot explain to anyone else, the single individual 'places himself in an absolute relation to the absolute' (1983: 62). Why is this relation one of the absolute to itself? Because in sin, that is, in the historical point of departure from the universal and the eternal, the difference is present as passion or interest. In the passion the understanding seeks its own downfall against immediacy *and* the passion (the difference) (already) wills that downfall so that each comes to learn of itself as already the relation to the other. Now the teleological suspension of the ethical is just such a passionate self-relation because his placing himself higher than the universal is precisely the downfall of the understanding that will learn of its dependence upon the universal, and of the dependence of the universal upon the downfall. This is the 'absolute difference in the absolute equality' (1985: 47) that Johannes Climacus spoke of earlier. The absolute relation of each to the absolute is in the teleology of the impossibility of faith, a fact that is upbuilding precisely because of its teleological necessity as the single individual.

This choosing of necessity is faith as philosophy's higher education. Either faith has its own truth, in itself, as our higher education about learning the truth (which is Johannes' project), or it is both arbitrary in what it chooses and is never, in any case, true to its own difficulty. Understood as our higher education it becomes, now, the key now to understanding other themes in the *Upbuilding Discourses*. For example, there is a law of the inner being that expresses the upbuilding faith of the single individual. 'Only the person who has abandoned his soul to worldly appetites' (1990: 84) uses this law for his own ends 'in the service of the moment' (1990: 84). But the person who knows faith as education recognises its choosing or necessity as his own. This person has the courage 'to assume the responsibility of the master by submitting to the obligation of a servant' (1990: 85) and has 'the humility to be willing to obey in order to learn how to rule and at all times is willing to rule only insofar as he himself obeys' (1990: 85). The law of inner being is the same passion seen above that meets itself when trying and failing to understand its relation to itself. The upbuilding nature of this inner law is that it strengthens the inner being.

It does this because as much as the single individual is strengthened, so he learns of himself as the absolute relation to the absolute. The passion of learning is, as Johannes Climacus testifies to, doubt. But, and here is why mediation falls to the repetition of recollection, doubt cannot give itself to itself. Doubt is always, *always* an historical point of departure. As *Philosophical Fragments* revealed, the 'condition for understanding' (1985: 14) cannot be present for if it has always existed then it has never existed. In reflective terms doubt may well be stronger than everything else. But as philosophy's higher education, doubt always lies in wait 'to disquiet him still more' (1990: 127). Doubt's higher education is that it cannot overcome itself, yet its passion is always to do so. Doubt is not stronger than itself. So what is strong enough to be able to 'give' doubt to itself? Kierkegaard's answer is 'that every good gift and every perfect gift is from above' (1990: 129, James 1:17). As I hope is clear from what we have explored above, this is not simply a dogmatic return to Scripture. On the contrary, and unlike Johannes de Silentio, this is the single individual Kierkegaard speaking philosophically of the impossibility that is aesthetic and religious. It is precisely the upbuilding character of the knowing of the unknown that is being expressed here. If you refuse to read the *Upbuilding Discourses* because they 'presuppose' God, then you are suppressing the other aspect of philosophy's higher education, that He also presupposes you. 'Every human life is planned religiously... But in our time who troubles himself to think of such things... one has no time... one grasps only what lies nearest' (1967: 94). Our education is in and through the 'pain' (1990: 128) of the knowledge according to the passion that is 'honest enough to want to be educated rather than to be deceived, out of the multiplicity to seek the one, out of the abundance to seek the one thing needful, as this is plainly and simply offered precisely according to the need for it' (1990: 128-9). Thus, says Kierkegaard, 'to need the good and perfect gift from God is a perfection' (1990: 136) because it is the absolute relation to the absolute wherein the need and the necessity meet each other in their absolute equality. 'The condition is a gift of God and a perfection that makes it possible to receive the good and perfect gift' (1990: 137). And, summing up the educative significance of the teleological suspension of the ethical, as well as the absolute relation that is philosophy's higher education for Kierkegaard, he says, 'false doubt doubts everything except itself; with the help of faith, the doubt that saves doubts only itself' (1990: 137).

To choose oneself is to choose to be the receiver of the gift that comes to us as necessity. Philosophy's higher education is to learn that we are 'obliged to receive' (1990: 144). But this does not mean that we should not learn within this necessity how to give. Give not to receive; give to recognise receipt of the gift. But 'keep an eye on it,' (1990: 147) and 'do not do as the person who knows how to make his gift yield even more after he has given it away' (1990: 147). Learning to give and to receive is learning to 'be trustworthy as a steward' (1990: 148) and that means learning that in the absolute relation you are 'more insignificant that the gift' (1990: 149). Of philosophy's higher education in general, and in particular to those whose temporal work is for others in the service of the gift— especially teachers—Kierkegaard advises

> If you have any truth to offer mankind, reduce the impact of yourself, nullify yourself, sacrifice yourself when offering your gift, lest people take you instead of the gift... Then you are indeed the giver, but nevertheless more insignificant than the gift, and every good and perfect gift is from above, even though it came through you (1990: 151).

As the absolute relation fosters equality between need or passion for the unknown and the necessity of the downfall of that need and of the unknown, so here the person who receives the gift and the person who gives it share 'equality in insignificance in relation to the gift' (1990: 157).

The upbuilding nature of faith or choosing oneself as necessity is also expressed in Kierkegaard's treatment of patience and impatience. Repeating the insights regarding recollection, Kierkegaard asks how is it possible to gain one's soul in upbuilding education if one already possesses one's soul? As with recollection, the contradiction appears that one 'cannot simultaneously possess and gain' (1990: 163) the same thing. To gain it is not to possess it; to possess it is not to need to gain it. Just as the paradox of recollection was not solved in the finite but rather revealed itself as part of the inner law of necessity, so now the soul reveals itself within the same higher education. As recollection had educational significance as repetition, and as infinite resignation had educational significance as faith, so the soul has educational significance as patience.

Like consciousness, the soul 'is a self-contradiction between the external and the internal, the temporal and the eternal,' (1990: 166) or between being (not) possessed and (not) gained. The soul, like doubt, is already an historical point of departure and, therefore, is already a repetition of itself. And, as the teleological suspension of the ethical was only teleological because faith expresses the mutual downfall of the unknown and the understanding, so the soul is only gained and possessed in the repetition that it is not gained or possessed in recollection.

The soul is most at risk when it is protected or hidden from the higher education of the eternal. This is achieved in 'impatience' which, like the aesthete, abandons faith for negative gratification, and in both cases negative gratification means earthly gratification. The person loses his soul 'who was infatuated with temporality and worldly desires,' (1990: 187) who seized 'the certainty of the moment' (1990: 187) and who 'danced the dance of pleasure until the end' (1990: 187). Such a person sees his soul 'come to standstill in the monotony of self-concern and self-preoccupation' (1990: 207) and suffers from what Kierkegaard calls 'soul-rot' (1990: 207). This impatience in the face of doubt and collapse before the unknown, becomes a 'cold fire that consumes the soul' (1990: 196). To begin with it is indulgent and sympathetic but it 'finally becomes loud mouthed, defiant and wants to explain everything although it never understood a thing' (1990: 196). Its certainty that an understanding of the absolute is 'impossible' (1990: 248) Kierkegaard likens to the earthly education that overcomes childhood. 'The child is astonished at insignificant things. The adult has laid aside childish things... there is nothing new under the sun and nothing marvellous in life' (1990: 226). As we grow older, so 'it is a long way to heaven, and the noise on earth makes it difficult to hear the voice' (1990: 243).

Yet, as we have seen, dread is exactly the continuity between the innocence of wonder and our wonder of innocence. Dread is what makes it possible for the child to know wonder and for the adult to be the child who knows. But impatience challenges dread with the earthly solace of temporal rewards. Thus what dread makes possible has to be chosen by and as the single individual. *Contra* impatience, Kierkegaard argues that in patience we gain the soul that we already possess. Whereas 'impatience is always untrue,' (1990: 216) patience is the steward of the gift that doubt cannot give itself, yet is. Patience begins not with an earthly goal, but on the contrary with a loss. What is gained in the loss is patience itself. As with choosing oneself as repetition, patience knows that what is lost is actually its gain, for patience grows 'through patience' (1990: 169).

> The first requirement is that he have the patience to understand that he does not possess himself, that he have the patience to understand that a gaining of his soul in patience is a work of patience... [that] patience comes into existence during this gaining (1990: 169-171).

Patience gains that which is already possessed but in the losing of it. As such, it shares the same educational structure of faith, the teleological suspension of the ethical, doubt and repetition. Each in their own way are examples of the work in which the gift is received by itself, from itself, within the absolute relation whose presupposition this work is, and whose work is the presupposition. As with proportionality in reflective judgement and with positing in the notion, so now within Kierkegaard's higher education, the perfect 'can be gained with full certainty, because it can be gained only by coming into existence within its own presuppositions' (1990: 169).

There are other examples we could give from the *Upbuilding Discourses*— death, expectancy, time, salvation, uncertainty, decrease—but there is one final repetition I want to draw attention to, one that serves to return us to the impossibility of our historical point of departure at the beginning of the chapter.

When Kierkegaard is quoted on marriage it is often from *Either/Or* or *Stages on Life's Way*. But in fact he returns to marriage as philosophy's higher education in an upbuilding discourse from 1845 entitled 'On the Occasion of a Wedding'. Seen now from within the educational significance of the repetition of recollection, the 'new immediacy' (1988: 162) that Judge William announces as the reconciliation in marriage of faith and love, is clarified. The collision between the seducer and the ethical man, like all collisions between immediacy and mediation that we have explored, has an educational significance that offers us a higher education. Within this higher education the question is no longer 'is it right to marry' for 'marry or do not marry—you will regret both' (1988: 156). To ask this question of another is to ask a third person 'for something one can never learn from a third person' (1988: 156). Just as 'one human being cannot teach another true wonder and true fear [for] only when they compress and expand your soul...

only then are they in truth for you,' (1993: 25) so the resolution required for marriage can only come from the higher education (the patience) that gains the soul.

The covenant requires a relation to eternity for it seeks, demands, an 'eternal resolution' (1993: 44) in 'the union of love through time' (1993: 44). So Kierkegaard's discourse seeks to explore the resolution of the betrothed and in particular to ask 'whether you have consulted God and your conscience' (1993: 44). This issue is the same one that began our chapter on Kierkegaard. If erotic love is immediate and 'unacquainted with work' (1993: 47) how, then, can it also be made a choice, a life of freedom, when this requires the work of resolution?

Kierkegaard sees marriage as upbuilding not in the infinite resignation that it cannot be true to love, nor in the 'faith' of Judge William that the ethical assimilates the aesthetic. Rather, marriage is upbuilding as the repetition of the recollection that the either/or of resignation and faith is a dualism of reflection, i.e., that it is a contradiction. Any resolution made which is not understanding of the necessity of difficulty as presupposition and presupposition as difficulty is not resolution at all.

> The resolution of marriage is that love conquers everything. Yes, it conquers everything, but it does perish in adversity if no resolution holds it firm... it is stifled in imagined importance if no resolution humbles it... Erotic love... goes astray when the resolution does not guide (1993: 62).

So Kierkegaard's advice to those proposing marriage is to 'know thyself' in order, then, to make a resolution that is in full awareness, even expectancy, of the difficulty and contradiction. The resolution of marriage is to resolve to know oneself in and as the relation that is difficulty or to know marriage as repetition. 'The first condition for a resolution is to have, that is, to *will* to have a true conception of life and of oneself' (1993: 52). This upbuilding education requires of the couple that before attending the ceremony they 'go to the house of sorrow' (1993: 52) so that they may first 'come to know the difficulties' (1993: 49). In this way marriage is a resolution, upbuilding and a repetition. When a marriage is not repetition, well, 'there is among us many a marriage that divorce has marked' (1993: 53) and for whom, married and unmarried, 'the binding covenant has become a curse' (1993: 53).

> Do I dare to deny that the sorry outcome may also have its basis in this, that in the time of youth and hope and surprise and rashness one lacked the direction or earnestness to renounce sentimentality and the lure of the moment and the illusion of fancy in order to subject oneself to the rigorous upbringing of resolution (1993: 55).

In that resolution as repetition or as oneself, not only can marriage 'provide a secure abode' (1993: 56) but it can also be the work, the repetition, of philosophy's higher education, that is, of our absolute relation.

> A true conception of life and of oneself is required for the resolution of marriage; but this already implies the second great requirement, which is just like the first: *a true conception of God*. The one entirely corresponds to the other, because no one can have a true conception of God without having a corresponding conception of life and of oneself, or a true conception of oneself without a corresponding conception of God, or a true conception of life without a corresponding conception of oneself (1993: 63).

Such is philosophy's higher education. Such is the absolute relation to the absolute. Such is resolution, faith and repetition. They are 'the only language in which God will involve himself with a human being' (1993: 63). But who will marry under such circumstances? Who will bring sorrow with them to the altar as the truth of their resolution? Does philosophy's higher education not make marriage too difficult? Is not that one of the reasons why so many people do get married, precisely and impatiently to skip the difficulties involved in choosing it or choosing themselves? And those who choose not to marry, isn't their infinite resignation also a failure of resolution? This, of course, is precisely the point. Choosing to marry or not to marry is not the issue. Choosing the higher education that comes from the dilemma, and therein choosing oneself in faith and in teleological suspension of the ethical, choosing to gain in time what is lost in eternity and to gain eternally what is lost in time, *that* is the issue. As Kant noted in his *Critique of Pure Reason*, if the size of a book be judged not by the number of pages but by the time needed to master it, then many a book 'would be much shorter if it were not so short,' (1968: 13) so marriage, as all occasions for philosophy's higher education, would be less difficult if they were much, much harder.

NOTES

[1] 'Hegel is a Johannes Climacus who does not storm the heavens... but climbs up to them by means of his syllogisms' (1985: 231, from a letter, January 20th, 1839).

[2] See Climacus, 1982.

[3] But, to anticipate, he says in the *Concluding Unscientific Postscript*, 'the subjective thinker is aesthetic enough to give his life aesthetic content, ethical enough to regulate it, and dialectical enough to interpenetrate it with thought' (1968: 314).

[4] SK became engaged to Regine on 10th September, 1840. In October of the following year he broke it off.

[5] In November, 1847.

[6] This is not the teleological suspension of philosophy's higher education however. We will return to this later in the chapter.

[7] We will return to the upbuilding or educative significance of faith below.

[8] Meaning, the watchman of Copenhagen.

[9] I am not therefore continuing to explore the aspect of teacher and learner in parts I and II. However, in place of a longer study we can note that Climacus reasons that the condition of the possibility of learning the truth is untruth. Untruth is realised by the learner when what he recollects from his (new state of) knowing is that he now knows that 'previously' he did not know. Indeed, it was 'his own fault' (1985: 15) that he did not know. In this new state now of knowing that he was in untruth, he is nevertheless still in untruth, for now all he knows is that he did not know, and by knowing that he did not know, he is removed from or 'excluded from the truth, even more than when he was ignorant of being untruth' (1985: 14). This education into his own prior and present untruth Climacus describes as a journey through sin, in that it is his own fault, repentance and sorrow at having been in the former state, but also a conversion from 'not to be' to 'to be', and a rebirth in that 'he enters the world a second time' (1985: 19) and is now a 'new person' (1985: 18).

But what of the teacher? Climacus argues that the teacher of recollection must be the god. It is his truth that is being learned in untruth for it is he that has provided the condition for learning. And in providing the condition for learning, he provides the condition for his being known. 'What moves him to make his appearance?' asks Climacus. The answer is love, for only love can find equality or unity in what is unequal. In this case it is love that is eternity fulfilled in time as the moment, and love that is the moment 'swallowed by recollection into its eternity' (1985: 25). Obviously this work cannot be done by an ordinary teacher. Such a teacher cannot be the unity of what is equal and different. Indeed the teacher must beware even of teaching the truth of untruth, in case he takes 'away the wrath that lay over the incurred guilt' (1985: 17) and becomes the 'reconciler' (1985: 17) of the opposition of truth and untruth. What the philosophical teacher can be, however, is the moment and eternity in and as the work of learning or philosophy's higher education.

[10] from pp. 44-8 of *Philosophical Fragments*

[11] my phrase

[12] i.e., unless god is a teacher

[13] It is the same mutuality noted above in chapter 2 between the slave and the thing in Hegelian phenomenology.

[14] Particularly the plethora of interpretations of Hegelian 'mutual recognition' which ignore its collapse into and collision with the political. See above, chapter 2.

[15] In fact he was completing his Master of Arts diploma, but in 1854 all those holding such degrees from the University of Copenhagen were upgraded to doctors of philosophy (see Kierkegaard, 1989: xii-xiii.

[16] Kierkegaard would be better putting this as indifference cannot learn from the 'nothing at all'.

[17] As we will see in the next chapter, this might more accurately be expressed in Nietzschean terms as forgetting to remember to forget.

[18] This is the self-determination of illusion, seen above in chapter 2, and returned to again in later chapters.

[19] As experience for Kant was a representation of a representation and philosophy for Hegel always arrived on the scene after actuality (Hegel, 1967: 12).

[20] We will return to philosophy's higher education as the philosophy of history in chapter 6.

[21] But not the teleological suspension!

[22] This is a difficult sentence but expresses the contradiction of repetition that faith means choosing itself as its own lack of choice, a choice that has already been made in having, then, to make the choice!.

REFERENCES

Climacus, J. (1982) *The Ladder of Divine Ascent*, New Jersey: Paulist Press, trans. C. Luibheid and N. Russell.

Hegel, G.W.F. (1967) *Philosophy of Right*, Oxford: Oxford University Press.

Hegel, G.W.F. (1969) *Science of Logic*, London: George Allen and Unwin Press.

Hegel, G.W.F. (1975) *Hegel's Logic*, Oxford; Oxford University Press.

Hegel, G.W.F. (1977) *Phenomenology of Spirit*, Oxford, Oxford University Press.

Kant, I. (1968) *Critique of Pure Reason*, London: Macmillan.

Kierkegaard, S. (1967) *The Concept of Dread*, Princeton; Princeton University Press, trans. W. Lowrie.

Kierkegaard, S. (1968) *Concluding Unscientific Postscript*, Princeton: Princeton University Press, trans. D.F. Swenson and W. Lowrie.

Kierkegaard, S. (1983) *Fear and Trembling/Repetition*, Princeton: Princeton University Press, trans. H.V. and E.H Hong.

Kierkegaard, S. (1985) *Philosophical Fragments/Johannes Climacus*, Princeton: Princeton University Press, trans. H.V. and E.H Hong.

Kierkegaard, S. (1987a) *Either/Or I*, Princeton: Princeton University Press, trans. H.V. and E.H Hong.

Kierkegaard, S. (1987b) *Either/Or II*, Princeton: Princeton University Press, trans. H.V. and E.H Hong.

Kierkegaard, S. (1988) *Stages on Life's Way*, Princeton: Princeton University Press, trans. H.V. and E.H Hong.

Kierkegaard, S. (1989) *The Concept of Irony*, Princeton: Princeton University Press, trans. H.V. and E.H Hong.

Kierkegaard, S. (1990) *Eighteen Upbuilding Discourses*, Princeton: Princeton University Press, trans. H.V. and E.H Hong.

Kierkegaard, S. (1993) *Three Discourses on Imagined Occasions*, Princeton: Princeton University Press, trans. H.V. and E.H Hong.

Lowrie, W. (1944) *A Short Life of Kierkegaard*, Oxford University Press.

Plato, (1956) *Protagoras and Meno*, Harmondsworth: Penguin.

Plato, (1992) *The Republic*, London: Everyman.

CHAPTER 5

NIETZSCHE: WILL TO POWER AND ETERNAL RETURN

Deleuze, in his book *Nietzsche and Philosophy*, challenges philosophy's higher education with a different kind of speculative experience. Before drawing out philosophy's higher education from Nietzsche, then, we will summarise Deleuze's reading, keeping in mind that despite its speculative rigour and logic, it brooks 'no possible compromise between Hegel and Nietzsche' (Deleuze, 1983: 195).

1. *RESSENTIMENT* AND NIHILISM

Chapter 5 of *Nietzsche and Philosophy* sets out Deleuze's case *for* Nietzsche and *against* the dialectic. There are several aspects to this opposition. First, the dialectic itself and its constituent parts—'universal and singular, changeless and particular, infinite and finite' (1983: 157)—are 'nothing but symptoms' (1983: 157) of a deeper condition. 'Dialectic thrives on oppositions because it is unaware of far more subtle and subterranean differential mechanisms' (1983: 157). In fact, this misrecognition is a kind of *camera obscura*. Seen from the reactive standpoint, 'the differential element is inverted, reflected wrong way up and turned into opposition' (1983: 159). Thus, 'the dialectic is the natural ideology of *ressentiment* and bad conscience' (1983: 159).

Second, this natural ideology of the reactive is 'the authentically Christian ideology' (1983: 196) and the authentically scholastic ideology of 'the theoretical man' (1983: 196). Both employ the negative to establish and preserve their own power, established by turning life against itself and preserved through a 'phantom of affirmation' (1983: 196) where 'whether as overcome opposition or as resolved contradiction, the image of positivity is radically falsified' (1983: 196). In this falsification the goal of the reactive man is nothingness, for the separation of 'active force from what it can do' (1983: 64) overcomes affirmation. As such, 'the foundation of the humanity in man' (1983: 64) is itself only a product of an endemic failure by that which is positive in man to affirm itself. Humanity therefore only knows itself in 'the reactive man as the failed or deified expression of reactive forces and [in] the active man as the essentially abortive product of an activity which falls short of its goal essentially' (1983: 168). As such, dialecticians 'were prisoners of symptoms and did not reach the forces or the will which give to these sense and value' (1983: 197).

Third, this deeper condition which the dialectic inverts is 'difference'. To comprehend what Deleuze means by difference, and to understand its structure and its logic, we have to explore Deleuze's model of the relation between will to power and eternal return. But to be able to do this we first have to analyse the characteristic that, for Deleuze, defines active and reactive standpoints.

The active force is a relation between 'active and reactive forces such that the latter are themselves acted' (1983: 111). This means that the active man 'expresses the "normal" relation between a reaction that delays action and an action that precipitates action' (1983: 111). Reaction acts to hinder, delay or obstruct. The active forms 'a riposte' (1983: 111). Thus the active man 'acts his reactions' (1983: 111) and his reactions obey that which is active in them. In the noble, the active is commander and the reactive is obeyer.

When the reactive prevails over the active, then the obeyer obeys a different form of force, the force of *ressentiment*. When the reactive obeys this force, it ceases to act. Deleuze makes clear that we should not define *ressentiment* 'in terms of the strength of a reaction' (1983: 111). It is not that *ressentiment* re-acts and triumphs, it is rather that it does not act. 'Reactive forces prevail over active forces because they escape their action' (1983: 111). In this escape, active forces 'are separated from what they can do' (1983: 114) and reactive forces become the (ideological) whole. That is, freed from having to act, reaction is nevertheless perceptible as *ressentiment*, as ceasing to be acted. Deleuze expresses this perception as the 'invasion of consciousness' (1983: 114) by memory which suppresses the faculty of forgetting which, previously, has itself suppressed activity as a memory (i.e., a non-activity or moment). This is why reactive forces, for Deleuze, are nihilism or a will to nothingness. They are not a stronger reaction than activity, they are non-activity. As Nietzsche makes clear in *Untimely Meditations*, the man of prodigious memory is the man farthest from activity and the man therefore of deepest *ressentiment*. Since this is not a 'doing,' it is, says Deleuze, 'felt instead' (1983: 115). As such, its relation to the object is one of revenge, for (again ideologically) it blames the object for the 'infinite delay' (1983: 115) in activity, rather than its own state of mind. Thus, 'the man of *ressentiment* experiences every being and object as an offence in exact proportion to its effect on him' (1983: 116). Deleuze concludes,

> *Ressentiment* is the triumph of the weak *as* weak, the revolt of the slaves and their victory as slaves. It is in their victory that the slaves form a type. The type of the master (the active type) is defined in terms of the faculty of forgetting and the power of acting reactions. The

type of the slave (the reactive type) is defined by a prodigious memory, by the power of *ressentiment*... (1983: 117).

The victory of *ressentiment*, of the reactive, is nihilism. When life as active is opposed by the negative as value, then the negative has already triumphed. Opposition is already memory; memory is already *ressentiment*; *ressentiment* is already other than activity and takes the form of value. Negativity as value defines and determines humanity thus far. But Deleuze finds in Nietzsche a transvaluation of all values, one in which a new freedom is released. This transvaluation can only be understood through Deleuze's conception of the will to power. But before there is transvaluation there is the absolute victory of nihilism.

Deleuze distinguishes negative nihilism from reactive nihilism. The former is at least a will to power for it retains itself in and as the will to deny. The latter, derived from the former, establishes denial as principle and as value. But it too stagnates into a passive nihilism, or into mere pity. Even God, the epitome of the higher value, is put to death by pity, for there can be no witnesses of the hostility to life, even those created by that very hostility. 'It is better to have no values at all than higher values, it is better to have no will at all, better to have a nothingness of will than a will to nothingness. It is better to fade away passively' (1983: 150). And Deleuze adds, 'told in this way the story still leads to the same conclusion: negative nihilism is replaced by reactive nihilism, reactive nihilism ends in passive nihilism. From God to God's murderer, from God's murderer to the last man' (1983: 151).

Thus, says Deleuze, whilst Hegel bets on the cross, Nietzsche 'mistrusts the death of God' (1983: 156). Hegel's 'suspended opposition' (1983: 156) works from within the fiction of the dialectic; it works only with symptoms. It is therefore 'unaware of the real element from which forces... derive' (1983: 157). 'Opposition can be the law of the relation between abstract products, but difference is the only principle of genesis or production' (1983: 157). Thus dialectic and contradiction are only a 'perpetual misinterpretation of difference itself, a confused inversion of genealogy,' (1983: 157) or where difference is 'turned into opposition' (1983: 159). As such, the dialectic is 'the natural ideology of *ressentiment* and bad conscience' (1983: 159) and the death of God occurs in 'the din of reactive forces and the fumes of nihilism' (1983: 159).

2. WILL TO POWER AND ETERNAL RETURN

Against the victory of nihilism, Deleuze finds the overman and transvaluation to be Nietzsche's twofold positive task. Overcoming and transvaluing, says Deleuze, are a new way of feeling and thinking. It is not even the higher man, for it differs 'in nature' (1983: 163) from all men, yet it is from man that overcoming and transvaluation will emerge. This double aspect or ambivalence of *ressentiment* is very important in Deleuze's reading of Nietzsche. The reactive mode is both essence and deformity. Indeed, the becoming of forces 'always requires... the presence of the opposite quality,' (1983: 167) that is, the becoming of forces in general is also 'the becoming reactive of all forces' (1983: 167). This is why, as we saw above, reactive force is not a *re*-action but rather it is activity opposed by itself in the form of denial. In negative nihilism this denial is still in a sense active, but as reactive and then passive nihilism it is absolutely opposed to activity. Thus reactive forces are not 'grafted' (1983: 167) onto the activity, they are two sides of the same coin.[1]

There is a reconciliation here—of the reactive man as the form of reaction with the active man who always fails. The form of failure and the formation of failure are reconciled as failure in the ambivalence of the higher man. But even the higher man is not Zarathustra. The higher man, who claims to convert reaction into affirmation, in fact remains within the fiction of values. He might change the values, but unlike Zarathustra he does not change 'the element from which the value of values derives' (1983: 171). Only when 'the element is changed, then, and only then, can it be said that all values known or knowable up to the present have been reversed' (1983: 171).

So, how is nihilism defeated? Who or what is Zarathustra? What is the new way of thinking and feeling that is overcoming and transmutation? Deleuze has the same answer to all three questions. They are the defeat of nihilism by itself, or its completion. To explain how this is the case Deleuze makes a crucial argument. The will to power, as knowledge, is the essential failure of will to power—its essence and deformity. Will to power as knowledge is therefore always its own opposition. This knowledge, manifest as nihilism or the will to nothingness is the foundation of all values that are and have been knowable up to the present time. 'All known and knowable values are, by nature, values which derive from this *ratio*' (198: 172) of the will to power as negative. But, if we know (sic) that such knowing is only 'one form' of the will to power, only 'one of its qualities' (1983: 172) then we are already 'thinking' the will to power 'in a form distinct from that in which we know it' (1983: 173). Thus, the '*ratio* in terms of which the will to power is known is not the *ratio* in terms of which it exists' (1983: 175).

Let us pause for a moment. We have come across this kind of distinction and relationship before. Kant distinguishes subsumptive knowing from reflective knowing, and includes 'feeling' in the latter. Caygill's reading of Benjamin finds a relation between the condition of knowing that is held by a particular surface (transcendental) and the particular configuration of knowing that is conditioned by the surface (speculative). Deleuze's ratio of will to power includes both aspects. The transvaluation is from the knowledge of values to the value of knowledge. The transmutation is both from the element of knowledge to the element of its deeper genealogy—will to power—'and' the transmutation is not a simple abstract or 'knowledgeable' overcoming. It is rather a transmutation where the will to power 'teaches us that it is known to us in only one form' (1983: 172). Or, we might say, where the will to power teaches us that the conditions of its being known (reactive) are also configured as only one of its possible forms of being known (active), and that the two conditions, together, see nihilism defeated by itself.

In the defeat of nihilism by itself the *ratio cognoscendi* of the will to power, our knowing it, is overcome by the *ratio essendi* of the will to power, our thinking of our knowing it, such that the will to power as a whole is affirmed as surface and configuration. There is no negation here. This is not merely another knowing that remains unthinking about knowledge as value. On the contrary, this overcoming is the affirmation of new values, values which are no longer in denial of their own genealogy in and of the will to power. Now 'the legislator takes the place of the "scholar" [and] creation takes the place of knowledge itself' (1983: 173).

Who lives this transmutation? It is the man who wills his own downfall, or who actively destroys himself as nothingness. This means he must become more of what he already is, not less, for his will to nothingness must destroy itself. Here is the irony of Deleuze's Zarathustra, or of any creator of the new values. He must be even more negative than the higher man. In such a man 'destruction becomes active to the extent that the negative is transmuted and converted into affirmative power: the "eternal joy of becoming"' (1983: 174).

> Nihilism reaches its completion by passing through the last man, but going beyond him to the man who wants to perish. In the man who wants to perish, to be overcome, negation has broken everything which still held it back, it has defeated itself, it has become of affirming, a power which is already superhuman, a power which announces and prepares the overman (1983: 175).

Deleuze, in a manner again similar to Caygill, characterises this thinking of knowledge as an 'excess' (1983: 175) or as a negation or not-knowing that is manifested 'above man, outside man' (1983: 177). This cannot be dismissed as a crude transcendental or *a priori*, for Deleuze stresses that this excess, this beyond, is also within the totality of the will to power. This is the current attraction of philosophies of excess, that they take us beyond our current limits but without eschewing our contingency within the confines of limits altogether. The relation of excess, therefore, is both transcendental and speculative, 'raised to its higher degree at the same time as it defeats itself' (1983: 179). We might say the will to power exceeds its own particular surface but limits all excess to surfaces *per se*.

Also, *contra* the dialectic, Deleuze's Nietzsche destroys the value of truth that resides in the bad conscience of the reactive and is 'opposed to every form of thought which trusts in the power of the negative' (1983: 179). The latter merely says Yes 'to everything which is no' (1983: 183). Its only positivity is that it says Yes to denial. For Deleuze, this is Hegel's 'positivity of the negative' (1983: 180). True affirmation, the Dionysian Yes, 'knows how to say no' (1983: 185) to all forms of *ressentiment* in which the No masquerades as Yes. Only this no can overcome the reactive Yes to all Nos. Only this No affirms itself through the denial of denial.[2]

Our final question regarding Deleuze's reading of Nietzsche must be to ask why, now, is the affirmative denial of denial not the positivity of Hegel's negation of the negative? The answer for Deleuze lies in eternal return. 'The lesson of the eternal return is that there is no return of the negative' (1983: 189). From the standpoint of reaction, opposed to creativity and affirmation, it looks as if it is the negative that eternally returns. Indeed it seems 'to compromise or contaminate' our essential reactivity 'so gravely that it becomes an object of anguish, repulsion and disgust' (1983: 65). The overman, however, bites the head off this coiled snake. Formerly the object of disgust, 'the eternal return overcomes disgust and turns Zarathustra into a "convalescent"...' (1983: 68).

In a physical sense, says Deleuze, 'it is not being that returns but rather the returning itself that constitutes being' (1983: 48). 'Identity in the eternal return does not describe the nature of that which returns but, on the contrary, the fact of returning for that which differs' (1983: 48). Again within the characteristics of Caygill's transcendental and speculative self-relation, Deleuze argues that eternal return is a synthesis, not a whole. The nature of this synthesis is a 'double affirmation' (1983: 48) of a kind that a merely mechanical cycle could not explain. The latter could not account for 'the diversity of co-existing cycles and, above all, the existence of diversity within the cycle' (1983: 49). This is much the same as Benjamin's double infinity of 'the transcendental infinity of possible marks on a given surface... and the speculative infinity of possible bounded but infinite surfaces or frameworks of experience' (Caygill, 1998: 4). As a physical doctrine, then, will to power is the force that both divides and is the difference. To differentiate is to be itself. It is as such always the destruction of the mechanism of the same or of experience, because even to express the characteristic of force as differentiation overcomes the predicate that is its reactive inversion or fiction. Thus the will to power is the principle of the synthesis of forces, and the eternal return is the synthesis which has as its principle the will to power.[3]

Deleuze argues that eternal return as a physical doctrine of being is the 'new formulation of the speculative synthesis' (1983: 68) where conformity to a law of identity is now overcome by the principle of selection in difference and repetition that constitutes will to power. In addition, 'as an ethical thought the eternal return is the new formulation of the practical synthesis: whatever you will, will it in such a way that you also will its eternal return' (1983: 68). But what can be willed eternally? Only difference itself or, as we have seen it above, the No-saying to all negativity, all reaction. Only in thinking, in the 'thought of the eternal return,' (1983: 69) is willing also creativity. 'Only the eternal return makes the nihilistic will whole and complete' (1983: 69). As Benjamin has a 'new concept of experience' (Caygill, 1998: 24) so, now, Deleuze offers 'the relation of the will to power itself with the eternal return, and the possibility of transmutation as a new way of feeling, thinking and above all being…' (1983: 71). He concludes,

> Nietzsche's speculative teaching is as follows: becoming, multiplicity and chance do not contain any negation; difference is pure affirmation; return is the being of difference excluding the whole of the negative… Nietzsche's practical teaching is that difference is happy; that multiplicity, becoming and chance are adequate objects of joy by themselves and only joy returns… The death of God needs time finally to find its essence and become a joyful event… This time is the cycle of the eternal return (1983: 190).

3. THINKING THE AFFIRMATIVE, AGAIN.

Our task now is to read philosophy's higher education out of Nietzsche's work for ourselves, and in doing so to show how it is 'different' from Deleuze's reading. We are not seeking to 'deny' what Deleuze has said, but rather to follow through the relation (the thought) of will to power and eternal return as our education. At the very point where he finds it necessary to employ the notion of education—where, he says, the will to power 'teaches' us to think (1983: 172)—he avoids the difficulty in and for itself of doing so.[4]

We will now explore four different but inextricably related 'moments' in Nietzsche's work which themselves explore the affirmative. Each moment, of course, consists of the excess and return of a dualism, the Apollinian and the Dionysian in *Birth of Tragedy*, the historical and forgetting in *Untimely Meditations*, the active and the reactive in *The Genealogy of Morals*, and the eternal return of will to power in *Zarathustra*. We will find that each of these moments contains and reproduces the logic and structure of philosophy's higher education. In each of the dualisms, then, we are looking for the immanent self-relation of form and formation in the first instance, the abstraction of that relation into and by negative and reactive experience, and our higher education regarding the formation and finality which is our experience of the relation of the relation.

3.1 *The Birth of Tragedy.*

The Birth of Tragedy opens with the themes of duality, reconciliation and struggle. These are the components of Nietzsche's philosophy throughout his work. The duality and opposition here is between the Apollinian and the Dionysian; the reconciliation is tragedy; and the struggle is art as will to power. The Apollinian offers the individual the illusion of calm and repose, the calm of the dreamer who knows he is dreaming, in the face of 'the incompletely intelligible world' (1968: 35). What this individual gains is trust and faith in the principle of the individual *per se*, for through him and in his stability the world is known and is anchored. But, says Nietzsche, when terror seizes this individual and the repose of the world is suddenly cast into chaos, then the cognitive form of phenomena, 'the principle of sufficient reason… seems to suffer an exception' (1968: 36). Alongside the collapse of the reason, and the terror, there is also a joy, a feeling of intoxication and even ecstasy at our downfall. This latter combination of collapse and revel is the nature of the Dionysian. Nietzsche makes grand claims for the positivity of this collapse. 'Everything subjective vanishes into complete self-forgetfulness' (1968: 36). 'Now the slave is a free man… Now, with the gospel of universal harmony, each one feels himself not only united, reconciled and fused with his neighbour, but as one with him' (1968: 37). 'He is no longer an artist, he has become a work of art… the highest gratification of the primordial unity' (1968: 37). [5] Indeed, the artist himself never enjoys this affirmation for in his work he can only 'imitate' the Apollinian dreams or Dionysian ecstasies. He sits 'alone and apart from the singing revellers,' (1968: 38) able to enjoy only symbolic affirmation.

But this symbolism was the fate that awaited Greek culture as a whole. In a sense, to protect itself from the barbarian influence of the Dionysian, the Apollinian took the destructive force as its own. This fusion of the will to stability and the will to destruction produced a 'witches' brew' (1968: 40) of pain and joy. But above all, what this fusion called forth was the artistic as the loss of the affirmative or, the same, the victory of symbolism over the self-forgetfulness and freedom of the dream and the ecstasy. This symbolic Apollinianism has the same structure as the internalisation of will to power in *The Genealogy of Morals*. It now endures terror and inverts joy, by controlling nature symbolically, as the slave revolt controls will to power by morality. In both cases nature is distorted into a convulsive self-enmity, but it is not 'overcome'.

The gods that Apollinian art creates and the visions of unity that it perpetrates are thus soaked in blood. But the necessary illusion here is that suffering has a 'higher glory' (1968: 43). Thus, as morality 'justifies' force by setting force against itself and calling it 'right,' so the gods that owe their genealogy to terror now 'justify' terror by living out the struggles themselves as higher struggles on behalf of man. In this 'transfiguring mirror' (1968: 43) lies the notion of the reactive where nature is denied by an art which claims to affirm it. Romantic notions of reconciliation are only so many more naive misrecognitions of the 'complete victory of the Apollinian illusion' (1968: 44).

But at this point Nietzsche makes an observation about nature that is highly significant, not only for the birth of tragedy but for all moments of affirmation in his work and indeed for Deleuze's reading of the double affirmative. Nietzsche says that the reactive transfiguring of nature into the artistic is 'one of those illusions which nature so frequently employs to achieve her own ends' (1968: 44). He continues, 'the true goal is veiled by a phantasm: and while we stretch out our hands for the latter, nature attains the former by means of our illusion' (1968: 44).

So what is the true goal of nature and why does it employ illusion? It does so because illusion is the work of nature as both repose (Apollo) and revel (Dionysus). When nature uses such an illusion as beauty to entice man into a reconciliation, it is in fact to *teach* man of the illusion therein, or to disappoint him. In each disappointment, in each failure, as illusion is forced into recognition of its true nature, so man is returned to nature as the relation of the individual (Apollo) and its downfall (Dionysus), and not as the overcoming of one by the other. The Apollinian vision of the calm and repose of the *principium indivuationis* is only art, a 'pleasurable illusion' (1968: 45). Art itself is part of the illusion, securing the identity of the individual against the terror of its downfall. Greek culture, like modern man, is already reactive, or artistic, and has no access to the 'complete self-forgetfulness' (1968: 36) that is posited by Nietzsche as the pure relation of Apollo and Dionysus. For us, a different relation is manifest, where nature is both the individual and its downfall, and this is the tragic, or as Nietzsche puts it, where the two great impulses, Apollinian and Dionysian, 'found glorious consummation' (1968: 47).[6] The true goal and end of nature is not any kind of 'pure' reconciliation between itself and man, not any kind of mutual recognition, but rather the primeval movement of nature as an internally disrupting force of formation and finality.[7]

However, the joy of this intoxication in Greek tragedy was wrecked by a new opposition, the Dionysian and the Socratic. Now, 'to be beautiful everything must be intelligible' (1968: 83-4). The optimism of knowing everything destroys the dream world of Dionysian intoxication and restores subjectivity as 'the theoretical man'

(1968: 94), a man who has an 'unshakeable faith… that thought is capable not only of knowing being but even of *correcting* it' (1968: 95). The 'mystery of union' (1968: 48) is present here too. On the one hand the Socratic is Apollinian because it acts as a universal 'panacea' (1968: 97) against the lawlessness of an 'entire solar system' (1968: 96). On the other hand, Socratic reason destroys its own basis by being the cause and the effect of 'the incompletely intelligible' (1968: 35). As Nietzsche says, Socratic man comes to see, with honour, 'how logic coils up at [its] boundaries and finally bites its own tail' (1968: 98). Here, says Nietzsche, 'a new form of insight breaks through, tragic insight, which, merely to be endured, needs art as a protection and remedy' (1968: 98).

Whilst the forms of the Apollinian and the Dionysian are different here, the logic of their relationship is the same. The repose is shattered, and the revel of the shattering itself requires repose. Can there now be a Socrates who practises music, another mysterious union of Apollo and Dionysus, another 'glorious consummation' (1968: 47) in which the joy of subjective annihilation can be expressed in music? Again Nietzsche answers affirmatively, finding the consummation in the images of 'a rebirth of tragedy' (1968: 121) and, of course, with Wagner as its apotheosis.

Again, however, Nietzsche makes clear that the consummation is not a relation of overcoming of one impulse by the other. Nature repeats its primal unity; it does not do anything other than itself. In the new tragedy the Apollinian still privileges repose over revel, deluding man 'into the belief that he is seeing a single image of the world' (1968: 128) and making music appear the servant of cognition. In return, the Dionysian, forced to use symbols and images in the Apollinian realm, nevertheless forces revel over repose. In the total effect of tragedy

> the Dionysian predominates again. Tragedy closes with a sound which could never come
> from the realm of Apollinian art. And thus the Apollinian illusion reveals itself as what it
> really is—the veiling during the performance of the tragedy of the real Dionysian effect
> (1968: 130).

The Dionysian cannot overcome the Apollinian for the Dionysian is forced to work in the world of images, of concepts and of representations. Equally the Apollinian cannot overcome the Dionysian for every representation will be destroyed by the will that created it. The desire for peace is also the eternal desire for war. It is, says Nietzsche, 'an eternal phenomenon: the insatiable will always finds a way to detain its creatures in life and compel them to live on, by means of an illusion spread over things' (1968: 109). Only as the mysterious union passes away again into the components of its relation, are the conditions of the possibility of the union repeated. Thus 'Dionysus speaks the language of Apollo; and Apollo, finally the language of

Dionysus...' (1968: 130). Art is already speculative because nature is determinative of itself in and as the *principium individuationis*. But the principle contains nature as both revel and repose. Thus art is both the veiling and the unveiling of nature, by nature itself. Art must die at its own hands in order to repeat the conditions of its own possibility. This death is the birth of the individual who is not only Dionysian, for every Dionysian birth must also be an Apollinian illusion. Without the latter, the revel has no participants; no one gets drunk, and no death and destruction results. Nietzsche is absolutely clear here, in identifying the Apollinian as the *principium individuationis*. As such, he is recognising the determination of nature in and by property relations. Property relations are the illusion of nature as the secure individual and the downfall of his world. This relation of thought to its object is the very relation and the very illusion in which nature achieves its goal. Property therefore is the condition of the possibility of nature, a truth both hidden by yet actual as the individual. This insight never waivers in the rest of his work, indeed, as we will see, Nietzsche's philosophy is a logical and consistent critique not only of the illusion of property relations, but of the illusions of those illusions and their essential relation to each other. What Nietzsche offers us is a critique of philosophy misrecognised as nature and a higher education regarding the necessity that has its possibility or actuality in illusion. Finally, and we will return to this later, we should note that it is precisely the uncompromising rigour of this relation in Nietzsche that drives him through Deleuze's interpretation. Whilst Deleuze's new man has a new way of thinking, feeling and being, Nietzsche's Dionysian man recognises his predetermination in and repetition of the eternal. At root their notions of primordial unity, 'the primordially One' (1968: 132) are not the same. In Deleuze illusion is overcome, in Nietzsche illusion 'overcomes' overcoming and is the true.

3.2 *Untimely Meditations*

Two years after *The Birth of Tragedy* Nietzsche published his essay on history, entitled 'On the uses and disadvantages of history for life'. As *The Birth of Tragedy* explores the actual and living relation of the two great impulses of the Apollinian and the Dionysian, so this 1874 essay explores the same difficulty of affirmation, this time as the relation of the 'untimely' that is the historical and the unhistorical, or remembering and forgetting. Nietzsche admits an element of revenge in writing the essay. His *ressentiment* begins with the ruminating cows. Man envies these creatures their happiness: 'they do not know what is meant by yesterday or today... [they are] fettered to the moment and its pleasure or displeasure, and thus [are] neither melancholy nor bored' (Nietzsche, 1983: 60). So much is the beast in the moment that when man asks it to speak of its happiness, the animal would say 'I always forget what I was going to say...' but forgets to say this and remains silent. There is nothing Apollinian or Dionysian about the cow. It neither soothes a troubled life nor undermines its own stability. No symbolism is required of that which lives so purely in the moment.

Our envy and our *ressentiment* in regard to the cow is that it appears 'like a vision of a lost paradise' (1983: 61) or like a child playing 'in blissful blindness between the hedges of past and future' (1983: 61). As such, 'the animal lives unhistorically,' (1983: 61) enjoying its capacity to forget and remember in and as the one moment. But the self-consciousness of nature, our self-knowledge and its offspring, culture, cannot live in and as the moment as the cow does. For us, the moment is always already corrupted by the past, which itself is only another corrupted moment. Each moment that has been lost 'nonetheless returns as a ghost and disturbs the peace of a later moment' (1983: 61). To remember the moment is to have lost the moment. Thus the moment is present only as 'it was' which, as Nietzsche says, is a 'password which gives conflict, suffering and satiety access to man so as to remind him what his existence fundamentally is—an imperfect tense that can never become a perfect one' (1983: 61). As such, being is never itself, it is only 'an uninterrupted has-been, a thing that lives by negating, consuming and contradicting itself' (1983: 61).

The man who lives purely historically, unable ever to forget, lives in the Heraclitean stream of eternal becoming, or rather, does not 'live' in any way that he would be able to recognise for he would 'lose himself' (1983: 62). Without at least an element of forgetting in our lives we would 'in the end hardly dare to raise a finger. Forgetting is essential to action of any kind' (1983: 62). As the Apollinian and the Dionysian are mutually dependent in a relation of opposition, so now (sic) the historical and the unhistorical, or remembering and forgetting, are also mutually dependent but in a relation of opposition against that mutuality. We will look briefly this relation now from within (and as) the logic and content of philosophy's higher education. Whilst it is the unhistorical in particular that constitutes 'the foundation upon which alone anything... truly human can grow,' (1983: 63) nevertheless only by 'imposing limits on this unhistorical element by thinking, reflecting, comparing, distinguishing, drawing conclusions... did man become man' (1983: 64). An excess of the historical as much as an excess of forgetting freezes man into inactivity. 'The unhistorical and the historical are necessary in equal measure for the health of an individual, of a people and of a culture' (1983: 63).

What then are the characteristics of the man who can live out such an opposition in himself? At times Nietzsche calls him 'historical' (1983: 65).[8] Such a man can incorporate into himself what is past and 'transform it into blood' (1983: 63). Such a man, we might say, lives in and as the contradiction that action means remembering to forget. He can draw an horizon around himself, remembering that which he can incorporate, forgetting that which he cannot, and being free to act from within this, his own boundary. Such a man 'forgets most things so as to do one thing' (1983: 64). On the surface this looks unjust, for shouldn't the just action take everything into account? How can a just action selectively forget? But this is Nietzsche's whole point. All action requires a forgetting. If there is no forgetting there is no action and that is also unjust. There is no greater *ressentiment* than, in the name of justice (or in the name of remembering everything) not to act at all, for that is merely to become petrified by the impossibility of the 'perfect'. The unhistorical and historical man 'is the womb not only of the unjust but of every just deed too' (1983: 64). He stands in the 'service... of life' (1983: 65) by incorporating into himself the oppositions that spring from life.[9]

The nature of the horizon that the historical and unhistorical man draws around himself is necessarily formative. A living thing, says Nietzsche, 'can be healthy, strong and fruitful only when bounded by a horizon' (1983: 63) which divides the 'bright and discernable from the unilluminable and dark' (1983: 63). Only by means of this division is an individual or a nation 'just as able to forget at the right time as to remember at the right time' (1983: 63). At first glance this description looks anything but untimely. It suggests that strength is the measure of right and that the strong man draws his own boundary without 'the conscience of method' (1968: 238).[10] The strong nation can act by forgetting its 'historical' relation to or memory of others. This boundary between self and other which is established by the forgetting remembers only that which can be incorporated into the forgetting. In other words, the boundary is already the difference between self and other, or between nation and alien, where I am not the other and the other, also, is not me. Forgetting, seen in this way, emerges as an arbitrary form of judgement power which is able to ignore history in the name of this living entity. It is reminiscent of the *Augenblick* of anticipatory resoluteness seen above in Heidegger, where Time is *this* Dasein. Equally, remembering here might mean the *ressentiment* of the slave against activity, against forgetting and thus against health. But Nietzsche is not privileging the historical or the unhistorical. He is expressing the necessity that is self-determinative within and as the relation of their relation. In fact Nietzsche is displaying here the self-opposition of the will to power. An action cannot begin with forgetting, for that 'action' remains undifferentiated. A beginning can only be made within a memory of not forgetting. Thus the beginning is already the boundary that determines action within the relation of remembering *and* forgetting. The beginning is already the result of forgetting. But it is also the memory of what was forgotten. Thus, in remembering to forget, will to power is active and self-determining. The historical and the unhistorical are both present in remembering to forget. This expresses the relation of the relation of the historical 'and' the unhistorical, and of remembering 'and' forgetting. Activity is always already a remembering to forget.

Understood in this way as philosophy's higher education, the boundary that the historical and unhistorical man draws around himself does not have an unknowable that lies beyond it, nor a self defined in opposition to that beyond. On the contrary, the boundary is a self-determination where forgetting is already remembering (an action is already known) but remembering is not forgetting (knowing the activity is the loss of activity). Activity determines itself in and as the relation of remembering to forget. This has the same substance as Kierkegaard's teleological suspension of the ethical. In both cases it appears as if activity is petrified by (its own) contradiction. In fact, the contradiction is the truth of activity. It does not prevent us from action; on the contrary, it is already activity.[11] It expresses the necessity that is already the condition of the possibility of the dualisms in and through which the relation of the historical and unhistorical man is, indeed, this man.

This reading of the historical and unhistorical man as philosophy's higher education is not being grafted onto Nietzsche. It has been found already in the illusions of the Apollinian and the Dionysian. We saw above that this illusion for Nietzsche is another of nature's artifices. Art, religion and philosophy are Apollinian in their transfiguring of nature into culture. But Dionysus himself is determined in and by his working with these representations. Thus, the historical and unhistorical man is not superman. He is not the overcoming of illusion nor is he the Dasein of Being Time. He is not creative of new values, only of the truth of all the old values. His higher education is that he understands illusion and dualism as value, but he does not, then, abstract the conditions of the possibility of his education from the necessity that repeats it and whose repetition it already is.[12] This historical and unhistorical man, the man of philosophy's higher education, is the relation of the relation of dualism, in this case remembering and forgetting. He is not just the illusion of Apollinian philosophy, art or religion, nor just the undifferentiated or unrepresented Dionysian chaos. He is the substantial relation of their relation. As such, his activity is also modernity's own will to power, viz, its self-determination in and as remembering to forget. The man who is strong enough to will this as his own freedom, and to relive it as himself, this is the man of Nietzsche's higher education. Not an overman, for the relation is not overcome, it is re-learned in the difficult experience that is this freedom. As such, justice is not mastered, it is practised. 'It requires a great deal of strength to live and to [remember to] forget the extent to which to live and to be unjust is one and the same thing' (1983: 76).

In another essay from 1874 the mysterious union that is the untimely is Schopenhauer. Here Nietzsche finds a tragic hero who puts service to life above the more common impulses that characterise the scholar. Schopenhauer, says Nietzsche, can be distinguished from Kant, and other 'rabid dialecticians' (1983: 141) because whilst the latter had a 'living and life-transforming influence on only a very few men,' (1983: 140) Schopenhauer stands as an example of philosophy as higher education in his life and his identity, not just in his books. Indeed, the example that Kant bequeaths is a 'gnawing and disintegrating scepticism and relativism' (1983: 140) whereas Schopenhauer as educator leads us 'from the heights of sceptical gloom or criticising renunciation up to the heights of tragic contemplation, to the nocturnal sky and its stars extended endlessly above us...' (1983: 141).[13]

Nietzsche is clear that the ideal which Schopenhauer stands for is that all education, and philosophical education in particular, should serve life. Every great philosophy should enable its students and teachers to 'descend into the depths of existence with a string of curious questions... why do I live? what lesson have I to learn from life? how have I become what I am and why do I suffer from being what I am?' (1983: 154). Indeed, the challenge of every great philosopher is to say 'this is the picture of all life, and learn from it the meaning of your own life' (1983: 141).

The Schopenhauer essay is a continuation of the relation of remembering and forgetting that emerged in the essay on history but with one critical addition. Where in the history essay the historical and unhistorical man is the power that can remember to forget so as to be able to act, in the Schopenhauer essay we see Nietzsche's demonstration that 'this ideal *educates*' (1983: 156). The stasis of remembering becomes, in educational terms, the scholar who serves calculation, enjoyment and security. Whilst the ruminating cow can do this through and as its own forgetting, such an immediacy is not available to the man in whom nature seeks itself as something higher. The scholars who forget to remember to forget are several times savaged by Nietzsche. Such men fear solitude lest 'when we are alone and quiet something will be whispered into our ear,' (1983: 159).[14] They seek refuge in the academic community that maintains itself in so-called pure knowledge, losing 'sight of truth altogether' (1983: 144) and becoming petrified in the face of life itself. Such men could not distinguish between serious philosophy and journalism. They enjoy thinking as some do fox hunting, pursuing the thrill of the kill. They choose truth according to the level of salary it procures. They choose and applaud colleagues who will return this recognition. And they ensure that whatever they think it never actually touches or affects them personally. 'The only critique of a philosophy that is possible and that proves something, namely trying to see whether one can live in accordance with it, has never been taught at universities' (1983: 187). Abstracted from meaning and significance, those who only remember, who collect information and call this education, serve and contribute to increasing barbarism.

> The sciences, pursued without any restraint and in a spirit of the blindest *laissez faire*, are shattering and dissolving all firmly held belief; the educated classes and states are being swept along by a hugely contemptible money economy. The world has never been more worldly, never poorer in love and goodness... Everything, contemporary art and science included, serves the coming barbarism (1983: 148).[15]

Why should an untimely educator feel so strongly about the suppression of philosophy's higher education? Because, says Nietzsche, 'he realises that he is in danger of being cheated out of himself' (1983: 154). His strength 'lies in forgetting himself' (1983: 155) for remembering to forget will free him from the myriad distractions that lead him away from life. Like the Dionysian man, 'he himself is his first sacrifice to himself' (1983: 155). Like the historical and unhistorical man, the untimely educator draws a boundary around himself by remembering to forget and says now I can live, now I can act. But this freedom is a suffering for this boundary, this life, this untimely man cannot spare himself. The boundary is not his salvation; it is his undoing, for it creates him as the relation of remembering and forgetting, the Apollinian and the Dionysian, and not the overcoming of that relation. He must now suffer these oppositions as himself. But he knows and feels—learns—that the suffering is of higher significance than a mere failure to rise above the animal desire to hang on to life. If man merely imitates consciously what the animal does instinctively then the imitation is in bad faith. The animal serves life, but man denies life, for in consciousness nature expresses its own purpose for man.

> If all nature presses towards man, it thereby intimates that man is necessary for the redemption of nature from the curse of the life of the animals, and that in him existence at last holds up before itself a mirror in which life appears no longer senseless but in its metaphysical significance (1983: 157).

These are revealing passages in Nietzsche, and their significance is carried through into his later works. The Apollinian and Dionysian impulses are here revealed in life as *thinking*. In thinking, life affirms itself, and the opposition is in consciousness and self-consciousness, or having to remember to forget. This is life's commandment to itself, and why, as Zarathustra later points out, it is commander, obeyer and avenger of its own law. When life is petrified as memory, then we 'fail to emerge out of animality [because] we ourselves are the animals whose suffering seems to be senseless' (1983: 158). However, 'there are moments when we realise this: then the clouds are rent asunder and we see that, in common with all nature, we are pressing towards man as towards something that stands high above us' (1983: 158). The untimely man who takes this commandment upon himself learns that life is this learning. 'What was' no longer suppresses 'what is,' rather, 'what is' is that which will be again. But we are advancing our argument too quickly here, for eternal return is not yet spoken by Nietzsche. At this stage the eternal return of will to power takes the form of the redemption of life through its own enlightenment of higher education. 'Nature needs knowledge' (1983: 158). This is life as will to power, or is, as Zarathustra will say later on, life's secret, that everything must be overcome. But it is terrified of the knowledge it needs, for it knows that its higher significance must destroy it. The Apollinian dream world of symbolic destruction will be shattered by the destructive impulse of the Dionysian, yet together nature makes a creative leap and enjoys a 'great enlightenment as to the character of existence' (1983: 159). Without the notion of eternal return this education could be interpreted as overcoming, for the untimely heroes are the true men, 'the philosopher, the artist and the saint' (1983: 160) in whom, for the first time, nature 'has reached its goal' (1983: 159). It knows its own higher significance because it has created men who live as this significance. Yet even here Nietzsche cautions that the victory is also, and inevitably, a defeat and is actual only in the untimely man who can contain himself in the opposition of remembering to forget what was. This untimely man does not become any kind of pure forgetting. Indeed, to forget to remember to forget belongs to cows and overman. It does not belong to those who understand that this ideal educates, and that this education is nature's own impulse, formation and finality.

3.3 On The Genealogy of Morals

Thus far the affirmative in Nietzsche has appeared in and as the relation of Socrates with music, the historical and unhistorical man and the tragic untimely educator. In the Genealogy of Morals the affirmative is another mysterious union, a 'redeeming man of great love and contempt,' (1968: 532) a 'man of the future who will redeem us not only from the hitherto reigning ideal but also from that which was bound to grow out of it, the great nausea, the will to nothingness, nihilism' (1968: 532). This affirmation is Zarathustra. However, his relation to the Genealogy of Morals is itself significant. In the 1887 text it is the ideal that again shows itself to be educative, not only about itself, but in and for itself. We have seen above that Deleuze attaches great importance to our understanding of the active/reactive dualism in relation to Zarathustra and to the 'double affirmative' that sees nihilism defeat itself. Our path, then, like Deleuze, is through an analysis of the active/reactive coupling to learn about Zarathustra, even though he is present in *The Genealogy* only implicitly as our education.[16]

In a sense *The Genealogy* is art, for it represents the representation that is morality as destruction, i.e., nature's self-relation of the Apollinian and Dionysian is symbolised, this time as critique. But critics who wish philosophical critique to be art, be it a new aesthetic or whatever, suppress the fact that this symbolism, this will to power, has a still higher form. But this, as we will see, is not art without representation (Deleuze), it is art as the relation of its own relation, or the circle in which eternal return is known, and which is philosophy's higher education. The *Genealogy* is a propaedeutic for this higher education, one which prepares our thinking for being able to speak of itself as its own formation and finality, or as Zarathustra. The critique of morality is educative regarding the illusions that obstruct philosophy's higher education, but it is not yet in and for itself the truth of that higher education.

The question that underpins *The Genealogy* is 'under what conditions did man devise [the] value judgements good and evil? and what value do they themselves possess?' (1968: 453). Nietzsche's answer is well rehearsed. In questioning the value of these values which act as the foundation of all value judgements, Nietzsche finds their genealogy to lie in the attitudes associated with victory and defeat. That is to say, he finds the value of all values grounded in relations of power and more specifically in the ways in which the will to power resolves itself into human character traits and attitudes. What is valued as good represents the character of the noble, but the noble is only he who has established himself above another. Equally, what is valued as bad is that which is ignoble, or merely that which is defined as less than or different from those who enjoy themselves as the Archimedean point of all values.[17] To understand that definitions of good and bad are merely political opens up the abyss of nihilism. If there are no absolute values, but only the ideology of the victors over the vanquished, then there is no absolute right or wrong. But this 'value' of nihilism, as we have already seen above, is just as political as the one it seeks to expose. Just as definitions of good meaning strong, powerful and commanding merely embody the character traits of those with the power to enforce them, so definitions of this as 'immoral' stem from the same process.

Nietzsche describes a slave revolt in morality which has several phases. First, in an act of spiritual revenge, the good are recast as evil, and good itself is seen to lie in the sufferers rather than the oppressors. This is the first inversion of values, and is itself political in that it represents the revolt of the vanquished. What is significant about this inversion of values is that it does not conquer its oppressors by physical force and subdue them as they have subdued others. Rather, the battle is fought out from the position of the vanquished. The war is now to redefine strength, ego, and will as bad, and to acknowledge the denial of power, victory and war as truly good. Here says Nietzsche it is the attitude of the oppressed that becomes creative, which is wholly different in character from the creative will of the noble. With the latter, good is affirmative of self and of will. With the former, good is the suppression of self and of will. It is not, says Nietzsche, that the denial of will *is* good, even though current moral sensibilities still hold to this. It is that this definition of good arises out of a spirit of *ressentiment* against those who have enjoyed the creative power of their will over others. This becomes morality grounded in *ressentiment*, and creates values which reproduce this attitude.

> The slave revolt in humanity begins when *ressentiment* itself becomes creative and gives birth to values... While every noble morality develops from a triumphant affirmation of itself, slave morality from the outset says No to what is 'outside,' what is 'different,' what is 'not itself;' and this No is its creative deed (1968: 472).

The second phase of this inversion of values is that *ressentiment* becomes an instrument of culture. We have seen this theme before. Apollo symbolises nature so as to domesticate it; memory serves to deny action in the *ressentiment* that the fate of all action is already 'it was'; modern scholarship and education ensures that the teacher is never a living example of his own ideas. Each of these marks the victory of *ressentiment* as a cultural force, such that the 'tame man' has learned 'to feel himself as the goal and zenith, as the meaning of history, as "higher man"' (1968: 479).

To emphasise the most significant phase of the inversion of values, Nietzsche pays particular attention to the way the relation of creditor and debtor characterise the inner moral 'nature' of man. Guilt and the bad conscience are not just the character of *ressentiment* and denial turned into memory and accountability. They have a life of their own as self-hatred. This is not just the consciousness of the animals who have had their natural instincts and infallible drives 'disvalued and suspended' (1968: 520). It is also the self-consciousness of this transformation, whereby man becomes aware of the world as other than himself. We saw above how Nietzsche writes of nature as having its own true goals and ends, (1968: 44) and how, in pursuing these ends it produces illusions and phantasms which re-present its Dionysian will to power always in relation to representation. Equally we saw how nature, again pursuant of itself, is terrified of the knowledge it needs (1983: 158) but that its redemption or enlightenment lies in both a recognition of metaphysical significance and its destruction in the mysterious union of the ideal that educates (1983: 156). The self-consciousness of this animal is precisely the internalisation of that relation, or of nature, such that man now suffers from himself. That he does so before God, is a symbolic representation of his suffering as guilt and debt. That he finally kills even that spectator is the final victory of the inversion of values. It is the victory of nihilism, where denial has grown tired even of itself, and finds in itself only a will to nothingness.

But before the death of God, the internalisation of man's forgetting such that he remembers to forget to forget, takes form as asceticism. Despite its strength and as a denial of self, of life, of impulse and of will, nevertheless asceticism is a form of strength, and is still a will to power. This is misunderstood in Kant, says Nietzsche, when beauty is described as pleasure without interest, but better understood by Schopenhauer who also saw beauty as arousing interest. The great ascetics were not without interest. On the contrary, overcoming 'love of luxury and refinement... was the dominating instinct whose demands prevailed against those of all the other instincts' (1968: 544-5). Such men can be seen in the light of the three metamorphoses that Zarathustra describes early in his teachings. As camels, they withdraw into the desert, taking upon themselves the greatest burdens of guilt and self-hatred. Such men are not disinterested. They are a will to power, determined to do this 'for the truth' (1968: 547) of themselves rather than suffer publicly as the martyr who feigns his condition as not his own. In the desert is the quiet where one risks that 'something will be whispered into [his] ear' (1983: 159). How is the camel to become a lion? The ascetic adds a further burden to his load, namely that he turns against himself as a carrier of burdens. Now he seeks the will to power of the man who came into the desert, which means that will to power now turns against itself, accusing the camel of the 'martyrdom' of carrying a burden that is not his own. This, now, says Nietzsche, marks a 'cruelty towards themselves, inventive self-castigation—this was the principal means these power-hungry hermits and innovators of ideas required to overcome the gods and tradition in themselves, so as to be able to believe in their own innovations' (1968: 551). Or, in the language of the metamorphoses, the spirit 'becomes a lion who would conquer his freedom and be master in his own desert' (1982: 138). The inversion of will to power that will to power has to overcome here is the asceticism that suffers 'thou shalt' as its truth. This guilt now faces its positive counterpoint, the will to power that affirms that this burden is not disinterestedness at all, but a domination of affirmation by the inversion of values; precisely a victory by a resentful form of will to power that denies it is even involved in a struggle. What the lion now demands of the camel is honesty; the ascetic must admit that his burden was his own will. To come to know the camel as will to power is to become the lion. 'Thou shalt' is the name of the inversion of values in the camel, but 'the spirit of the lion says "I will,"' (1982: 138-9) meaning 'I will' is 'I am'.

Seen in this way we understand the importance of the ascetic for nature in preserving itself and in working for its own ends and goals. Nature is involved in such work by seeking the value of seeking, but is terrified of this need (1983: 158). It requires to know the value of suffering, a requirement that is already a suffering without value. Hence the ascetic that takes on the burden of others comes to see that the value of disinterestedness is already overcome by his will to be burdened. Nietzsche notes that,

> It must be a necessity of the first order that again and again promotes the growth and prosperity of this life-inimical species—it must indeed be in the interest of life itself that such a self-contradictory type does not die out. For an ascetic life is a self-contradiction: here rules a *ressentiment* without equal, that of an insatiable instinct and power-will that wants to become master not over something in life but over life itself... (1968: 553).

Indeed, it is a necessity of the first order. It is a necessity or a law that has underpinned all of the aspects of Nietzsche's work that we have explored so far. Nature is preserved in the self-contradiction of the modern Dionysian man, in the historical and unhistorical man, and in the self-contradiction of the will to power that remembers to forget. Now it is preserved in the self-contradiction of the ascetic who turns against himself as the inversion of values. But is the ascetic now able to learn of new values? Is he now the untimely man who transforms his reactive will to power into something affirmative? 'To create new values—that even the lion cannot do' (1982: 139). Even though the ascetic now knows of the genealogy of morals, and thus creates the freedom for new values, he is not himself yet these new values. The lion is life's self-contradiction and knowledge, even of itself as never more itself than when it is opposed to itself, but this alone is not the higher education that awaits this philosopher. What is it then that this higher education can do that the lion cannot? It can experience the 'necessity of the first order' as its own law. But even here the law determines that the law itself be denied. The lion as the philosopher who says 'I will' is again only the ascetic inversion of values. He takes the view that in the law of 'I will' all that 'unconditionally posits truth' (1968: 554) is error. 'The entire conceptual antithesis "subject" and "object"—errors, nothing but errors' (1968: 554). This is what Nietzsche calls the 'lascivious ascetic discord that loves to turn reason against reason' (1968: 555). Much as nature requires the ascetic for its own goal and end, nevertheless the ascetic philosopher will not affirm the truth of will to power, only deny it. And precisely the law is that in the denial, life is preserved. 'The ascetic ideal is an artifice for the preservation of life' (1968: 556). 'This ascetic priest, this apparent enemy of life, this denier—precisely he is among the greatest conserving and yes-creating forces of life' (1968: 556-7). The wound that he inflicts upon himself when his will to power turns on itself, 'compels him to live' (1968: 557) because in attacking itself it preserves itself. Or put another way, the denial of the value of the disinterested is, again, the true interest even of the latter value, and preserves or retrieves that value.

For the last man of ascetic philosophy, then, there is not truth for all is his will, a will he can never free himself from. Thus he says 'I am sick of myself' (1968: 558). When this nausea inspires *ressentiment* in the form of pity, then the inversion of values produces the monster of the last man with his 'will to nothingness, nihilism' (1968: 558). The sickness becomes the inversion of values that denies even the truth of the camel and the lion. Here even denial is denied. This is not a new value; it is the totality of the spirit of all the old values.

We have seen above that for Deleuze this is the sickness that creates the overman whose strength of *ressentiment* is manifest in and as the will to perish. This final No must be said to the consent, the Yes, that has underpinned all previous Nos. Only such an absolute No can free man from the totality of *ressentiment* that determines the camel and the lion. Nietzsche ends the *Genealogy of Morals* with a similar thought.

> As the will to truth thus gains self-consciousness—there can be no doubt of that— morality will gradually perish now: this is the great spectacle in a hundred acts reserved for the next two centuries in Europe—the most terrible, most questionable, and perhaps also the most hopeful of all spectacles (1968: 597).

This self-consciousness, for Deleuze, is the transmutation into 'a new way of thinking, feeling and above all being' (Deleuze, 1983: 71). For Nietzsche, this self-consciousness, which is 'the will to truth become [ ] conscious of itself as a problem,' (1968: 597) has the potential to produce the 'man of the future' (1968: 532). Such a man will

> Redeem us not only from the hitherto reigning ideal but also from that which was bound to grow out of it, the great nausea, the will to nothingness, nihilism; this bell-stroke of noon and of great decision that liberates the will once again (1968: 532).

Such a man is Zarathustra. It is to him that we must now turn if we are to draw out the ways in which this self-consciousness is philosophy's higher education, and how above all it can be said to be the self-consciousness 'of the child' who is the third metamorphosis.

4. ZARATHUSTRA AND THE ETERNAL RETURN OF WILL TO POWER

At the end of *The Genealogy of Morals* Nietzsche restates the law of nature that, in obedience to itself, commands in man a new self-consciousness.

> All great things bring about their own destruction through an act of self-overcoming: thus the law of life will have it, the law of the necessity of "self-overcoming" in the nature of life—the law-giver himself eventually receives the call: "patere legem, quam ipse tulisti (submit to the law you yourself propose) (1968: 597).

This is the same law of formation and finality, of master and slave, or in sum of the necessity of the conditions of possibility applied to themselves, that constitutes philosophy's higher education in previous chapters. When Deleuze states that Nietzsche is not a dialectician, (1983: 8) that his philosophy is fundamentally anti-dialectical (1983: 8) and that his 'concept of the overman is directed against the dialectical conception of man,' (1983: 8) it follows that there can be 'no possible compromise between Hegel and Nietzsche' (1983: 195). Equally, then, his conception of the overman and of difference stand opposed to philosophy's higher education. However, as we will see now, philosophy's higher education is in Deleuze's thinking, but misrecognised as the overman. In the end it is the opposition of Deleuze's Nietzsche to Hegel that brings him into philosophy's higher education.[18] The affirmation of 'difference' is again *ressentiment*. It is in the destruction of this Yes to No-saying, implicit but restricted in Deleuze, that the law of nature is fulfilled. It is not therefore a different truth or a new value that opposes and completes Deleuze's higher education, it is his own truth.

However, to make this clearer we must now explore the law of self-overcoming as it works in and on Zarathustra throughout the four books of *Thus Spake Zarathustra*. We meet him first coming down from the mountain having been in solitude for ten years. Clearly the camel has taken his burden into the desert, but now the lion descends determined to show others that their obedience to 'thou shalt' can be transformed into an obedience to 'I will'. The whole of Zarathustra's story can be seen as the educative truth of the relation between the camel and lion. As the lion must come down to teach because he is already 'I will,' so the lion will return to the camel, again taking upon himself the greatest difficulties of 'I will' as a burden. This is the same story as that of the ascetic who is already saying Yes to No-saying, and who, in attempting to say No to No-saying, can only do so by saying Yes to *that* No-saying. In this circle lies Zarathustra's self-consciousness of will to truth and, implicitly, of philosophy's higher education, but this only becomes explicit when the forces at work in this circle themselves become and are the law of his own self-consciousness, or will to power and its eternal return.

On each occasion that Zarathustra as the lion teaches 'I will' the result is a palpable failure. To teach 'I will' is already reactive, already a No-saying to his pupils. The teaching is full of the necessity of its own contradiction, or, to say the same thing, of its own freedom. Teaching students *contra* 'thou shalt' is to engage in a pedagogy of 'thou shalt'. If 'I will' becomes 'thou shalt' in education then the teacher of 'I will' can only fail. Each failure of Zarathustra deepens his own burden, returns him to solitude, and increases his nausea. *The Prologue* is an exemplar of how this failure is played out and Deleuze is right that 'it 'contains the premature secret of the eternal return' (1983: 70). The teacher teaches the overman, the man who has overcome himself in the hour of his greatest contempt. He tries to use the courage of the tightrope walker as an example of the qualities of the overman, a man who perishes from his own will. But the crowd ask Zarathustra to give them the overman and Zarathustra concludes 'I am not the mouth for these ears' (1982: 130). Even when Zarathustra finds disciples, the relation of the camel and the lion repeats itself. 'Man,' he says to them, 'is something that shall be overcome' (1992: 160) and this 'highest thought you should receive as a command from me' (1982: 160). The higher education here is not the disciples', but rather in the circle that Zarathustra now repeats again and again. Realising that he had taught them of themselves before they had yet sought themselves (1982: 190) he tells them to go away, to 'resist Zarathustra. And even better: be ashamed of him! Perhaps he deceived you' (1982: 190). We have seen this logic of destruction and creation throughout Nietzsche's philosophy. Now it is revealed as the truth of the teacher whose 'I will' is also, and already, 'thou shalt'. What lies ahead for Zarathustra is this truth and this logic realised as his own education in teaching it as the truth of others. He is already the others, and they are not him. The circle that is proving to be the contingency, i.e., the condition of the possibility and impossibility of the lion's teaching, will soon become the absolute necessity that is Zarathustra himself.

Within the circle of the camel and the lion and its repetition of solitude and teaching, or work, it is important now to understand the different but related content that Zarathustra experiences. Of these, three are of most significance. In book 2 he learns of life as will to power; in book 3 he learns of will to power as eternal return; and in book 4 he learns of his own self-consciousness, his own being, as this self-work, this necessity, of life. What we witness at these crucial moments is not Zarathustra teaching, but Zarathustra being taught, and being taught by 'something unstilled, unstillable… within me [which] wants to be voiced' (1982: 217).

The first lesson is from life. Zarathustra learns of life as the force that turns the circle from lion to camel and from camel to lion.

> Life wants to build itself up into the heights with pillars and steps; it wants to look into
> vast distances and out toward stirring beauties: therefore it requires height. And because
> it requires height, it requires steps and contradiction among the steps and the climbers.
> Life wants to climb and to overcome itself climbing (1982: 213).

The same lesson is found in the Schopenhauer essay. Life needs knowledge, but is 'terrified of the knowledge it has need of' (1983: 158). When we are in common with nature we are 'pressing towards man as towards something that stands high above us' (1983: 158), and courageous enough to raise our heads above the stream 'in which we are so deeply immersed' (1983: 159). To know life thus, and to know ourselves as this life, is nature's own 'great enlightenment,' (1983: 159) its own truth and goal regarding itself. In Zarathustra life must become itself through this great enlightenment, this self-consciousness of itself as the will to truth. *The Tomb Song* speaks of life out of its own death. Life *is* when and because it overcomes or annihilates itself. What lives, says Zarathustra, also obeys itself, for only then is life its own command. Even in those who serve, says Zarathustra, 'I found the will to be master,' (1982: 226) even in the camel I found the lion. But life prepares Zarathustra for the lesson that is more terrible than the fact that the camel is already the lion. At the end of book 2 life affirms that 'I am that which must always overcome itself' (1982: 227). This affirmation contains the contradiction that makes it true. It will overcome even the affirmation of the lion, or 'I will,' for it to be true to itself. Life must even overcome itself as that which must be overcome. But this, we know, even the lion cannot do. For this, a third metamorphosis is required, one where this contradiction, this circle, is life's own self-consciousness.

The second lesson then is the most abysmal, for it is the self-consciousness in Zarathustra not only that the lion must be overcome if the lion is to be true, but that it is always already overcome. In the lesson of the eternal return Zarathustra learns not only that the lion returns to the camel, always and already, but that this unbearable contradiction is already the law of the necessity of the relation of the camel and the lion. What is always already the case is that the law of overcoming has already, and will always, overcome itself. Or, put another way, that the will to power is also the eternal return of itself, upon itself.

This education of Zarathustra into the eternal return of will to power has several parts. First, at the end of book 2 the soothsayer teaches the law of commanding and obeying as the steps and contradiction by which life overcomes even itself. 'All is empty, all is the same, all has been' (1982: 245) says the soothsayer. Zarathustra now recalls that he has been the guardian of death, protecting the overcoming of life as if it were an event which could be held in stasis, or as if it were a victory without also a defeat. However, emerging from the dream Zarathustra teaches his disciples something that Nietzsche himself taught some 10 year earlier. The event of a victory is, by its own law, just as quickly always defeated, for the very idea of an 'event' is a *ressentiment* of the will against that which has victory and defeat as its own law. The victory of an event is an inversion of values, or will to power turned against itself. In *Untimely Meditations* Nietzsche taught of the 'moment, now here and then gone' (1983: 61) and of the man who envied the cow that could forget and for whom every moment 'is extinguished for ever' (1983: 61). For man on the other hand, the moment is not forgotten, it is remembered as 'it was', which, says Nietzsche, 'sets the seal on the knowledge that being is only an uninterrupted has-been, a thing that lives by negating, consuming and contradicting itself' (1983: 61). What Nietzsche sought in the historical and unhistorical man, remembering to forget, is now for Zarathustra the lesson of the eternal return. Zarathustra notes,

> To redeem those who lived in the past and to recreate all 'it was' into a 'thus I willed it'—that alone I should call redemption. Will—that is the name of the liberator and joy-bringer; thus I taught you, my friends. But now learn this too: the will itself is still a prisoner. Willing liberates; but what is it that puts even the liberator in fetters? 'It was'— that is the name of the will's gnashing of teeth and most secret melancholy. Powerless against what has been done, he is an angry spectator of all that is past. The will cannot will backwards; and that he cannot break time and time's covetousness, that is the will's loneliest melancholy (1982: 251).

The point of course is that to wish to will differently *is ressentiment*. Redemption here is defined by *ressentiment*, in the spirit of *ressentiment*. '"That which was" is the name of the stone he cannot move' (1982: 251). Within the inversion of values this creative law must be denied, hence a 'solution' or a 'liberation' must be found. What the inversion says No to is that what has happened had to happen, according to the law of commanding and obeying. In experiencing the moment as 'it was,' as 'a vision of a lost paradise,' (1983: 61) nature is overcoming even itself. This is the highest conformity to itself that it can perform. Life, because it must overcome, can only be victorious, again, in its eternally repeated defeat of itself. As its 'great enlightenment' this is our experience of the law of nature, in contradiction, and as a Yes-saying to its eternally repeated No-saying to itself. Eternal return is our experience of nature as the law of will to power, experienced not just negatively, and as loss, but also, always, as conformity to and affirmation of what 'it is'. The eternal return of will to power is the recognition of the experience of *ressentiment* and revenge as 'thus I will it; thus shall I will it' (1982: 253). To ask how experience can be turned into a creative will is to ask a revengeful, and wrong, question. The point is, experience is already the creativity of will to power. To try and separate them is only again to set one's teeth gnashing against the stone that will not be moved, or to wish that will were other than itself as experience.

Zarathustra's reaction (nb) to the recognition of will to power as experience and of experience as will to power is terror. The implications here are universal. A voice tells him 'you know it Zarathustra, but you do not say it' and he answers, 'yes, I know it, but I do not want to say it... let me off from this. It is beyond my strength' (1982: 257). This education is higher even that that found in *The Genealogy of Morals*. In the latter all conception of right and wrong, all moral categories, are relativised within a context of power and domination, and the will to power of victor and defeated. For Zarathustra, even that genealogical understanding pales beside this most abysmal education. Now, not only can moral categories be understood as the law of commanding and obeying, now even our response to genealogy is understood within the same law. We saw above that Nietzsche admitted that revenge moved his *Untimely Meditations*. Now we see that revenge is the whole of the law of nature in its need for knowledge. This abysmal thought means that man himself is neither the person he appears to be, nor is he the ascetic negation of himself. He is their relation; he is the rope between them. And, worse, he is only that rope when he knows that he is neither of them. The desire to overcome commands; the failure to overcome obeys the commandment. The truth of the relation is that the law both precedes itself and therefore follows itself. This eternal return of will to power is philosophy's higher education. It is the same comprehensive necessity seen in Kierkegaard's recollection and repetition, in Kant's formation and finality, in Hegel's mater and slave, and implicitly in Heidegger's being and time. But where the latter overcomes the relation, Nietzsche's philosophy suffers it eternally.

By book 3 Zarathustra is ready to tell the dwarf of this abysmal idea. The path leading backwards into the past and the path leading forward into the future come together as the gateway called 'moment'. But the moment does not and cannot hold out against the two pathways, for the moment is not their union, it is their repetition (as they are also its repetition). As such, even the moment is lost, for it too is only repetition, or the experience of 'it was'. The higher education of this experience, its recognition as the law of commanding and obeying, is that in our revengeful attitude is the repetition of all that has happened and will happen (is happening) again. Softly Zarathustra recognises 'must we not eternally return?'(1982: 270).

The truth of this experience and the truth of experience in and for itself, Nietzsche plays out in the remainder of Zarathustra's education. Of absolute significance is the misrecognition of eternal return that Zarathustra enjoys at the end of book 3, which was originally intended to be the conclusion to the work. 'Thus I willed it! Thus I shall will it' (1982: 310) becomes the creation of new 'virtue,' (1982: 324) 'new values on new tablets' (1982: 325). Now Zarathustra returns to the mountain, replete in the knowledge that 'eternally the ring of being remains faithful to itself' (1982: 329) and he is able to dance, like Socrates with music, in and as this newly discovered creative will. Book 3 ends with Zarathustra performing the song of the Yes-sayer. 'How should I not lust after eternity and after the nuptial ring of rings, the ring of recurrence... I love you, O eternity' (1982: 341). And to prove this he says Yes and amen to eternity. He is able to tell life what he knows—that life is that which must overcome, even itself, and that the truth of this will to power is eternal return. 'You know that,' life replies, 'nobody knows that' (1982: 339). This is a beautifully ambivalent reply. Certainly life believed that nobody knew that, for life has lived inverted against itself in memory, promise and morality. But equally, this is life's own *ressentiment*. The view that 'nobody can know it' is the view of life that remains terrified of the knowledge it needs for its own truth and goal. Even its great enlightenment is denied by itself. The denial stands as the return of struggle and suffering for both life and Zarathustra that is book 4.

We find Zarathustra again after several years of dancing and singing on his mountain. But now he is disillusioned. 'My happiness is heavy' (1982: 349) he tells his animals, because he squanders what is given to him. We remember that in *The Prologue* the teacher had 'gathered too much honey' and needed 'hands outstretched to receive it'. Now, however, Zarathustra has 'spent and squandered the old honey down to the last drop' (1982: 353). How are we to explain the missing years between the end of book 3 and the beginning of book 4? What has happened to the dancing Zarathustra? Why did Nietzsche need to write book 4? We will answer this by returning to Deleuze. If we apply his version of eternal return to the end of book 3 we find a vision of Zarathustra as 'the cause of eternal return and the father of the overman' (1983: 192). Here Zarathustra's dance is no longer a trust 'in the power of the negative' (1983: 179). It is not a dance that celebrates 'the positivity of the negative' (1983: 180). It does not say Yes to No. On the contrary, it says a final No to denial. This No is to all the Nos of *ressentiment* and the inversion of values. Now it is the inversion itself that is finally inverted. 'This is why,' says Deleuze, 'affirmation in all its power is double: affirmation is affirmed' (1983: 186). He continues, 'affirmation is the enjoyment and play of its own difference' (1983: 188) and is 'the being of difference as such or eternal return' (1983: 189). Suffering the opposition that belongs to the negative is overcome in and as the play that is difference's own affirmation. Zarathustra no longer suffers, now he sings and dances on his mountain. For him, 'there is no return of the negative' (1983: 189) for the negative is excluded in and by return (1983: 190). This, for Deleuze, is 'transmutation' where the negative 'ceases to be an autonomous power' (1983: 191).

But if Zarathustra has thought of himself as the overman at the end of book 3, then by the beginning of book 4 it is clear that all such optimism has been destroyed. Deleuze offers a reason why this might be the case. Zarathustra, he says, 'is always in an inferior position in relation to the eternal return and the overman' (1983: 192). He is the lion who utters the final No, but he is not the child for whom the final No is a self-creative Yes. Zarathustra, says Deleuze, is only able to 'posit' (1983: 193) the child, for, in the life of Zarathustra, it is always 'the entanglement of causes or the connection of moments, the synthetic relation of moments to each other, which determines the hypothesis of the return of the same moment' (1983: 193). However, in relation to Dionysus, the relation is 'the unconditioned principle' (1983: 193) or the 'relation of the moment to itself' (1983: 193). Thus the 'yes of the child-player is more profound than the holy no of the lion... Zarathustra is not the whole of affirmation, nor what is most profound in it' (1983: 193). Zarathustra wants to be overcome, and is the cause of eternal return, but Dionysus is the 'absolute principle' (1983: 193) that gives power to the conditions. If Zarathustra is the will, Dionysus is power *per se*.

In this explanation it is no surprise that Zarathustra in book 4 comes to realise that he is the lion 'who still lacks a final metamorphosis' (1983: 192). However, Deleuze applies this account not to the end of book 3 but to the end of book 4, which means that Zarathustra takes us this far and no further. Nihilism turns on itself; reactive forces implode and create the conditions for the transmutation of the negative into the affirmative. But the overman, this 'new way of feeling... of thinking... [and] of evaluating,' (1983: 163) 'that even the lion cannot do' (1982: 139). What we learn from *Thus Spake Zarathustra* then is that difference is 'the highest power,' (1983: 197) one that is the unconditional principle of the will, but is not itself present as past, present and future in the conditions that 'posit' the unconditioned. We must conclude then that when Zarathustra leaves his cave at the end of book 4, ripe and glowing as the morning sun, he is still the cause of eternal return but not, like Dionysus, also its effect.

5. PHILOSOPHY'S HIGHER EDUCATION

Deleuze's explanation rests on a suppression of the law of the relation between conditioned and unconditioned. As such, Zarathustra can only posit the 'synthetic relation of the moment to itself' (1983: 193) which, from Dionysus' perspective, is already the unconditioned principle of difference determining 'its relations with all other moments' (1983: 193). This presupposition is itself a denial of a higher principle that underpins the relation between the conditioned and the unconditioned. This higher principle is not difference, for difference in Deleuze is only the unknowable posited as the principle of difference. Difference is not and cannot be the determinate principle of the relation between the conditioned and the unconditioned because it does not speak of the whole of the experience of that relation. It does not speak of the universality, the law, of the relation that is our experience of its own necessity.

Indeed, Deleuze's explanation is itself reactive, for it denies the necessity of contradiction, preferring to posit a necessity of play. But the experience of necessity or law as play belongs to no one for it is no one's actual experience of law. To deny contradiction and negation as and in experience is to say No to the principle that returns eternally in experience. What experience affirms repeatedly and always already is that we cannot say No to No-saying, and to affirm this is to affirm the higher principle that is at work. *Ressentiment* judges this higher education to be the 'abstract conception of universal and particular' (1983: 197) who are merely 'prisoners of symptoms' (1983: 197) which they cannot overcome. It is a judgement of *ressentiment* because it denies the very thing that life tells us—life is that which must be overcome. The 'must' is unequivocal (or better, unequivocally equivocal). To be true to itself life cannot achieve a victory in the child, in the Yes-saying, or in the creation of new values that Deleuze argues for. He argues that in the child we find 'the negativity of the positive' (1983: 180). If this were true then the child's own truth would be that, once and in victory, he is not himself, whereas really he is not himself in the eternal return of his defeat. The child knows this, not in a 'new' way, but in all the old ways. He re-cognises that he is not and never was what he appeared to be. It is to this absolute contingency that he must say Yes, but it is a Yes that is constituted by and in the negative experiences wherein victory and defeat struggle with each other as the one divided relation. Only for the child 'who knows,' who is the experience of remembering to forget, is his being the eternal return of will to power. Only the child who is never a beginning nor an end can be 'a new beginning' for only the experience of victory 'and' defeat is a 'self-propelled wheel, a first movement, a sacred "Yes"' (1982: 139). How can the child 'who knows' be 'innocence and forgetting?' (1982: 139). Because what he knows is that in the relation of victory and defeat, in the experience that is life's will to power as eternal return, he repeatedly becomes what he is—a No-sayer who is already a Yes to being this No-sayer. This is philosophy's higher education.

Seen in this way, book 4 of *Thus Spake Zarathustra* has a somewhat different outcome. The whole idea of the overman that Zarathustra celebrates at the end of book 3 is itself defeated in and as the eternal return of will to power in book 4. Zarathustra learns, again in and as the relation of the camel and the lion, that the dancing Zarathustra, in celebrating 'I will', is still denying his own will. Zarathustra the lion has made dancing into a victory of the will. Zarathustra the camel knows this victory as a No-saying to the defeat of the victory and understands again that he must take up this burden ascetically. If the lion says Yes to this, this victory will also undermine itself. There is a higher education here for the soul that is willing to will this circle. In this education the Yes-sayer is the relation of the No-sayer to himself, a relation whose necessity is the eternal return of will to power.

This is Zarathustra's higher education. Previously he taught one half of a broken middle. He taught the death of God and the coming of the victory of 'I will'. But equally throughout the book he learns of the defeat and the death of 'I will' in and as the return to the ascetic and, as such, the return of God. We have seen this relationship before in *The Birth of Tragedy* where the Apollinian will to power offers the illusion of calm, control and reconciliation. Apollinian will to power as art perpetrates the illusion that suffering has a higher glory. The Dionysian will to power which undermines such illusions is experienced as the terror wherein exceptions are found to the rule of reason. But in *The Birth of Tragedy* the 'unity' of intoxication and control is 'complete self-forgetfulness' (1968: 36). As such, this unity lacks the higher education that Zarathustra gains, namely that of eternal return. Through the traumas of remembering to forget, the historical and unhistorical man, and the will to power of the ascetic, Nietzsche moves inexorably towards learning of this relation of unity as the eternal return of will to power. Zarathustra is the unfolding of this higher education. Eternal return was implicit in all of Nietzsche's early writings explored above. Indeed, it is his own life which, as Zarathustra, says to him, 'you know it… but you do not say it… speak your word and break' (1982: 257-8). In doing so he sees into the truth of the illusion, and speaks its truth as eternal return.

As eternal return the illusion that is nature's own work and goal is philosophy's higher education. The illusion is known not merely as a dialectic of terror and reconciliation but as the eternal return of will to power. We saw above that nature employs illusion in order to achieve her own ends, and we know now from Zarathustra that life must overcome. Nature, then, is never what we know as 'natural law'. Nature is always a return to itself by its own work. It is eternally overcoming all notions of natural law, even its own. As such, it is actual as illusion. The illusion of overcoming is that it has an end or a result other than itself. To know will to power as this illusion is to know will to power as eternal return. In this respect, philosophy's higher education is nature's own 'great enlightenment' (1983: 159) and it is the truth of illusion.

Why then is this enlightenment not just another Apollinian illusion that suffering has a higher glory? Surely this is just another reconciliation and collapse? Precisely. This is what is learned in God's death and return, that this 'nature' is eternity. To argue that the illusion is or is not its own truth is merely to posit that illusion can or cannot be overcome. Such a positing is against the necessity of illusion that determines even this positing. The point is that the truth of illusion is already and again both of these. In Nietzsche, then, and for Zarathustra, we can say that the death of God, the coming of the overman, the death of the overman and the return of God are the whole of the illusion that nature employs to achieve its knowledge of itself. Whereas we judge truth from the illusion of beginnings and ends, philosophy's higher education teaches us how this very judgement is itself contingent upon that which is its own beginning and end. This is our absolute contingency within and upon the truth of that which obeys and commands itself as the necessity of its own conditions of possibility. It is nature, but not as we abstractly posit it from within the illusory stance that nature has predetermined for us. It is God, but not as we posit for or against Him within the illusory stance that His work has already created. Why call this 'God'? Because it is as God, and in the death and return of God, that the commander and the obeyer realises itself. It is part of the higher education of Zarathustra that God is how we know nature, for it is how we know law and necessity. That which is its own beginning and end is so in a way that creates for us the illusion of its impossibility, but whose possibility, precisely, is the illusion.

God necessarily returns on the mountain in two senses. The first is in the sense that the failures of the overman means we turn to God again as the truth of our No-saying, or the truth of slave morality. Previously the failures of the overman have been explained away by the misunderstandings of others—the townsfolk, his disciples, his animals—but time has run out for that *ressentiment*. What Zarathustra learns in book 4, as he is visited by seven forms of the higher man, is that each of these men represent a form of *ressentiment* that Zarathustra has left behind: a dishonoured teacher, a conscientious teacher, a confessional teacher, a pious teacher, a revengeful teacher, the gift giver and the obeying teacher. These last men still embody the ascetic, which is, as we saw above, 'a necessity of the first order... an insatiable instinct and power-will' (1968: 553). Equally, on the mountain, the higher men, at one moment able to laugh at themselves, at the next fall to their knees and worship the ass who, like the camel, never says No to taking upon himself the will of others, or to No-saying itself. In worshipping the ass, these last men reveal only what Zarathustra had feared all along, that they need something to follow, they need the will of another to say Yes to, be it Zarathustra, the overman, the ass or God. This is the return of God in the first sense where No-saying is already the other and the other *is* this No-saying. This return of God is the one that Zarathustra the dancer has overcome. However, in book 4 he recognises that his own life of dancing has become too 'perfect' (1982: 388). He has found a kind of happiness, but has no work, no experience, no defeat, and therefore no victory. What looks like the absence of *ressentiment,* the dancing overman of the ring of rings, is a No-saying to precisely the kinds of experiences that have educated him this far about will to power and eternal return. His soul is tired of the 'long voyages and the uncertain seas' (1982: 388) but these are the struggles of will to power wherein eternal return has been its truth. He realises, 'did not the world become perfect just now?' (1982: 389). If so, like the truth of the moment, it is experienced as 'it was'. It is only in a kind of half sleep that Zarathustra believes that this much happiness is good for him, when really he knows, from all that he has learned, that it is 'little happiness that makes the best happiness,' (1982: 389). Up, then he says to himself, 'you sleeper' and asks 'cheerful dreadful abyss of noon! When will you drink my soul back into yourself?' (1982: 389-90).

This marks the return of God on the mountain in a second sense, that of philosophy's higher education. Zarathustra's return to the abyss, to the search and to the ascetic, marks the truth for Zarathustra of the eternal return of will to power that he thought he had understood. He comes to experience the pity in himself when he sees how God returns to the higher men again. As God died on the mountain for the sleepful Zarathustra, so now again God returns to the mountain as the struggle of victory and defeat, the will to power, of the teacher and the taught. It is the second sense of return which is our higher education now regarding the totality of the first sense of return. Now, as the suffering which suffers itself, contra pity, Zarathustra is able to say Yes to the necessity of saying No to No-saying, a necessity which is the relation of the relation of overcoming 'and' return. Here, as Yes-sayer to the No of the No-sayer, as Yes to the eternal return of will to power, the No-sayer is already other and the other is not him. It is this that marks the truth of the return of God, namely that He was always already misrecognised in his own death *and* in his return, and that He is the whole of this relation appearing as (not) itself. God has survived Zarathustra's dancing song because the dance was not only the death of God, it was the misrecognition of the return of God before and after His death. God eternally returns in and from His defeat by *ressentiment.* The last men mark the truth of Zarathustra's experience of teaching, of what he teaches, and of the teacher himself, for in the return of God is the return of the 'insatiable instinct and power' that is life. To be the commander of this obeying, to will the return of God as the overcoming of the overman, is philosophy's higher education, and is the 'final' education of Zarathustra on the mountain. It is where he is already other, and the other is not him. It is only his pity for the last men which has prevented Zarathustra from being the commander and obeyer. He has sought to save them precisely from that which they already are and must become. He has sought to save them from their own asceticism, from the need to overcome which is expressed as God and His repeated murder and return. As at the beginning of Zarathustra, so at the end, Zarathustra asks the sun, 'what would your happiness be had you not those for whom you shine?' (1982: 436). Put another way, what would the eternal return of will to power be if it did not create and destroy itself? God is the need to overcome expressed as the ascetic. God is also the victory of overcoming expressed in His death. God is also the defeat of overcoming, by itself, in the return of God as the need again to overcome. As we seek the transcendental other, so we seek at the same time to overcome ourselves. This is *ressentiment*. But to seek to overcome *ressentiment* is itself just another *ressentiment* and God is present as much in his denial as in His affirmation. God, in and as the necessity of *ressentiment,* is a will to power which knows itself, or is eternity.

If Zarathustra does not learn this in book 4 then he leaves his cave hoping, still, for the overman. But that is not the case. He leaves his cave without pity for the higher man who still seeks. 'That has had its time! My suffering and my pity for suffering—what does it matter? Am I concerned with *happiness*? I am concerned with my work' (1982: 439)—and this work is to return to the vocation to teach life, to teach the eternal return of will to power, and to teach the truth of overcoming overcoming as God's own victory and defeat, or God's will. This is not, let us be clear, 'the lie involved in the belief in God' (1968: 596). Atheism is 'the most spiritual formulation' (1968: 596) of the ascetic ideal. Its will to truth is, as *The Genealogy of Morals* displays, a will to power. But as a will to power, it is universal, and as such always against itself. Experienced as slave morality, the ascetic is punishment without meaning. Experienced as nihilism, the ascetic is meaninglessness without the significance of eternal return. Experienced as atheism the ascetic is the eternal return of will to power. And, experienced as the eternal return of will to power, this higher education knows necessity not as the overman, but as relation; not as difference, but as formation and finality; not as unconditioned principle but as the unconditioned conditioned by itself; not just as the death of God, but as the truth of God in the eternal return of will to power.

NOTES

[1] This ambivalence says Deleuze is important to Nietzsche. 'All the forces whose reactive character he exposes are, a few lines or pages later, admitted to fascinate him, to be sublime because of the perspective they open up for us... they separate us from our power but at the same time they give us another power, "dangerous" and "interesting"' (1983: 66). This is why, again mentioned above, the dialectic fails and must fail. Its goal misunderstands that, for example, the reconciliation of theory with practice becomes impossible precisely in and because of the attempt to unify them. It 'fails essentially' (1983: 168).

[2] I have kept upper case for Yes-saying and No-saying, and for their requisite Yes and No, but I have not amended translations in quotations.

[3] I don't think it is going too far, again, to liken this relation to Caygill/Benjamin's double infinity. The will to power is the principle of what can be known, this is the transcendental condition of the possibility of what can be known, and the eternal return is the synthesis that has difference, or this possibility, as its own difference from any one form of the will to power and its reactive form. When will to power, or the transcendental, is thought as eternal return, then the reactive itself is finally overcome for difference and its repetition are now one creative thought. Interestingly, it is just such a synthesis that Caygill works hard to avoid in Benjamin, but finds for example, in 'voice', divine violence and pure language (Caygill, 1998: 6).

[4] Deleuze's reading of Nietzsche has not been interpreted within educational thinking as speculative. Educational theorising not only misses the educational significance and import of Deleuze's interpretation of Nietzsche, it does not encourage philosophical interpretation to seek the educational aspects of Deleuze's speculative work. For example, in a recent book within the philosophy of education, the double affirmative is named as 'the multiple'. This is an attractive yet flawed misrecognition of the 'negativity of the positive' (1983: 180). See Peters, (1998).

[5] Hegel too describes the true as the Bacchanalian revel in which all are drunk and entwined in and as the repose of the whole (1977: 27-8).

[6] We will return to their 'child' below.

[7] This cannot be art for art is only symbolic imitation and appearance. It is part of the illusion. But the redemption of art rather than of nature, this is the higher education regarding the relation of man to nature. Knowing what art is, is our education regarding the truth of nature, and our education is nature's true goal and end, that it should be known for what it is—dualism, reconciliation and struggle. And because this is the redemption of art it is not knowing without feeling. On the contrary, it is, now, the knowing of the truth of feeling. At different times this 'mystery of union' (1968: 48) takes different forms. The identity of the lyrist and the musician is both Dionysian and Apollinian, able to re-present the primordial contradiction and pain (1968: 49) with the primordial pleasure of mere appearance not merely subjectively but objectively, or 'from the depth of his being' (1968: 49). He may say 'I' but as 'the only truly existent and eternal self resting at the basis of things...' (1968: 50). Again Nietzsche emphasises that appearance is not overcome by the Dionysian individual, it is 'released' (1968: 52) to its own truth as appearance and destruction. Music, says Nietzsche, symbolises this 'primal unity' (1968: 55) which 'ever anew discharges itself' (1968: 65) in the chorus not by 'Apollinian redemption through mere appearance' (1968: 65) but by 'the shattering of the individual and his fusion with primal being' (1968: 65).

[8] But when he calls him 'the historical man' he includes the quality of being unhistorical, that is, freed from the petrification of historical memory. I therefore refer to this man as the historical *and* unhistorical man. When used separately, then historical means inactivity and unhistorical means without the education of reaction.

[9] 'Incorporate' here is too voluntaristic, sounding as if it is a decision that this man can make. But with Zarathustra we see that when this is understood as our higher education, what we learn is that this incorporation is already within us and determining us even without our 'knowing' it.

[10] From *Beyond Good and Evil*, section 36. Nietzsche uses the phrase to remind us that the notion that the world—defined and determined according to its intelligible character—is will to power, is itself a thought experiment. This conscience of method is the will to power turned against itself, and is already the relation of the relation of the will to power.

[11] As such, 'what ought I to do' is determined by the truth of 'what is'. As we saw in chapter 1 above, the separation of practical and theoretical reason is itself the necessity of our conditions of possibility. The ought is not a categorical imperative of subsumptive judgements, it is the formation and finality of reflective judgements. Living the truth of philosophy's higher education is the re-cognition of the misrecognition of the ought and the is.

[12] An analysis of this as eternal return comes later in the chapter.

[13] Of course Kant was himself partial to looking to the stars. 'Two things fill the mind with ever new and increasing admiration and awe, the oftener and more steadily we reflect on them: the starry heavens above me and the moral law within me.' Kant, I. (1956) p. 166, para. 162.

[14] As life does to Zarathustra in his moments of stillness.

[15] Just to note here that the sentence preceding this one states 'the nations are drawing away from one another in the most hostile fashion and long to tear one another to pieces' (1983: 148). As I write this modernity is 20 days into an 'illegal' war with Iraq. Again the ambivalence of modernity is clear. Modernity acts for freedom, and against freedom. But, failing to learn of freedom from within this relation, it is the master who is not slave. As such the war remembers that the other is not free, but forgets that freedom is the other. Even bourgeois social relations have a 'nobility', *forgetting* the self-determination of freedom in the name of its self-determination.

[16] We are taking seriously here Nietzsche's own comment in 1887 that for the reader of *The Genealogy* a reading of Zarathustra is also necessary (1968: 458).

[17] This is similar to Rousseau's argument in the discourse on the origin of inequality which sees those benefiting from a surplus of possessions instigating the rule of private property. They offer the rule to safeguard the possessions of all, and offer it therefore under a cloak of equality, but in truth they offer it only so that their advantage can be safeguarded by law. As the standpoint of the victors is passed off as the equality for all of private property law, so for Nietzsche, 'popular morality also separates strength from expressions of strength, as if there were a neutral substratum behind the strong man... but there is no such substratum... the deed is everything' (1968: 481).

[18] And, therefore, into Hegel.

REFERENCES

Caygill, H. (1998) *Colour of Experience*, London, Routledge.

Deleuze, G. (1983) *Nietzsche and Philosophy*, New York, Columbia University Press, trans. H. Tomlinson.

Kant, I. (1956) *Critique of Practical Reason*, New York: Macmillan.

Nietzsche, F. (1968) *Basic Writings of Nietzsche*, New York, The Modern Library, trans. W. Kaufmann.

Nietzsche, F. (1982) *The Portable Nietzsche*, New York, The Viking Penguin Press, trans. W. Kaufmann.

Nietzsche, F. (1983) *Untimely Meditations*, Cambridge, Cambridge University Press, trans. R.J. Hollingdale.

Peters, M. (ed.) (1998) *Naming the Multiple: Poststructuralism and Education*, Westport: Bergin & Garvey.

CHAPTER 6

ROSENZWEIG: FIRE AND RAYS

1. INTRODUCTION

Philosophy's higher education as we have presented it has concerned the substance and the subjectivity of illusion in the relation between thinking and the object. In modern political terms this refers to the relations between thought and universal private property relations, or between religion and the state. Yet philosophy's higher education has another essential element. It concerns not only politics and social relations but also history. More precisely, philosophy's higher education is the philosophy of history and, just as the absolute is retrieved in this higher education, so the absolute is also retrieved in the philosophy of history. Here are two quintessentially modern blasphemies, that the absolute can be known, and that its being known is teleological. It leads to a third blasphemy which we will return to in a moment, that the education which is formative of the absolute and the philosophy of history is world spirit. This will be explored below around the relation of law and learning. We will argue that philosophy's higher education is both the law of learning and the learning of law or again, a relation of formation and finality that is true to itself only as our education.

The ubiquitous critique of the philosophy of history centres on the unacceptable domination of difference by the imperialism of western logocentrism. However, this domination and this imperialism are only actually negated when risked and in this risk lies learning about the relation to and as the other. In previous chapters, the dualisms of philosophy's higher education—formation and finality, master and slave, being and time, recollection and repetition, and eternal return and will to power[1]—have to varying degrees revealed their import for the relation to the other. In this final chapter, dealing with the philosophy of history, we have to be even more ambitious. We will argue that the relation to other carried within philosophy's higher education and manifest as the philosophy of history, is teleological, but in a way very different from its abstract formulation as 'total' or 'closed'. This latter misrecognition of teleology is determined in and by modern social relations and from the point of view of the master. Its deconstruction into pluralism is equally masterful. Philosophy's higher education however learns about teleology as the formative relation of self and other, a learning that itself constitutes a subjectivity which can be in and of the world and not merely master *or* slave.

One way to approach world spirit is through notions of eternity and method within the Judaism of Buber and Rosenzweig and the philosophy of Hegel.[2] This brings out the differences between the eternal people and the peoples of the historical nations, but it also reveals their shared higher education regarding dualisms, both internal and external. Our chapter now will take us briefly through Buber's and Rosenzweig's thoughts on dualisms in Judaic life, to a more detailed analysis of eternity and method in the latter's *Star of Redemption*, and its comparison with the philosophical dialectic in Hegel. This is then used as the basis for a discussion of the concept of world spirit as it appears within philosophy's higher education. It is argued that world spirit is the absolute contingency of the philosophy of history, a living, learning relation of self to self and to other. It is the Idea present in and as learning. The chapter ends by arguing that it is the Idea that is present but suppressed in all dualisms, and that it is the conjunction 'and' in which this presence and suppression are to be found. As such, it can be argued that the relation Rosenzweig 'and' Hegel already embodies a view of history as the formative experience of the absolute where the manifestation of truth, in and as the law of learning and learning of law, is in itself a relation—one of many—that constitute world spirit.

2. BROKEN JEWISHNESS

Buber and Rosenzweig, writing in the first quarter of the twentieth century, share a particular spiritual concern, namely the lack of unity in Jewish life. For Buber, whilst 'lasting substance,' 'immortal being' and constancy of existence' (1967: 14) are to be found in the blood of the community, or his people, for the western Jew in particular 'the world of constant elements [environment] and the world of substance [inwardness] are ... rent apart' (1967: 17). The tragedy of the self-affirmation of the Jew is that he must find his way 'from division to unity' (1967: 21) for his soul and his people to be one.

Yet Buber also argues that Judaism is 'a polar phenomenon' (1967: 23) riven by contradiction and dualism. This, he says, is what always ensures that the Jew, striving for unity, is also a phenomenon of mankind as a whole. It 'transforms the Jewish question into a human question' (1967: 25). God Himself 'emerged from the striving for unity' (1967: 27). Thus, 'just as the idea of an inner duality is Jewish, so is the idea of redemption from it' (1967: 27). Importantly for Buber's notion of unity and the eternal, 'the Jew was denied immediate unity, an immediate, artless, original experience of unity within the I and within nature. He did not start out from, he arrived at, unity' (1967: 28-9). This has many important implications, not least the status of the Law as human or divine.[3] Buber is clear in his correspondence with Rosenzweig that 'it is only through man in his self-contradiction that revelation becomes legislation' (Rosenzweig, 1955: 111). Thus, he says to Rosenzweig, 'I cannot accept the laws and the statutes blindly,' (1955: 114) nor can he accept 'the Law as something universal' (1955: 115).

This kind of broken relationship to immediacy we have seen to be determinative of philosophy's higher education. Buber also turns to education, and specifically to teaching, as the truth of this brokenness. However, he turns not to the barren intellectualism of liberalism but to a 'renewal'—a return to and transformation of—Jewish spiritual life. For Buber here, one thing is needed above all else, and that is the desire for unity. This desire is creative in and as religiosity, even though it 'induces sons, who want to find their own God, to rebel against their fathers' (1967: 80).[4] This return to religiosity, driven by the desire for unity, represents a decision and a deed to choose spiritual being over the immediate environment of contents. This return, this decision, is the 'religious act: for it is God's realisation through man' (1967: 83). There is, says Buber, 'no meaning and no truth for man anywhere except in that authentic life which unifies and liberates the world. He who walks on the way, walks in the footsteps of God' (1967: 69).

Decision, return and deed, then, represent renewal in the sense of a reinvigorated and transformed notion of education as the desire for unity. Buber turns his attention to the teaching of the youth as a vital component of this renewal of the Jewish community. Intellectualisation has turned God into a Kantian idea. But God 'is not a Kantian idea,' (1967: 109) says Buber, He is 'an elementally present spiritual reality' (1967: 109). It is the destiny of every man to be religious for 'at some time or other, be it ever so fleeting and dim, every man is affected by the power of the unconditioned. The time of life when this happens to all,' he says, 'we call youth' (1967: 151). However, since many men deny this unconditionality to themselves, it is our responsibility, argues Buber, to help youth 'not to miss its metaphysical self-discovery by being asleep' (1967: 152). It will not be achieved outside the Jewish community—outside the deed—in the 'depressing loneliness' (1967: 158) of the intellectual climate of Europe. Indeed, the danger is that this 'negative loneliness of the abyss experienced by the lost and the forlorn' (1967: 159) leaves youth open and ready 'to surrender to any phantom of community' (1967: 159). Against this, Buber stresses that 'only a genuine bond with the religiously creative life of its people can still this longing of Jewish youth, and overcome the loneliness of its intellectualization' (1967: 159).

Buber sees two ways in which this educational commitment can be achieved: through Jewish teaching and Jewish Law. The danger is that both elements have lost the vitality and creativity that are required for renewal. The teaching can become abstract and formulaic when removed from the context of individual life and appear finished and unequivocal. Observance of the Law can become empty when it is merely heteronomous and lacking an inner unity. As such, the Law appears closed and immutable. Against both of these Buber advocates the return, transformation and deed of Jewish spirituality and a commitment to 'the primal forces, to the living religious forces which, though active and manifest in all of Jewish religion, in its teaching and its law, have not been fully expressed by either' (1967: 169). He concludes that these eternal forces never 'permit one's relationship to the unconditional ever to wholly congeal into something merely accepted and executed on faith...' (1967: 169).

For Buber, then, renewal recognises that 'God's original tablets are broken' (1967: 169) and seeks to 'restore the blurred outlines of divine freedom on the second tablets, the tablets of the teaching and the law' (1967: 169). This reunification of the dualism of spirit and 'world' requires commitment to the primal forces of Jewish life. *Contra* what teaching and law have become within the 'world' of the nations, renewal means recovering the inner forces of Judaism, transforming a life lived in the other's world into a life lived in and for itself. 'It is not at all the intention of the new teaching to be new; it wants to remain the old teaching, but a teaching grasped in its absolute sense' (1967: 46). He continues, 'only then will the Jewish people be ready to build a new destiny for itself where the old one once broke into fragments... but the house can be built only when the people have once more become builders' (1967: 54).

Rosenzweig, writing around the same time, shares many of Buber's concerns about broken Jewishness, and also argues the need for 'the builders'. The Jewish sphere of life now exists only in the synagogue, says Rosenzweig, it having been abandoned in the home. The struggle for equality in the non-Jewish world has distracted from the more central concern of the decline of the Jewish community. Thus a Jew may possess a Jewish world but only does so 'surrounded by another one, the non-Jewish world' (1955: 29). He may be given equality of rights, but would therein have attained as an individual 'what would have been denied to us as a community' (1955: 52). Such a man may be renowned in book learning, but 'from the point of view of inner life... [this] is not only no advantage for the community, but a loss...' (1955: 54).

What is required, says Rosenzweig, is a 'renaissance of Jewish learning' (1955: 55) under the watch of a new form of teacher-scholar who will restore to Jewishness the notion not of Jewish 'nationality' but of 'Jewish human being' (1955: 57). This form of learning is to be found in the presentiment of the current moment, between past and future.[5] It will not be found in books but in 'life itself,' (1955: 60) for 'that which is distant can be reached only through that which is nearest at the moment' (1955: 65). This teacher-scholar will learn and practise a pedagogy of 'readiness' offering the learner the opportunity, the risk, of saying 'we Jews' (1955: 65). 'With the simple assumption of that infinite "pledge" he will become in reality "wholly Jewish"... the Jewish human being arises in no other way' (1955: 66). For the teacher-scholar and for the pupils this readiness is a confidence which needs no plans or recipes. 'There is one recipe alone that can make a person Jewish... [and] that recipe is to have no recipe' (1955: 66).[6] Thus the teacher-scholar 'cannot be a teacher according to a plan' (1955: 69). He must listen, first, in order then to join together the learner with their desires, in order to retrieve that Jewish human being who lives, at that moment, in front of him.[7]

Rosenzweig explains the relation of his educational ideas to the Law in a piece addressed to Buber written in the summer of 1923. He is supportive of Buber's critique of intellectualisation and its damage to Jewish life. Buber has shown that teaching has become defined by what is 'knowable' instead of being defined by the transformative capacity of the primal forces or inner power. In liberating Jews from the whole sphere of what is knowable, says Rosenzweig, Buber has 'removed us from the imminent danger of making our spiritual Judaism depend on whether or not it was possible for us to be followers of Kant' (1955: 77). However, Rosenzweig is less supportive of Buber's notion of Law. Buber relieves teaching from the shackles of what is knowable, but fails to relieve Law from the shackles of what is 'doable'—and here doable means permitted or forbidden.

Rosenzweig, however, is able to extend Buber's critique of Law into a philosophical education regarding the conditions of the possibility of Law. In the case of the teachings, he says, the way to Jewish human being is through the knowable, or in the loss of the knowable where 'the goal lay a step beyond' (1955: 80). This is a path without a path and a recipe for no recipes. It is pathlessness, literally, aporia—no way—and it is the way that leads to Jewish teachings. Why can pathlessness lead to Jewish teachings? Because this working through 'knowable Judaism' faces its own precondition, or the condition of its own possibility and the necessity in experience of that condition. The nations, says Rosenzweig, do not know this precondition 'for the nations have a face still in the making... their faces are not moulded whilst they are still in nature's lap' (1955: 81). This enables the nations to possess what they learn.[8] But the Jews were born of a different nature, not unknowable because unformed, but unknowable because already formed. The Jews were led forth 'a nation from the midst of another nation' (Deuteronomy 4:34). Even before it was born, says Rosenzweig, it was known. This precondition, known but not in the bookish sense of knowing, is Jewish 'being'. Only he 'who remembers this determining origin can belong to it,' (1955: 81) a remembering that, in Nietzschean terms explored above, is present in forgetting the historical memory of the nations. 'That is why this people must learn what is knowable as a condition for learning what is unknown, for making it his own' (1955: 81). Thus, to Buber's critique of the possibility of teaching in an un-Jewish environment is added Rosenzweig's philosophical analysis of its truthfulness and its own inner necessity.

Rosenzweig now extends this philosophical insight to Law. As the non-path through what is knowable led to the truth of the relation of the teachings to Jewish human being so, too, the non-path through what is doable leads to the Law. In its 'Western Orthodox' form the unity of the Law has fallen into the dualism of the forbidden and the permissible.

> Wherever the Law is still kept among Western Jewry it is no longer a living 'Jewishness,' one that while largely based on legal paragraphs, was taken naturally and as a matter of course. This sort of Judaism has acquired a polemical point that

quite contrary to any original intent—is turned, not against the outsider, but mainly against the large majority of those within Jewry who no longer keep the Law. Today the Law brings out more conspicuously the difference between Jew and Jew than between Jew and Gentile (1955: 61).

Rosenzweig argues that just as the dualism that separated the knowable and the unknowable 'should no longer exist,' (1955: 82) so 'in the sphere of what can be done the difference between the forbidden and the permissible... must cease to exist' (1955: 82).[9] Indeed, what was 'permissible' has been rendered external, whilst only the prohibitions are left to define the Jewish sphere. Thus has the Jew taken into his identity the duality that opposes the oneness of his community. But this should not be read as Rosenzweig arguing that oneness can overcome duality. 'Zionism fails us' (1955: 65) he says. On the contrary, he argues that in an educational sense—a sense that we will explore more fully in the remainder of this chapter—the Law must return to the custom of the people and itself be changed by that living relation. This is not to have some posited unity overcome the Law; it is to see an educational relation between the two poles of the Jewish Question which learns of itself in and through its own difficult and aporetic conditions of possibility. If unity is read as necessity without learning, then unity is dogma. If unity is read as necessity with learning, in learning, and as learning, then it is not dogma, but nor is it merely dualism. It is its own necessity. This education Rosenzweig calls 'naturally grown freedom' (1955: 84). In other terms, its structure is the higher education that results when the conditions of possibility— the Jewish Question— are subject to their own necessity. At the risk of returning Rosenzweig to Kant, but to a different Kant than the one Buber liberated him from, this naturally grown freedom is the formation and finality that is Law.

In Law as freedom, then, 'not the negative but the positive will be dominant' (1955: 84). Read unphilosophically this merely asserts the domination of the Yea over the Nay. But in presenting this relationship in *The Star of Redemption*, Rosenzweig shows there is a third partner is this relationship, the Nought. The educational and philosophical significance of this is explored in a moment. But it is in this context that we must read the end of 'The Builders' where Rosenzweig states that Law can again become commandment as 'living reality' (1955: 85) when it stops being content 'and becomes inner power...' (1955: 85). This means nothing unless the latter is its own content, and is reduced to dogma unless this content is its own formation and finality. It is, therefore, not to reduce Rosenzweig again to intellectualism that we explore its logic and substance as philosophy's higher education. It is to find within it its own necessity as Jewish learning, and its relation to the necessity of the nations' propertied learning. The former necessity, argues Rosenzweig, is to be found not in the content of what must be done, but in what can be done. It is ability that carries the difficult relationship of outer law and inner commandment. Knowledge and deeds can be formative of (the teleology of) teaching and Law, but it cannot be known in advance which will be so. 'We do not know the boundary, and we do not know how far the pegs of the tent of the Torah may be extended, nor which one of our deeds is destined to accomplish such widening' (1955: 87). That is why the Jewish human being, and the Jewish teacher-scholar, must risk the desire for unity expressed by both Rosenzweig and Buber, so that in readiness and confidence (Rosenzweig) and in religiosity and renewal (Buber) the Jew may become the builder—formative and teleological.

3. THE CONFIGURATION

To understand the higher education of philosophy in Rosenzweig we will now compare 'method' in Hegel and in *The Star of Redemption*. For Hegel, method is form *per se*, for which all content that is *other* is only the illusory being of 'form-determinateness' (1969: 825). We will argue that the Star is configured by a similar phenomenology. It will be argued that in the differences of method lies the significance of those differences as philosophy's higher education. This is not a unification of Hegel and Rosenzweig, but it is the truth of their relation as the absolute necessity that is free contingency, free and absolute as formation and as finality. Put differently, in both Hegel and Rosenzweig, the truth of their relation is the truth of relation *per se,* a truth of learning and law where the 'and' becomes two 'ofs', learning of law and law of learning.

The first point of comparison is the triune representations of relations to truth which abound in Rosenzweig. The Star itself consists of two sets of triadic relations. God, world and man form one triangle; creation, revelation and redemption form a second triangle; and together they form the configuration of the Star.

Each point on the Star is related to other points. God is the creator who reveals himself. Revelation is 'the means for confirming creation structurally,' (1971: 161) an act of the lover so that each moment is a new stability for love as experience. But the present is therefore a gift. To say Yea to the gift and to the present is to know more than the present, it is to know that the present is contingent upon creation and revelation. Such a unity of God and man is, for us, redemption.

But the 'for us' here is obviously crucial. For the God that is, and for the man that is, the order of events, outside of world-time, is that creation precedes its revelation. But revelation is world-time and, says Rosenzweig, 'this temporal relationship is reversed' (1971: 218). As such, for us, creation is the world that is renewed in each moment, or, again, for us, creation is 'creature' or providence. Here (and now) the relation between God and man is known not as it is in itself but as it is for us in world time. The illusion here is that we take the creature to be the beginning and see God and man as something to be achieved in the future. Rosenzweig says 'to put it paradoxically: the world manifests itself as creature in creation, but the substructure for this its self-"revealing" must await its being-"created" in redemption' (1971: 219). Because creation is God and man *as creature*, then God and man are misrecognised as 'for' the creature. 'For God and man, redemption was preceded by the sweeping erection of their own being which their own act had then only to consolidate from within and to unify structurally. For the world, however, it was followed by this' (1971: 218). 'While God and man are older in essence than as phenomena, the world is created as phenomenon long before it is redeemed for its essence' (1971: 219).

God, man and world, therefore, are phenomenologically related to creation, revelation and redemption. The world is the third party to God and man which experiences their relation as separation. This experience or the for us of God and man, is the knowledge of separation as the here and now of world-time, and in this time, by definition, there is no redemption. That which is creation and revelation, for us, is yet to come. Or, to put it another way, the gift, or the present, is never received by the beloved as it was given by the lover. In fact, the beloved receives the wrong gift, intended as a present of the eternal, but received as a promise of the eternal.

Before exploring this as philosophy's higher education, we will examine the implication of this creaturally misrecognition for the rest of *The Star*. It is clear that Rosenzweig must be writing *The Star* having recognised creaturely misrecognition. He has re-cognised eternity and retrieved it from its earthly appearance so that now Rosenzweig can state that the 'unity into which the fragments of the All now enter' (1971: 254) is not an Hegelian circle but is the configuration of the Star, or God's becoming. Eternity is present and is a present.

> God has not simply been once upon a time and now hides modestly behind eternal laws... God is not merely in the moments when someone is wholly blissful with the heavenly glow of feelings... What eternity does is to make the moment everlasting; it is eternalisation (1971: 258).

But what then of eternity for man and for the world? For them, eternity is present, as present and as promise, or not-present. In the relation of this Yea and Nay is the actuality of eternity. If

> the possibility of a separation must be sustained on the certainty of a connection [ ] then the world-day of the Lord must already bear within itself the predisposition to eternity's day of God. For God, redemption provides this assurance of eternity despite the temporality of self-revelation... But this direct equivalence of assurance and fulfilment of eternity is not valid for the other 'elements'; it is this, indeed, which makes them the 'others' and God the One (1971: 259).

Consequently, for man, it is creation that beholds eternity for creation is the relation, the 'And' (1971: 259) between God's love for man 'and' man as loving, or between 'the creature of God "and" the image of God' (1971: 259). For the world, on the other hand, revelation is the 'and' between the seemingly contradictory elements of God who created the world and the man who endures it. For Rosenzweig this is not, however, an eternal contradiction (an Hegelian circle), for revelation, as seen above, is already the present of redemption.

> Thus Gods revelation to man is the pawn given to the world for its redemption. It is the basis for the world's certainty that its doubts will one day be resolved... For the world, revelation is the guarantee of its integration into eternity (1971: 260).

The fact that the eternal is present is not a contradiction for Rosenzweig. It provides the foundation now for his reading of the differences between Judaism and Christianity, readings which cross the threshold 'from miracle to enlightenment' (1971: 261). Clearly if world-time is the revelation of God and man as eternity, and if redemption is already present for the world in that revelation, the nature of the present will be seminal to Rosenzweig's account.

From 'our' point of view (and this 'our' will divide and collapse in a moment, as the moment!) the eternal has to be anticipated as something yet to come. But in God's time, the future is not anticipation. For man and the world decisions have to be made (prayers have to be said) about whether actions will accelerate or delay the kingdom of God. The sinner prays because he has missed redemption; the fanatic prays for redemption before its time. This is the appearance of the eternal, the present, in earthly time. But for God who is already present and eternally present in the present, (the gift of his love), 'redemption is truly as old as creation and revelation' (1971: 272).

But there is another voice says Rosenzweig praying within 'us'. Christianity holds to the appearance of the eternal as 'the way'. But Judaism knows the eternal as 'life'. The most significant feature of the difference between them is that whilst Christianity gains temporal life, Judaism is trusted with eternal time. Rosenzweig cites the difference in the responses to 'fate' or to necessity. The Christian prays a 'prayer to the personal fate' (1971: 277) rather than to the world as a whole. This means that revelation concerned not the presence but the absence of God in the world, which Rosenzweig refers to as Christian paganism. The Christian was forced to turn to an inner reality of faith whilst seeking also to convert the world. Conversion implies power over time, over earthly time, and also it implies that the eternal is not the nighest, not now, not 'this' revelation. For Rosenzweig, Christianity's paganism is precisely this, that God's creation and revelation are not to be grasped today, in the moment that is already creation, revelation and redemption, but rather, in the way through time. Christianity 'has made an epoch out of the present' (1971: 338) and its paganism is not only world history, but also the state, both of which symbolise 'the attempt to give nations eternity within the confines of time' (1971: 332). As such, Rosenzweig concludes, Christianity is always a middle or a mid point between beginning and end which it can never unite. His path, or the eternal way, is all middle for beginning and end are always equidistant. Indeed, the eternal is only a way; its departure and its goal are not the way. Thus, 'he who travels the current itself can only see from one bend to the next. For him who travels the iron tracks, the current [of time] as a whole is but a sign that he is still en route, only a sign of the between' (1971: 339).

The Jew, on the other hand, 'buys its eternity at the cost of its temporal life' (1971: 303). The Torah 'raises the people from the temporality and historicity of life, and deprives it of the power over time' (1971: 304). 'We have,' says Rosenzweig, 'struck root in ourselves... and it is this rooting in ourselves, and in nothing but ourselves, that vouchsafes eternity' (1971: 305). Later Rosenzweig says that God arched 'the bridge of his law above the current of time which henceforth and to all eternity rushes powerlessly along under its arches' (1971: 339).

Whilst admitting that the Jewish world is 'teeming with contradictions in every single thing,' (1971: 307) Rosenzweig eschews any dialectical or idealistic 'circle' for these paradoxes. Even though the Jew is loved by God (revelation) and unredeemed, nevertheless redemption is part of the 'present' that is God and man. But for us, 'for the present, all that is visible is the spilt' (1971: 308). The question of God exists in these paradoxes 'and thus cannot readily be answered at all' (1971: 308). But unlike the paradoxes, for the Jew the orbit of man's life within eternity, but out of history, is whole within the 'orderly pattern in the yearly rings of life' (1971: 308). These rings are not growth, for growth would imply time. Rather they are a suspension of contradiction and of resolution of contradiction. As such the suspended people 'lives in its own redemption' (1971: 328) for between creation and revelation is God and man as love. The renewal of the ring is to repeat the moment because 'the feeling that redemption is still unattained breaks through again' (1971: 328). 'The years come and go, one after the other as a sequence of waiting' (1971: 328) but a waiting that does not reduce eternity to time. Rather, 'eternity is just this: that time no longer has a right to a place between the present moment and consummation and that the whole future is to be grasped today' (1971: 328). If we stopped here, then, a relation between Rosenzweig's Judaism and Christianity would seem to be improbable, if not impossible, separated as they are by the different and opposed epistemologies and phenomenologies of life and the way.

However, the eternal life and the eternal way are related in the configuration of the Star. The Jew whose rootedness means that 'nothing may remain outside as something contradictory' (1971: 348) has an internal relation to the contradictions, 'harnessed,' says Rosenzweig, 'into the internal structures of God, world, man' (1971: 348). Christianity on the other hand, works in opposition to itself. Its expansionary mission to be all-embracing means that Christianity by definition is unrooted. Whereas Judaism 'was able to be one people, the eternal people,' (1971: 349) Christianity is the separation of one person from another. Christian brotherliness is found only on the way or in the middle, that is, in time. Jewish communion however is innate in the simultaneity at the boundaries of time (1971: 346). As such, Christianity's mission for all-embracing association is already determined by diffusion. For the Jew, contradiction is within God, 'it is in ceaseless connection precisely with itself' (1971: 349). For the Christian, however, the One has contradiction as external, that is, as his Son.

In the external diffusion of contradiction that is Christianity Rosenzweig finds its innate paganism. The Christian necessarily follows a dual path. He is related to the divine truth by divesting himself of 'everything personal' (1971: 350). But he is 'familiar' with God, or has him near, only through the Son. 'He cannot imagine that God himself, the Holy God, could so condescend to him as he demands, except by becoming human himself. The inextinguishable segment of paganism which is innermost in every Christian bursts forth here' (1971: 350). Rosenzweig says it is 'un-Christian' to confuse the two ways, that their differentiation requires great tact 'to know when it is proper to walk the one and when the other' (1971: 350).

So Judaism and Christianity are explored within Rosenzweig as different phenomenologies, that is as different experiences, internal or external, of the revelation of God where revelation, in the creatureliness of the world, is contradiction. But these different phenomenologies are *both* part of the Star of Redemption. 'The rays of the Star... break forth to the exterior, the fire glows towards the interior' (1971: 398). The rays of Christianity shine out but remain unconnected, unable to form a unity. But the fiery inner core of the Star, Judaism, 'by thus gathering its blaze inwardly, it in turn smelts the blazing, flashing contradictions more and more into a unitary, still glow' (1971: 403).

Both the fire and rays have their dangers. Christianity's dangers are that God is diffused into spirit, into the human and into the All, relieved thereby of the Oneness from which the rays emanate. The dangers of the fire for Judaism are that the nature of the innermost is constricted and 'too simple' (1971: 406). Says Rosenzweig, if the rays threatened the concept of God, the fire threatens 'his world and his man' (1971: 406).

> By radiating apart to the outside, Christianity threatens to lose itself in individual rays far from the divine nucleus of truth. By glowing towards the inside, Judaism threatened to gather its warmth to its own bosom, far away from the pagan reality of the world. If there the dangers were spiritualization of God, humanization of God, secularization of God – here they are denial of the world, disdain of the world, mortification of the world... All three of these dangers are the necessary consequences of an inwardness turned away from the world, as those of Christianity are the consequence of an externalisation of the self turned toward the world. (1971: 406-407).

But even in the dangers there is a crucial difference. 'In the final analysis,' says Rosenzweig, the Jewish danger is not such because the Jew 'cannot descend into his own interior without at the same time ascending to the Highest' (1971: 407).

Thus by nature the Jew's innermost leads towards himself whilst the Christian is by birth a pagan, and the rays lead the Christian on a path of contradiction which is away from himself, a 'self-renunciation' (1971: 407-8). Whilst the inner core of the Star has paganism on the outside, the Christian has it on the inside.

The phenomenologies, then, of core and rays share different dangers which, in themselves, exhibit a different significance and thus determine the relation between them. The significance of contradiction as innermost for Judaism is that commandment and the Now are the present of redemption. The significance of contradiction as self-externalisation for Christianity is that 'emotional satisfaction remains denied to it' (1971: 413). The construction of the fire is now expanded 'into the Whole... [it] has redeemed itself for the Unification of the One,' (1971: 411) whilst the latitude of the rays works against such unification. Emotion as fire illuminates 'the Innermost of the Jewish soul' (1971: 411); emotion as rays becomes something worldly and expresses the eternity of way without beginning or end.

Fire and ray, then, are different phenomenologies of triune relations. But for Rosenzweig they are also the relationship between Judaism and Christianity. The very existence of the Jew he says,

> constantly subjects Christianity to the idea that it is not attaining the goal, the truth, that it ever remains – on the way. That is the profoundest reason for the Christian hatred of the Jew, which is heir to the pagan hatred of the Jew. In the final analysis it is only self-hate... (1971: 413).

But this relationship, like that of God's time and world-time is 'a separation... sustained on the certainty of a connection' (1971: 259). The separation, as we have seen, is of the eternal people from the eternal way. The connection, however, is in their difference, viz. that because the former lacks the way and the latter lacks the whole, 'before God then, Jew and Christian both labour at the same task' (1971: 415). Rosenzweig continues, 'He has set enmity between the two for all time, and withal has most intimately bound each to each... The truth, the whole truth, thus belongs neither to them nor to us' (1971: 415-16). The Jew, looking to the interior, misses the rays and what they illuminate, whilst the Christian, always looking outward, misses the light. Thus says Rosenzweig, both Jew and Christian 'have but a part of the whole' (1971: 416) and are both creatures limited within and by the boundaries of life and humanity.

The *Star of Redemption* 'ends' by stating that the Star itself is the countenance of God, 'the divine visage,' (1971: 418) and that such a recognition is the 'consummation' (1971: 418) of our cognition of the Star. In this consummation, redemption which for world and man seemed to be 'another day' (1971: 419) is recognised as already the present of revelation, whether that be in the eternal life of the eternal people, or in the revelation of the second creation on the eternal way. Thus, Rosenzweig concludes the eternal life and the eternal way 'enter under one sign of the eternal truth' (1971: 421).

4. THE METHOD OF 'SLAVES TO THE FIRST COMMAND' (1971: 26)

What are we to make of this consummation in which the cognition of the rays and the fire are a recognition of redemption in creation and revelation for both Jew and Christian? Is this recognition similar to that found in Hegel and explored in chapter 2 above? Is consummation a higher education in any way similar to philosophy's higher education? To explore such questions requires us now to retrace our steps through *The Star*, this time locating the points at which the phenomenologies of revelation are stated as 'different'. Philosophy's higher education regarding these differences might offer, as Rosenzweig does, their 'consummation'. How different this is from Rosenzweig's consummation will be part of the consummation itself.

The Star begins by stating a difference between man as living man and philosopher as his subjugator. We might say here that the difference stems from the attitude of each towards the phenomenological experience of death. For Rosenzweig man knows death as something, indeed as 'fear and trembling,' (1971: 3) as a 'poisonous sting' (1971: 3) and withal as 'the cry of mortal terror' (1971: 5). Philosophy however seeks to turn death into Nought, denying man's fears, by 'weaving the blue mist of its idea of the All about the earthly' (1971: 4). Philosophy lies about itself in this triumph of the concept of the All over the lived terror of the singular, for philosophy 'creates for itself an apparent freedom from presuppositions' (1971: 5). In fact, for Rosenzweig, in presupposing the Aught to be the Nought, philosophy suppresses nothing less than divine freedom. Pride of place in this suppression goes to Hegel, whose conclusive system dragged revelation into the concept of the All and reconciled heaven and earth.

> Accordingly Hegel had to make of the history of philosophy itself the systematic conclusion of philosophy because thereby the personal point of view of the individual philosopher, the last thing which still seemed able to contradict the unity of All, was rendered harmless (1971: 52).

Against Hegel, Kierkegaard's 'Archimedean fulcrum' was individual and singular; it was 'the peculiar consciousness of his own sin and his own redemption...' (1971: 7). But only in Nietzsche does Rosenzweig find the unity of thinker and man who was able to step out of 'the All of philosophy' (1971: 10) by recognising in and as himself the 'unconditional vassalage of soul to mind' (1971: 9).

Of equal significance for Rosenzweig is the difference in the phenomenologies of positive and negative between himself and Hegel, or between their methodologies. For Rosenzweig, the beginning of our knowledge of God is not 'the presupposition of the one and universal All,' (1971: 25) it is 'ignorance of God,' (1971: 23) that is, 'God is therefore initially a Nought for us' (1971: 24). From this beginning there emerge two paths, the Yea and the Nay. The Yea affirms the non-Nought of the experience. The Nay negates the given, the Nought. They are two paths of the one experience, two ways of experiencing the Aught and the Nought, but two paths with very different significance. The Yea, as Aught, relates to the Nought as neighbour, for the Yea is the affirmation of everything that is not-Nought. Its identity is secured and it contains nothing 'which strives beyond the Yea itself' (1971: 28). It is says Rosenzweig freed to infinity and takes itself as the infinite realm of 'divine essence' (1971: 27). But the Nay is more troublesome. As the negation of the Nought it 'points to something limited, finite, definite' (1971: 24). The Nay, says Rosenzweig, is the experience of liberation from the Nought. It is 'as a runaway who just now has broken out of the prison of the Nought' (1971: 24). But it is no more than this one experience. It is action, but it is not essence.

The Nought can also be approached from the opposite direction, 'that of becoming Nought' (1971: 24) by the affirmation of the non-Aught, or the negation of the Aught. The latter 'is' the annihilation of the positive. In either case what is vital for Rosenzweig is that unlike in philosophy the Nought is not presupposed as 'a one and universal All' (1971: 25). On the contrary, the Nought that is known is only 'the individual Nought of the individual problem' (1971: 25). The only presupposition that is justified here is that the Nought is 'productive of definition' (1971: 25) but not therein defined. As such, in these limits, 'we have shattered the All' (1971: 26) for all (sic) concepts 'remain within this limit... essence [is] within God [and] action can never refer to an object thought of as outside God. We do not get beyond pure reflections of God' (1971: 26). In this 'magic circle' (1971: 26) 'every fragment is now an All in itself' (1971: 26) and we remain 'slaves to the first command' (1971: 26).[10]

The slave to the first command is really the question of method, or what Kierkegaard calls the historical point of departure. In its Heideggerian guise it is the Dasein that has enquiry into beginning and end as its ownmost being. In its Hegelian guise it is spirit that has beginning and end as Notion. But in both phenomenologies, as in Rosenzweig, what is at stake here is the relation of knowing to the first command, a relation in which the slave and the master share confused identities, both being the whole that is (absolute) contingency. If method were not the issue, then this command would merely be the night in which 'all cows are black' (Hegel, 1977: 9). That there is experience, that 'we have shattered the All,' (1971: 26) that there is Yea and Nay, that there are slaves to the first command, means that contingency becomes a methodological issue where the object of the enquiry and the contingency of the enquiry struggle for sovereignty.

It is precisely the pre-determined relation to the object that constitutes the methodological dilemma of any enquiry.[11]

The relationship of Yea to Nay, or knowing the first command, reveals for us, says Rosenzweig, both a divine nature and divine freedom. Divine nature is the 'Amen behind every word' (1971: 27) for every word is already the affirmation of infinity or the Yea. There is no word that is not already Yea and Amen, for 'the affirmation of the non-Nought circumscribes as inner limit the infinity of all that is not Nought. An infinity is affirmed' (1971: 26-7) as the right for everything to exist including the individual subject who is always and already 'simply "other," other, that is, than the Nought' (1971: 27).

If divine nature is endless affirmation of the Yea, divine freedom stems from the Nay. Affirmation is always of a restless Nought, for the affirmation had to 'well forth' (1971: 28) from this Nought. Equally, the Nought of the Nay is this Nought, conceived of 'as a Nought of knowledge, as a point of departure for reasoning about God, as the locus of posing the problem' (1971: 28-9). Thus the Nay is preceded by the Nought 'from which affirmation had to come forth' (1971: 29). Rosenzweig highlights that whilst the Yea is the neighbour next door who is affirmed as other, the Nay 'is intertwined in closest bodily contact with the Nought' (1971: 29). The significance of this will become clear in a moment.

Rosenzweig concludes his methodological relation of Yea and Nay, or essence and freedom, thus:

> Divine freedom confronts infinite divine essence as the finite configuration of action, albeit an action whose power is inexhaustible, an action which can ever anew pour itself out into the infinite out of its finite origin: an inexhaustible wellspring not an infinite ocean. Essence is constituted once and for all 'as is'; it confronts the freedom of action, a freedom revealing itself ever anew, but a freedom for which we cannot as yet contemplate any object other than the infinity of that everlasting essence. It is not freedom *of* God for even now God is still a problem for us. It is divine freedom, freedom *in* God and with reference to God (1971: 30).

The New Unity of the fragments that Rosenzweig finds in the face of God sets itself against any kind of Hegelian dialectic, or circle, or unification. Rosenzweig is stating a different unity of infinite and finite, of positive and negative, of Yea and Nay, and of essence and freedom than that which he finds in Hegel. In particular, the 'and' that links these pairings says Rosenzweig must 'assume an entirely different significance' (1971: 230) than it finds in Hegel. The key difference is that whereas for Hegel the synthesising 'and' is creative, for Rosenzweig synthesis can only draw conclusions. It is precisely the presupposition that synthesis is creative that lies at the basis of philosophical presuppositions of the concept of the one and all, that is, that mind can create the creator. Rosenzweig brooks neither dialectic nor transformation in the synthesis. The And he says is not original. 'No Aught originates in it; it is not, like Yea and Nay, immediate to the Nought; rather it is the sign of the process which permits the growth of the finished form between what originated in Yea and Nay' (1971: 229), In Idealism, synthesis reconstructs or re-cognises thesis such that *it*, the synthesis, becomes 'the actual creative principle of the dialectic' (1971: 229). Antithesis (of Yea and Nay) is reduced from its originality to mediation or mere transition. A category, says Rosenzweig, is not 'an inner force for its own propulsion' (1971: 230).

Thus for Rosenzweig, Hegel's idea of a unity is a creative synthesis which suppresses the originary first creative command. For Rosenzweig the circle is replaced by three points, creation, revelation and redemption, which exist on a line, but a line lacking 'a theorem of construction setting up an ideally and absolutely valid relationship' (1971: 255) between the points. The circle is replaced by the construction of the Star.

What I now want to attempt is to read a different Hegel against Rosenzweig, one where Hegelian philosophy is actual as philosophy's higher education and not as an abstract circle of reconciliation. In this 'different' Hegel, the philosophical circle is not ours either, and this is the countenance of the absolute. This unity or consummation sees nothing creative about philosophy's higher education except creation itself, revealed as work, and known as formation and finality, or necessity and freedom.

5. OF OF: OR KNOWING DIASPORA AS SELF

A comparison of the Yea and Nay with illusory being and the master and slave in Hegel is instructive regarding the structure of freedom and necessity in each thinker. We saw above that the Yea and the Nay are 'the two ways' (1971: 24) that lead to and from the Nought. From the perspective of divine nature the Yea—the neighbour—affirms the essence of the non-Nought whilst the Nay—the runaway—is an action 'in sharp delimitation' (1971: 24) from it. But from the perspective of divine freedom the Yea is attached not to a pure essence but to the non-Nought that has been provided by the action of the Nay. It is in this relation of divine essence to divine freedom that we are to understand not only the configuration of the Star, but also Rosenzweig's relation to Hegel, and through that, Judaism's relation to the (pagan/Christian) historical nations. This is learned when the relation of divine essence to divine freedom is understood as philosophy's higher education.

From the point of view of the master who is the Aught that is affirmed as 'all that "is" not Nought,' (1971: 24) the Nay is other. The latter is action, but the former is his ceaseless essence. The latter is the other of all that is, and that means it is nothing. We have seen this relation of master and slave before in chapter 2. We know that the perspective of the master is political in that he posits his own independence at the expense of the existence of the other, and we know that it is methodological in that the object is posited as external and for him (as owner).

But, as Rosenzweig points out, viewed from the perspective of divine freedom, this same methodological positing of the relation of Yea and Nay, or master to other, looks very different. Within divine essence 'Yea is the beginning' (1971: 26). But it is not the Yea of the Nought for even in immediacy[12] if the Nought were to be located 'it would be located before every beginning' (1971: 26). So even though Yea is the beginning, it is the beginning of the non-Nought or 'the beginning of our knowledge' (1971: 26). 'An infinity is affirmed,' (1971: 27) but known.

The question is, then, how is this infinity known in such a way that its 'creation' is not granted to the knower? How is the Yea the beginning of that which in some way is already begun? To avoid being the creative synthesis it cannot be originary as a concept. Yet what kind of relation can the beginning have to itself such that it is known as a neighbour and not as a runaway?

Rosenzweig poses the same question in different terms. What, he asks, brings the 'placid surface (1971: 28) of the 'unmoved, infinite being' (1971: 28) of the Yea into commotion? His answer amounts to a critique of the methodological presuppositions implicit in both the question and in the posited identity of the Nay. 'The Yea contains nothing which strives beyond the Yea itself; it is the "then." The commotion must therefore come from the Nay' (1971: 28). We know that the Yea affirms the non-Nought and is therefore dependent upon a movement or activity to inaugurate its departure. This 'activity' is the Nay. From the perspective of the master it is other than something. But from the perspective of the runaway it is a freedom and self-determination. It is true says Rosenzweig that this Nay is not preceded by a Yea, for indeed it is the Nay that provides the Yea with its point of departure, its non-Nought.

> Nay is the original negation of Nought. Yea could not have remained attached to Nought because the latter provided it, so to speak, with no point of contact; repelled by Nought, Yea therefore cast itself upon the non-Nought and, thus freed to infinity from its point of departure, it placed the divine essence in the infinite realm of the non-Nought (1971: 29).

In terms of methodology, and therefore in terms of philosophy's higher education, essence here is freedom. Just as in Hegel essence is both illusory being and the free self-determining positing of illusion by itself, so in Rosenzweig essence is both the illusory beginning and the free and self-determining departure of illusion from itself.

In terms of the master and slave relation the Nay, like the slave, has a dual significance which marks its educational import. It frees the Yea to affirm infinity but, crucially, it binds the divine essence to divine freedom. Although the infinite is other to it, i.e., *everything* is other to it, nevertheless 'the infinite' is already dependent upon freedom. Divine freedom is the 'finite configuration' (1971: 30) of infinite essence. The master who affirms everything, or is in-itself, and who has the Nay as purely dependent, learns here that in fact freedom works in opposition to its appearance. The master is dependent upon the slave's freedom of action for its own freedom, and as such 'the truth of the independent consciousness is accordingly the servile consciousness of the bondsman' (Hegel, 1977: 117).

The educational significance of the Nay, like the slave, is remarkable. The Nay is related to the Nought in the same way as the slave is related to the master, that is, through activity or work. The Yea leaves the Nay behind with the Nought. For the Yea of the non-Nought, the Nought is nothing and the Nay is the experience or event of nothing; it is *of* nothing. For the Yea, the Nought is non-Nought, or the point of departure for knowledge. As such, methodologically, the Nought cannot be affirmed. But this impossibility of affirmation, taken by the Yea to be the (lack of) truth of the Nay, is in fact precisely the (lack of) truth of the Yea. It is this master, this affirmation, that cannot be affirmed for it is already the result of the prior negative work of the Nay. As philosophy's higher education, the freedom of the slave is the essence of the master. This freedom is the truth of essence because the Nay is of itself. But this is a relation of self-determination, and of education, because the runaway is of the nothing that is himself. His affirmation is his negation. He is Yea and Nay, related in and by the self-determining 'and'. He is *of* of; he is his own child. He is the runaway who knows the necessity of his own conditions of possibility to be diasporic.

Rosenzweig states that the Nay 'contains no Yea' (1971: 29) and always has Yea as 'other'. This might be where Rosenzweig would distinguish his Nay from Hegel's slave. The Nay resists affirmation and therefore is not creative. It only concludes that essence is other, whereas in Hegel, perhaps from what we have seen above, Rosenzweig would criticise the freedom of the slave as being based on a synthesising 'and' of master 'and' slave. The slave has an affirmation and becomes all otherness.

It is difficult now to unravel these threads but we must do so. Rosenzweig is right; the Nay resists affirmation and is not creative, unless the Nay itself can be recognised as the self-formation and finality of creation. The Nay is itself. As such, the Nay of the Nought already expresses a creation for 'it bursts forth directly from the Nought, bursts forth, that is, as its negation' (1971: 28). If this is not an affirmation of the Nought in and by itself, it is so only for the Yea who judges affirmation from its own perspective. For the Yea, the Nought is only 'the point of departure and [is] therefore simply incapable of being itself affirmed' (1971: 26). Of course the Yea would say that. The Yea has left the Nought behind and is now universal as not-Nought. It is this universal viewpoint for whom the Nought cannot be creative. Universality destroys the Nought. But, just as the master falls to the slave, so the viewpoint of universality falls to its own contingency. The Yea is itself derived from the very activity of self-creation that, from its own point of view, is nothing.

Rosenzweig is wrong I think to say as he does that philosophy turns death into Nought and 'creates for itself an apparent freedom from presupposition' (1971: 5). What Rosenzweig is doing here is traducing the life and death struggle that is the birth of philosophy into the universal viewpoint of the Yea for which death is Nought, and the Yea is all not-Nought, or the once and for all universality. Philosophy he says 'plugs up its ears before the cry of terrorized humanity' (1971: 5). This is certainly true of philosophy that suppresses philosophy's higher education, for the suppression is precisely the misrecognition of death or the negative as nothing. It is this misrecognition of Nought as nothing that lies at the root of scepticism in its many forms as lacking subject and substance. The modern difficulty in thinking the absolute can be traced to the illusory being of essence for which the Nought is other than itself. In both Rosenzweig and Hegel, our higher education consists in the re-cognition of the true nature of the Nought, that it is Aught, but that the Nay, or self-negation, always has Yea as other and therefore as itself.

The life and death struggle, as outlined in the *Phenomenology of Spirit*, is posited as the misrecognition of 'this' consciousness or the 'I'. This 'I,' in surviving the trial by death, is immediately the Yea, and, as 'life,' knows everything that is not itself as other. In addition, since what is other is not life, other is mere thing. Put more dramatically, the life of the I is grounded in the death of death. The I is not-death in Hegel as the Yea is not-Nought in Rosenzweig. Both are models of absolute contingency. As in Hegel the death of death has life in the slave, so in Rosenzweig the Nay is the free work of the Nought. For both thinkers, all universal viewpoints of the negative (critical, post-modern, Marxist etc) must assert the negative as something, repeating its separation from itself as other, and suppressing the self determination that is its own necessity.[13]

It is not Rosenzweig's analysis of the Yea and Nay that we are criticising here. On the contrary, we are criticising Rosenzweig for reading Hegel from the universal viewpoint, the illusory nature of which Rosenzweig understands. Rosenzweig, in preserving the Nay against his view of Hegelian synthesis in fact preserves it from its own originary activity. Crucially, to recognise the Nay as the freedom of creation is not the same as saying that Yea and Nay are synthesised by the infinite or that the 'and' somehow creates (sic) something beyond the terms of the 'original' relationship. On the contrary, and here I think Rosenzweig and Hegel are in complete agreement, the 'and' of the Yea and Nay or of master 'and' slave, already contains within it both the misrecognition of freedom as essence and the recognition of essence as true only in and as the self-relation that is freedom. Creation is already misrecognition; that is its nature. Its necessity is its self-relation, and its necessity is absolute. We are other to this self-relation, and that is why it is our necessity and also our absolute. The necessity of freedom is that it opposes itself for that is its self-determination. Hegel's 'and' does not synthesis something new, it only re-cognises that its appearance is already its own misrecognition.

The comparison of master and slave with Yea and Nay leads to another interesting comparison. Rosenzweig says of the Creator that 'creating is the beginning of his self-expression' (1971: 113), a beginning in which Nay and Yea both share in a configuration of power and attribute. This beginning is a capricious act, a pure necessity, because 'its interior is pure caprice, unconditional freedom' (1971: 116). As such, creation is 'a becoming-manifest on the part of God' (1971: 159). But creation is only the first revelation, one in which God remains concealed. It is love become 'compulsion' (1971: 160). A second revelation is required, one where the once and for all nature of the first revelation is supplemented by a revelation 'at that very moment' (1971: 161). The latter is the 'means for confirming creation structurally' (1971: 161) and is the love of the lover, not the beloved.

In terms of sequence here, there are two versions of what is the same. For the lover and beloved, God 'first' loved man and man received the gift of this revelation. Here 'the once-and-for-all occurrence preceded that which happens momentarily' (1971: 218). But as we noted earlier, for the world 'this temporal relationship is reversed' (1971: 218). Here it is the world that is created with every moment. The world is creature and the creator is 'providence' (1971: 218). In the reversal that which was created 'must now await its being-"created" in redemption' (1971: 219).

Thus the life of God and Man and the way of the world are opposed to each other. But both are revelation. The life of the lover and beloved is lived each day eternally and eternally each day. The way of the world has love as infinitely other than the original Nay. As we saw above, the Jew and Christian share the same task, bound to each other with the whole belonging to neither. Yet here again the separation of fire and ray is not a separation without consummation. In the Star the dual aspect of Yea and Nay is the 'created truth,' (1971: 417) the countenance of God under 'one sign' (1971: 421).

Such a relation of life and the way, or Yea and Nay, can be found in Hegel between being and essence. Indeed, I suggest, illusory being is to be found as the work of the beginning and end in both Hegel and Rosenzweig. Illusory being is the positing by essence of being as nothing. In Rosenzweig's terms, illusory being is the perspective of the second revelation, a perspective which suppresses the first revelation. Illusory being is the misrecognition of the first revelation. It is love that has the Nought as absolutely other. This second revelation takes love to be the way of absolute consummation, that is, earthly, creatively, or as pagan. It suppresses the presupposition of the second revelation, or its positing, and therein suppresses the first revelation on which it is dependent. Illusory being re-cognises itself when it knows that its own positing is self-posited. This is its created truth. This re-cognition does not overcome illusion, it does not create as Rosenzweig claims, a new absolute. On the contrary, the recognition is of illusory being as determinative of precisely the illusion that being is nothing, or of essence. It is the relation that is determinative, not some new synthesis that mind 'creates' out of itself. Mind was always the Nay of the Nought and the Yea of essence. Now, where illusory being has the necessity of creation, or the negative as its own, the Nay affirms itself, but not as anything other than what it already is, viz. the relation to everything as other as to itself.

Rosenzweig's critique of Hegel's circle as creative and synthesising is, we might say, a dialectical misrecognition of the dialectic. The circle, in leading back to itself, is interpreted by Rosenzweig as paganism, for it is only the work of the Yea, an affirmation of infinity or essence by itself. Alone it is incapable of being other than the way, and always in the middle between beginning and end. It is not the life of truth as 'an inner force for its own compulsion' (1971: 230). The only Nay available to the Yea is itself a pagan one, a human mediation. The circle, in short, has no direct relation to God. But Hegel's philosophical Christianity sets itself to show exactly how the pagan is not itself, and that all assertions that it is, including Rosenzweig's, are a further domination of the illusory by itself. All beginnings for Hegel are abstract. This does not mean that beginnings cannot be known, in fact the opposite. It means that beginnings are known, and in being thought we become slaves to the first command. To now posit that because they are thought they are not known in themselves, or in their original state, is the presupposition that Hegel's corpus works against. It is this presupposition, that the contingency of thinking is less than absolute, that is the basis of the view that philosophy is free from presupposition. The denial is categorical, but this (contingent) denial *of* contingency is *of* itself. It is always already a presupposition. That is what experience learns of the necessity of its own conditions of possibility, that it undermines its own necessary and abstract pre-judgements about those conditions. Necessity is this knowing of the beginning as known, or it is mediation in its truth, not in its illusory guise as the necessity of everything except itself. 'Every beginning must be made with the absolute, just as all advance is merely the exposition of it' (Hegel, 1969: 829). This advance—our learning or our higher education—sees the absolute become for itself, that is, 'individual' (1969: 829). This advance includes the externalisation of itself, its Yea as non-Nought, as it includes the eternal but variously manifested relation, and downfall, of that Yea to the necessity of the Nay. Together 'and' apart they are the self-expression of freedom and necessity as a whole.

In Rosenzweig's dialectical interpretation of the Hegelian advance from absolute to beginning and end, the opposites are able to create something out of themselves that reconciles their opposition. I call Rosenzweig's critique dialectical for this reason. On the one hand it sees oppositions synthesised, but on the other hand, the synthesis remains antithetical to the present of eternity in the life of the eternal people. Rosenzweig would surely agree with Adorno in stating that Hegel's system is closed and is a 'positive infinity' (1973: 27). Yet where Adorno advises never to deny conditionality 'for the sake of the unconditional' (1991: 247) because this delivers the unconditioned to the world, Rosenzweig claims at the end of *The Star* that Israel and eternity lives, in full reality, and not merely as an idea. *The Star* is already a higher education than Rosenzweig's dialectical critique (and misrecognition) of Hegel. Where Adorno is sometimes seen to protect the unconditional from the world,[14] Rosenzweig knows already that the unconditional is worldly, even if neither Jews nor Christians have all of it. What in Adorno's dialectic is perhaps held open as hope and possibility, in Hegel and Rosenzweig is present and actual as necessity, both individually and collectively. This means that a different relationship emerges between Rosenzweig and Hegel than that presented at the beginning of chapter 2 between Adorno and Hegel. Method is actual in Rosenzweig and Hegel, recognising the full participation of the conditioned and the unconditioned in their relation to self as to other.

6. THE PHILOSOPHY OF HISTORY

What, then, can we conclude regarding the relation between Rosenzweig's Judaism and Hegel's modernity? Does one win out over the other? Is Rosenzweig right to cite eternity in the people who turn away from the world, and to cite universality in the world as the way with no beginning or end? Is Hegel usurping Rosenzweig by claiming that the way is the beginning and the end? In acknowledging the countenance of God as ever present and always on the way, has Rosenzweig moved towards Hegel? And, in acknowledging the necessity of the beginning and the end as the way, has Hegel moved towards Rosenzweig? Are they the pair of wrestlers (1971: 29) who are in fact the one? And if we want to claim a relation such as this between them, for whom is this relation a learning individuality? Who is it that has the experience of this relation as his own? It is the learning individual[15] for whom learning and law are individuality, or are the relation to self as to other, in this case Jew 'and' Christian, but neither Jew nor Christian. But the learning individual is also world spirit, the knowledge of contingency as the self, not just politically and socially but also historically. Other than as learning, as the formation and finality of world spirit, necessity is untrue to itself, illusory being is unrecognised, and the life and the way determine each other in ways which are not known as self-determination. Yet despite this, to talk of world spirit in this way still commits the greatest blasphemy of the post-foundational age. We must now explore the misrecognition of world spirit if we are to argue for such an educational relation between Rosenzweig and Hegel. In doing so, we must also finally explore the educational and philosophical nature of the 'and' that has accompanied us throughout the book, and which has held together the dualisms of each chapter, including now those of Rosenzweig 'and' Hegel, and Judaism 'and' modernity.

Let us not rehearse the criticisms of the philosophy of history as a western intellectual and teleological imperialism. Of course it is; what else could it be? However, there is an education that is suppressed in the very idea of the philosophy of history, an education regarding absolute contingency which lies at the heart of philosophy's higher education, and one which re-educates the philosophy of history about its relation to and as 'the other'. Obviously the very possibility of a philosophy of history rests upon a notion of a higher education. As such, if its own educational structure and the necessity of its own conditions of possibility remain misrecognised, then the philosophy of history can only ever appear as a transcendental schema detached from and dominant over that which it claims to understand. The philosophy of history is by definition a 'privileged' perspective. But the key to the philosophy of history is that its privilege lies in knowing that it is not privileged. It is our education about misrecognition, but is not itself 'immune' from the contingency of its own understanding (of contingency). It too is misrecognition. It too is also the relation that it understands. It is the same conditioned relation of the conditional to itself that constitutes truth and freedom. It is the history of modernity and it is the eternity of Judaism. Being different does not mean they are not also the same.

What, then, is the philosophy of history? It is philosophy's higher education of and as spirit. It is consciousness learning about itself as its own necessity, from itself, in and through the dualisms that are the condition of its possibility. It is the revel and the repose of the educating perspective and the educated perspective. The logic and method of the philosophy of history are the same as that of philosophy's higher education. They are both the experience of learning and the science of that learning. This self-relation is available to us only in the dualism of reflection and its content. As history this dualism is spirit and content. As the philosophy of history the content is spirit, and spirit is the content. To comprehend the philosophy of history, then, we have to comprehend not only its conditions of possibility but also the different ways in which those conditions determine themselves according to their own necessity, and appear to us within and as the illusion of such determination.

The philosophy of history can only be available to spirit, for spirit is the negation of the particular known as singular. The singular is an individual, but not in any abstract sense. It is the individual who is not merely a particular, but is universal in his particularity. He is already everyone else, but no one is him. This contradiction, wherein the I is the We, is spiritual in and as philosophy's higher education. But if this spirit is bounded by relations (for example, the state), how can it ever be wholly universal, or world spirit? Indeed, in an age where the certainty of the nation state is in decline, does this not make world spirit as the singular of particular nations even more unlikely? The answer is yes and no. Hegel, in the *Philosophy of Right*, captures this equivocation. The absolute in international law can only oppose the sovereignty of autonomous nation states. Yet the state 'is as little an actual individual without relations to other states as an individual is actually a person without a *rapport* with other persons' (1967: 212). The opposition of absolute (international) law to the state expresses the truth, the contingency, of the state. Here the truth of the master is always the slave.[16] World spirit is the negation of the state at the same time as this negation recognises and reinforces its particular nature. The singular is both universal *and* particular. World spirit is the self-relation of states, both in themselves and for others. This world spirit is the formation and finality of a perspective that is both distant to each individual and yet, also, the same as the individual. As Rosenzweig said, 'that which is distant can be reached only through that which is nearest' (1955: 65).

Too often the structure of world spirit is suppressed by its abstract appearance as either for someone (the West) or for no one and therefore irrelevant. However, the logic of spirit, whether between sovereign persons, or between sovereign 'free' nations is the same logic of philosophy's higher education. We saw in chapter 2 that all of Hegel's concepts share the logic of the master/slave relation. The same is the case now for world spirit. For spirit, being-known is also being not-known and includes the recognition that not-knowing *is* knowing. To talk of world spirit is to enter a threefold relation of self-consciousness, the state and the world. The I that is self-consciousness is not-myself. This not-myself is the I who experiences other not-Is. Together, 'we' who are all of us 'not-I' (the state) experience that 'we' (which is not-we) in relation to other not-wes. World spirit, the latter, holds all three negations—not-I, not-you, not-we—as its own negative substance and subject. It is precisely because world spirit is whole in its incompleteness that it is the work of these negations. World spirit is not a resolution, it is a formation and a teleology of philosophy's higher education where 'we' learn that we are already other and that the other is not us.

For consciousness, self-consciousness, spirit and world spirit the self-relation of experience is the same. Each knows that it does not 'correspond to its object' (Hegel, 1977: 54). Each also knows that the lack of correspondence is experience. 'Consciousness now has two objects: one is the first *in-itself*, the second is the *being for consciousness of this in itself*' (1977: 55). This is a universal occurrence, for wherever there are ideas, including and especially when there are ideas about (others) ideas, there is this movement. The philosophy of history is the development of the Idea, universally misrecognised up to the learning of itself, by itself, as the Idea of the Idea. But whilst this recognition of itself is of its truth, this truth is no longer what uneducated ideas of the truth assume it to be. The irony is that whereas modern reflective thinking, or illusory being, still takes truth to be a concept that is closed and final, the very existence of the philosophy of history shows this not to be the case. The philosophy of history is the perspective of an educated spirit which knows now of *its own* contingency. The perspective of the philosophy of history is not above contingency, it is absolute contingency. Here spirit is finally subject to (and as) the necessity of its own historicism. What the philosophy of history therefore means is that spirit is the true only as 'the-being-for-consciousness of this in-itself' (1977: 55). It is 'what experience has made of it' (1977: 55). And what has experience made of it? That the Idea, even of itself, is true only as the law of its own failure. This is the law of learning and the learning of law, and is the truth of world spirit and its own idea of itself, the philosophy of history.

Two things still require to be discussed. What does this mean for the relation between Rosenzweig's Judaism and Hegel's modernity and what, finally, is 'and'?

Rosenzweig and Hegel are the one truth manifested in one of its necessary forms of difference and dualism. Each recognises this and each therefore can be read as within philosophy's higher education. Rosenzweig knows Jew and Christian to be 'but a part of the whole' (1971: 416). The eternal core burns and throws its light out as time which has to be lived in the contradiction of their opposition, whether from the perspective of the eternal or the way. For the eternal, time and the nations are the eternally present reminder that those born a nation out of a nation can never wear their own face. Yet this is the face of that nation, the diasporic face, born in and of its absolute contingency. For the historical people, the Jews are the eternally present reminder of their (the formers) face that is still in the making. Yet this too is the face of the nations, always failing and always diasporic because of its absolute contingency upon a beginning that is also not its own. 'The truth, the whole truth, thus belongs neither to them nor to us' (1971: 416) says Rosenzweig, and this relation is the self-relation of the true, the face of God, 'the divine visage' (1971: 418).

Hegel's writings on the Jews are famously controversial. Jewish law, he states, since it is not given to themselves by themselves, is not free. 'On God the Jews are dependent throughout...' (Hegel, 1975: 196) and this is their fate. 'Against purely objective commands Jesus set something totally foreign to them, namely, the subjective in general' (1975: 209). The temptation always is to play the slavish Jew off against the free Christian, irreconcilable in their opposite views to freedom. But are these not precisely the parts that we have seen constitute Hegel's notion of freedom? *The Philosophy of History*[17] is a dangerous book, perhaps Hegel's most dangerous, because for the reader it assumes the work, the learning, which underpins it. Its premise, says Rose in *Hegel Contra Sociology*, is that the subject in history 'does not know that it is a determination of the absolute' (1981: 106). But this means that the subject in the philosophy of history does know that it is a determination of the absolute, and it knows that it misrecognises that determination in various ways according to its own Idea of itself, an Idea made actual in property law or as the relation to the object. Indeed, the whole philosophy of history is the way the subject misrecognises its determination. Judaism, in the philosophy of history, is described by Hegel as the moment when spirit is freed from nature and realised as 'the pure product of thought' (1956: 195).[18] The very fact that there is Judaism *and* modernity shows that the Idea of God in Judaism is part of its own philosophy of history (or its eternity). The nations' freedom and spiritual freedom oppose each other, both internally and externally, for both Jew and non-Jew. The misrecognition of their determination by the absolute is a shared fate, even if differently experienced. Rose says,

> The inner character of the absolute is negative. It is subject, because to be a subject means to be conscious of existing in a relation of opposition and to be conscious that what stands opposed, the finite, determination, may be excluded or suppressed. It is substance because the determination is re-cognized and not suppressed or excluded. This subjectivity means self-determination (1981: 106).

The aporia applies as much to the eternal people whose legal subjectivity opposes their spiritual subjectivity (in Rosenzweig and Buber) as to the people of the nations. In both cases the experience is of the dualism of freedom and nature. In Rosenzweig, Jews experience the freedom of their inner nature against the illusory freedom of the outer. Non-Jews experience the freedom of the outer against the inner morality of the conscience. But both experience this relation of law and learning. Seen in this way the philosophy of history does not merely separate the Jew and the non-Jew into slavery and freedom, or eternity and history, rather it recognises that such judgements are themselves constituted by those very separations. The philosophy of history does not dogmatically assert world spirit, it carries world spirit as law and learning. Nor, therefore, does philosophy's higher education side with Jew or non-Jew. It causes trouble for both, because it is the truth of their relation, of the very idea of otherness that constitutes that relation, and it is the work of that relation—uncomfortable for both because it is the truth of both, Judaism *and* modernity.

7. AND

So, finally, what is 'and'? And, related to this, who is the 'other'? We have been accompanied throughout each chapter, and now in this chapter, by the bearer of philosophy's higher education—*and*. Obviously and is the third partner in our experience of dualisms.[19] It separates and it conjoins; it holds apart and yet it holds together; it relativises its constituents with their opposites yet it affirms each in this opposition. But the secret of and is that it contains and hides its work as the bearer of our higher education.

When we speak of dualism—subject and object, theory and practice, self and other or, now, Judaism and modernity—we speak of knowing a separation. And therefore contains, implicitly and quietly, our negative experiences. We know something and we know its opposite. Dualism is the expression of negativity, or of the dialectic. But this and by which we implicitly know the negative is also the and of the experience of experience. The and is not just the relation of opposites in dualism, it is the Idea of their relation, or it is where the positing of illusory being is the condition of the possibility of the relation, the and. And therefore is already carrying our higher education regarding the determination of subjectivity in and by illusion, but in such a way as to hide this significance. Self and other, for example, looks like a construction that any thinking about human social relations must begin with. But the construction is not that kind of beginning. It is in fact already a negative experience of self, in relation to other, experienced by itself, but posited as if it were not already that contingency. Its appearance as a natural beginning is the Idea as illusory being and the and of its dualisms is already the repetition of that misrecognition. We saw above in chapter 2 that this Idea, posited as the certainty of the 'I', re-presents the already forgotten relation of the life and death struggle. The survivor has death-as-other as the Idea of himself. This I enjoys relation itself as relation to other—or as and—but not as self-determination. We have also seen that philosophy's higher education is the recognition of the self-determination of relation, wherein I am other and the other is not me. Within the Idea of (as) bourgeois private property relations the dualism of self and other appears neutral, a natural observation. The and appears to *be* relation, but really is the illusory being of relation, or is relation as the Idea that otherness has been overcome and is now only its object. The and of self and other therefore is not only politically charged for Rosenzweig and Hegel. As the misrecognition of its own configuration, its own education, it is also historically charged.

Put another way, one which offers a radical re-education for modernity about itself, and signifies the diasporic essence of modern reason. And is reason's home truth, the home of its own necessity. As the Jew is homeless and eternal, so reason is groundless and absolute. Recognising the diasporic truth of reason has been the subject of this book and continues to be the formation and finality of philosophy's higher education. The absolute can be known hidden within and precisely because the Idea can be known by itself. But here, truth has not suddenly overcome illusion. Redemption has not suddenly overcome doubt. That is not and never has been the teleology of the absolute. The teleology of the absolute has been to make itself known in and as the Idea that is consistently misrecognised, and misrecognised because the Idea (of the Idea) is always already the idea of the subject (in both senses). Philosophy educates us about the logic and structure of this experience of misrecognition in a higher way. Philosophy can enable us to have this process of experience-content-idea as its own experience, the experience of the experience. This involves us in wonderful, intriguing and already present contradictions which are contained in and. Indeed, here is where philosophy discovers thinking as its own vocation.

Instead of asking what or who is the other, philosophy's higher education understands the truth of the question to lie in a different question, namely how is the other already posited in and by the conditions of its possibility which are themselves only a positing? Put another way, philosophy's higher education asks, how is illusory being, separated into subject and object and conjoined by and, able to hide its role in positing itself as the conditions of possibility? Each chapter above has opened up this question, seeking the necessity of positing that is our higher education regarding the conditions of possibility. This is the aporia of modern reason. It can only repeat its form no matter what the content, unless the content is itself. Only this will be a genuinely higher philosophical and formative experience, but even then it will still, of necessity, be conditioned in, by and as illusion.

When the experience of content is examined, or to say the same thing, when the presupposition of the Idea is examined, two things are true. It can only be performed in another experience, and can only deliver another idea. This looks like the ultimate weakness of experience, that even its self-experience will not arrive at the true, but only at another content for us. In fact, this weakness is its ultimate strength, for here its diasporic truth is realised, both in the sense of known and formed. The groundlessness of truth in experience is now experienced truthfully. We saw above that this is the experience of the slave who is not true, and whose work is the truth of that not being true. Now the Idea is recognised by itself as an idea, it is known as not-true *and* it knows that this work, this idea, is the truth of being known as not-true. Here, even in this and, is the absolute nature of philosophy's higher education. It does not resolve the lack of truth in the first experience, but it does know the truth of that lack of truth. As such, it knows the true, but it still has not resolved the dualisms of the first experience. What has changed is not only our understanding of what dualism is, but also, and more significantly, our understanding of the idea of truth *per se*.

For dualisms in general, and is the political and historical misrecognition of the Idea and thus of its own relation of self-determination and content. This means that and is also the misrecognition of the identity of the 'I', or of the person. As we have seen at various points in previous chapters, what we learn about self and other is that I am already other, and the other is not me. This is the truth of reason's own work. Self and other is the positing of relation by the misrecognition of relation. Experience has worked on this content before it appears as a dualism, and the work it has carried out has been according to the idea of work (or property relations) that it carries with it at any specific historical moment and in any specific social and political relations. As we have argued before, in relations of universal private property, work, or the relation to object, is of owner to thing. The and of self and other therefore in modern social relations is not only independence from the other, it is indifference to otherness *per se*. Bourgeois freedom is freedom from a relation of dependence, suppressing the experience of relation in and as the idea that all are free. Thus, only in the re-experience of the and of self and other can the political idea which forms it be criticised in ways which do not hide, again, that very formation.

It is this education, this re-cognition, regarding the and of self and other, that has enabled us in this chapter to find philosophy's higher education in the relation between reason and the eternal. The configuration of contingency is the fire and the rays of the Star for Rosenzweig and it is the philosophy of history for Hegel. Thus Hegel and Rosenzweig are both within a logic whose formation and finality sees each as already other, and sees the other as not themselves. Rosenzweig's *Star* has Yea as other than Nay, but also has Nay as other to itself. Hegel's concept has master as other than the slave but also has the slave as other to itself in and as its work on the object. In both cases there is a Yea to the Nay, but it is a Yea in which all Yea's as other are determinative of the self-relation or freedom of the Nay. Divine freedom is younger that divine nature but that, precisely, is the nature and freedom of the divine. The slave is the truth of the master but that precisely is the nature and freedom of the absolute. When Rosenzweig reads necessity in Hegel as abstracted from itself and as a synthesising 'and' then the relation to the Creator is dissolved. But when Rosenzweig reads necessity in the Star as the separation of Yea and Nay wherein Nay is the Yea of Nay and Yea, then he shares Hegel's own understanding of necessity. Necessity does itself and that means it does itself once and for all and in every moment. If Judaism has moment as other, then it has other as itself. Similarly, if Christianity has the present eternal as other, it too has other as itself. Judaism and Christianity, thus understood, are the one truth of necessity, the one truth that is our higher education regarding contingency as absolute. To call this a philosophical higher education is perhaps unwelcome to both Jews and Christians, but unwelcome it must remain *as their otherness*. It is the truth of their relation, and demands itself as the work and vocation of its own self-determination.

Thus, the universal mind constitutes the relation that is Judaism and modernity[20] but it cannot be a mind of masters, for then the truth of world historical relations is suppressed. Yet in bourgeois social relations I am already master. Where, then, is the universal mind in modern social relations? It is in philosophy's higher education. In the downfall of the master is the truth of the slave, but the truth of the slave, as universal, is only available to us in and as this formative and philosophical experience, or as master *and* slave. We do not have to engineer this experience but we do have to learn how to learn from it that every idea is by definition already the contingency of the universal. Dualism is already the political misrecognition in experience of itself. This misrecognition can be experienced by itself. As such, the idea can re-cognise itself not only as the condition of the possibility of all knowing, but also as the knowing of the conditions. This unique, absolutely contingent and immanent work is reason's own self-education: to know its groundlessness groundlessly, to know its dependency dependently, to know relation as self, and to know contingency absolutely. This knowing is philosophy's higher education. It is the absolute, present and not-present as the learning of law and the law of learning. It is actual in and as spirit, including as world spirit, whose own absolute contingency is known as the philosophy of history and whose work is still in the learning that I am already other, and the other is not me.

NOTES

[1] We will discuss the conjoining 'and' of these dualisms in a moment.

[2] Please suspend judgement for a moment about the nature of the 'Gentile' who is writing about Jewishness. My lack of Jewishness, my not being a Jew, and perhaps your being a Jew, are precisely the subject of our higher education in this chapter.

[3] I have kept to Buber's and Rosenzweig's use of upper case for particular terms.

[4] And religion, Buber continues, induces fathers to reject their sons also. This religiosity can be opposed by religion when it transforms the Law into 'a heap of petty formulas' (1967: 92). Here religion no longer 'shapes but enslaves religiosity' (1967: 92).

[5] We return to the theme of 'time' in Rosenzweig below.

[6] We will explore in a moment the logic and method of this formulation of pathlessness or aporia.

[7] It is too early, yet, in our study to express this as 'who lives "before" him.'

[8] Even whilst thinking that they can achieve a non-propertied relation to knowledge. The critique of this misrecognition is the whole substance of philosophy's higher education presented in this book.

[9] This is a challenging way of expressing Rosenzweig's notion of 'unity'. In the essay of 1920 ('Towards a Renaissance of Jewish Learning') he states that 'there is no end to learning, no end to education. Between these two [past and future] burns the flame of the day, nourished by the limited fuel of the moment... (1955: 59). This does not suggest that the difference, the opposition, will cease to exist, but rather that their relation will be known in an altogether different sense. This reading is borne out more fully in the *Star of Redemption*, which we will examine shortly.

[10] At this point Rosenzweig promises the consummation of the fragments 'into the perfection of the new All' (1971: 26).

[11] It just so happens that currently the philosophy of history reveals reason as the methodological positing of the separation of consciousness from the object, ironically even and especially when that contingency is itself the object, for here it is that a knowledge of the Absolute is ruled out. Contingent consciousness is methodologically presupposed as separate from truth. As Hegel says in the *Phenomenology*, 'it takes for granted certain ideas about cognition as an instrument and as a medium, and assumes that there is a difference between ourselves and this cognition. Above all, it presupposes that the Absolute stands on one side and cognition on the other...' (1977: 47).

[12] Rosenzweig does not use this term here, presumably to avoid being implicated in a creative dialectic with mediation.

[13] The 'culture' of these determinations and suppressions is dealt with below in the final essay, 'The End of Culture.'

[14] See, for example, Rose's essay, 'From Speculative to Dialectical Thinking—Hegel and Adorno', in Rose, 1993.

[15] Described above in chapter 2.

[16] And here is why the USA and the UK were so maligned internationally for the recent war in Iraq. Not just that it was 'illegal'; but that their actions suppressed the deeper truth of their contingent world relation. It remains to be seen how the modern rational empire can survive the inevitable and necessary education—or negation—that is already the truth of the master.

[17] Of course taught some twenty years after Hegel's early essays on Christianity.

[18] It is, he says, when East separated from West, although compare this with Buber's argument that the Jew is of the Orient (1967: 56-78). Equally, it is of course this idea that thinking can be creative of God that Rosenzweig so mistrusts. I hope that the present work is showing both that this creativity in Hegel is in fact recognition of absolute contingency, and that Rosenzweig is presenting an experience of the eternal in his own work.

[19] I am aware that these sentences read awkwardly when the inverted commas are removed from 'and'. This disruption in the reading is itself a philosophical experience.

[20] I will suspend the ethical teleologically here and posit that it also constitutes 'other' world historical relations, for example between Islam and Judaism and between Islam and modernity. These relations require study from within the contingency of their 'and' if the relations are to be self-determinative (of both sides, as it were).

REFERENCES

Adorno, T.W. (1973) *Negative Dialectics*, London, RKP.

Adorno, T.W. (1991) *Minima Moralia*, London, Verso

Buber, M. (1967) *On Judaism*, New York, Schocken Books.

Hegel, G.W.F. (1956) *Philosophy of History*, New York, Dover Books.

Hegel, G.W.F. (1967) *Philosophy of Right*, Oxford, Oxford University Press, trans T.M. Knox.

Hegel, G.W.F. (1969) *Science of Logic*, London, George Allen and Unwin.

Hegel, G.W.F. (1975) *Early Theological Writings*, Philadelphia, University of Philadelphia Press, trans. T.M. Knox.

Hegel, G.W.F. (1977) *Phenomenology of Spirit*, Oxford, Oxford University Press.

Rose, G. (1981) *Hegel Contra Sociology*, London, Athlone.

Rose, G. (1993) *Judaism and Modernity*, Oxford, Blackwell.

Rosenzweig, F. (1955) *On Jewish Learning*, New York, Schocken Books.

Rosenzweig, F. (1971) *The Star of Redemption*, London, RKP, trans. W.W. Hallo.

THE END OF CULTURE

Within philosophy's higher education the 'and' of dualism is known to be the misrecognition of subjectivity, that is, both by subjectivity and of subjectivity itself. It is also the suppression of that misrecognition in that it reproduces the substance of the Idea to illusion as other than illusion. Put together we can say that the 'and' of dualism is the illusion contained in and carried by modern social relations. The higher education within philosophy regarding the political and historical work that 'and' carries is realised as self-determination. Remarkably, it is not illusion that has to be overcome, it is illusion that has to be understood as formative and self-determinative within this higher education. Philosophy's higher education teaches us that illusion is the truth of subject and substance and that as such the absolute, or God, not only can be known, but is already known.

It could be said, in conclusion, that the absolute lies in the 'and' of philosophy 'and' education. This separation is illusion, and the illusion is the self-determination of this truth as relation. But philosophy and education both repeat, in a multitude of ways, the illusion of their separation without the contingency of that illusion as constitutive of the judgement. Philosophy eschews the teleological implications of education yet presupposes that its practice has some kind of impact. Education too often presupposes the teleology of its practice at the expense of the philosophical aporias it perpetrates. Even the philosophy 'of' education shows little interest in or awareness of the property relations that are the condition of the possibility even of its nomenclature. The continuing domination of bourgeois property relations determines the unfreedom and the abstraction of both philosophy and education, and the higher education carried in the 'and' that joins and separates them is continually suppressed.

But recently there has arisen a new and even more powerful form of this mastery, one that seduces education itself out of the teleological and the philosophical. This new mastery has succeeded in re-forming the notion of culture by separating it from an idea of itself as re-formative. This domination by the pure abstraction of culture marks the end of culture in two albeit contradictory senses. It is the end of culture as education and it is the telos of culture, now, to realise that end. The end of culture thus marks one of the most significant victories of illusion over work. For culture, now, all content is seen as unessential, assuming therein the identity of pure contingency for itself. When re-formation, or culture, is re-formed without this idea of content and activity, i.e., without re-formation, then the absolute significance of education and self-determination in illusion is comprehensively threatened. The end of culture is thus the end of higher education, yet even this is a telos which the end of culture must suppress.

Hegel showed how the cultures of religion and art were re-cognised philosophically. It is well known that, in view of the end of religion and of faith as representations of the absolute, he advised religion to 'take refuge in philosophy' (1985: 162). Although in philosophy representation was now a higher education than either art or religion, nevertheless for Hegel, art and religion, like philosophy, seek to represent the highest ideas. He states that the immediate representation of truths in fine art is 'the first middle term of reconciliation' (1993: 10) between nature and reason. Fine art represents the third party, or spirit, sensuously such that the relation between subject and object is known. Art is a higher education here for it brings the mind to bear on the world of merely sensuous presentation. 'Art liberates the real import of appearances from the semblance and deception of this bad and fleeting world, and imparts to phenomenal semblances a higher reality born of mind' (1993: 11). Liberation, here, means precisely, brought into a knowing relation, the very achievement that then makes art vulnerable to the criticism that it is unscientific or merely the imaginative representation of the world. It is the strength of art here that is its weakness. In aiming to make known the highest ideas its own form restricts its capacity to do so. Criticism, in the age of reflection, sees the passing of a form of life in which the unification of nature and freedom is achieved in the imagination. There is a certain sadness when Hegel writes that

> the peculiar mode to which artistic production and works of art belong no longer satisfies our supreme need. We are above the level at which works of art can be venerated as divine... the feelings which they stir within us require a higher test and further confirmation... the beautiful days of Greek art, and the golden time of the later middle ages are gone by' (1993: 12).

Similarly for Hegel, the fundamental contradiction of modern art is that abstraction from the prevailing (political) conditions of the possibility of the relation between subject and object repeats precisely those conditions.[1]

A similar case is made by Hegel regarding religion. It too makes known to us the eternal truth of God as our highest idea. As such, 'philosophy is the same activity as religion... the service of God' (1988: 77-8fn). But although 'they are both religion' (1988: 78fn) the differences between them define them as in relation but not in any immediate unity. Theologians and artists alike are suspicious of philosophy in that it perhaps thinks too much about things, missing the spontaneity and the feelings of beauty and the inner truth of faith. The claim to objectivity offends those who hold that truth is a matter of inner conviction, either an immediate intuition of beauty in the imagination or of God in faith. Both are spiritual, both concern the contingency of the knower, both are a representation of the third party for whom the eternal is already the insufficiency of the human. To know God in faith is already to know that God is not knowable in itself as an object. Reason, says Hegel, is seen by religion as claiming to know God in ways that contradict faith, i.e. as cognition. Yet Hegel also argues that religion is making these moves within itself. The 'unknowable' in being rejected as myth (e.g. miracles, the virgin birth, the trinity) and faith is now concerned with the divine as it is represented in the human will. 'Thus Christ is dragged down to the level of human affairs' (1988: 82) and the more 'irrational' claims are treated historically rather than substantially. Here Hegel remarks it is philosophy that is seen as too weighty for a religion which concerns the immediate presence of God in us. Christianity now represents the conviction of modern religion 'that God is revealed immediately in the consciousness of human beings... that the human being knows God immediately' (1988: 85-6). Thus, 'all conviction that God is, and regarding what God is, rests, so it is surmised, upon this immediate revealedness in the human being, upon this faith' (1988: 86).

Of significance for the learning individual, the effect of rendering God personal 'is utterly to remove all external authority, all alien confirmation. What is to be valid for me must have its confirmation in my own spirit' (1988: 87).

> More precisely, the immediacy of this knowledge is supposed to reside above all, in the fact that one knows that God is, but not what God is... In this sense it is further declared that we can know only our relation to God, not what God himself is... God as such is not made the object [of enquiry] himself; God is not before us as an object of cognition and knowledge does not spread out within this sphere (1988: 88-9).

But faith in this case reveals religion to be a culture but not a telos, that is, relation without unity or substance and not a free self determination. Faith re-presents the separation of subject and object, in this case of human and divine, in such a way as to dominate the relation that it seeks to express. In other words, by representing the impossibility of knowing God in himself as (therefore) a matter of personal conviction, faith suppresses our knowledge of God. Worse still, the universal that religion offers forgets or cannot see how it represents its own conditions of possibility as other than itself, and as such remains unaware of the way its universal dominates those conditions. For us, the third party has faith as a negative experience and has religion as the return of unity to relation. As such, we see how religion is a culture, reformed in and by its own vocation, its own subjectivity. But religion itself does not recognise itself as a culture, and misses the higher education that is present when the representation of subjectivity, religion, is itself re-presented as illusion. Faith as a representation of the conditions of possibility is a lacking of faith in its own conditions of possibility, and in its actuality as aporetic experience. Our higher education of faith is philosophical, where faith's own sacrifice becomes substantial as the other, that is to say, where faith is recognised as freedom and God is present in such cognition. As such

> the result of the study of philosophy is that these walls of division [between religion and philosophy] which are supposed to separate absolutely, become transparent; or that when we get to the bottom of things we discover absolute agreement where we thought there was the most extreme antithesis (1988: 91-2).

Even so, Hegel admits that this reconciliation 'is itself only a partial one' (1985: 162fn). Philosophy does not have a spiritual community to offer religion in the way that religion (perhaps) still has one to offer philosophy. He notes that, at best, philosophy forms a 'sanctuary apart... an isolated order of priests, who need not mix with the world and whose work is to preserve the possession of truth' (1985: 162 fn). Like religion, there is no guarantee that philosophy will usher in the time of freedom against the prevailing social and political conditions that suppress it. Our higher education works 'for' truth by working 'for' freedom, where 'for' means both to work as their slave and, yet, to know them as other than master. The struggle is truth as our higher education, but even as struggle its attempts at reforming the world are always already a repetition of the form of the world as it determines our efforts. Unless, in philosophy, education is what is achieved and realised, struggle has no significance, work has no import and illusion cannot be known. But, in the spirit of our higher education regarding the community of learning individuals that does not exist, let us at least admonish Hegel's despairing protectionism of philosophy from its own fate, its own vocation. As higher education, philosophy is actual as education. The isolated community may educate themselves, but not each other – too many masters and not enough slaves.[2] This 'community' is actual when philosophy represents the truth of the educational relation between master and slave or teacher and student. It requires to be done, and it is not done by being protected from being done. Hegel feared that the philosopher might become priest, forced to impose its concept against a congregation who did not believe he shared their world. Isolation was to protect against imposition, and against the kind of misrepresentation Hegel himself suffered and continues to suffer. But this view is not borne out by Hegel's life as a teacher in which he exposed the need for the teacher to risk the educational relation.[3] Perhaps by 1821 he had already seen his own teaching re-formed by the very conditions of possibility that he sought to comprehend as determinative. Perhaps illusion was rarely if ever formative of itself, and always formally received by other as his absolutism, his apparent lack of re-presentation or culture or mediation. As early as 1801 Hegel was aware of philosophy's abstract appearance as 'general reflections... occasioned by the fact that presupposition, principles and such like forms still adorn the entrance to philosophy with their cobwebs' (1977b: 83).

What Hegel did not foresee, however, was the revenge of the abstraction of culture *per se*, and its domination of the whole notion of 'higher', of teleology and of formation. What price now art or religion if the very notion of culture itself is denied, if, that is, there is no re-formation or self-determination of representations of the absolute? We must now ask, how is it that representation is comprehended such that the West is again prepared to argue for, to *assert*, the impossibility of knowing truth and, therefore, the impossibility of knowing world spirit as the self-relation of the absolute? Where is the slave in modern society for whom work is formation and finality? Where is the learning individual for whom education is formation; for whom higher education is formation of the relation to the absolute; for whom culture is the representation of that relation; and for whom philosophy is the homecoming of that representation to its diasporic freedom? The answer is that the slave is obscured by the master or person in bourgeois social relations for whom equality with all means all otherness defined as thinghood. The master is removed from a relation to nature, from a relation to death, and as such, from a relation to himself formed in his negativity to others. All work has been formalised, emptied of any content that is self-determining. This is the condition of the impossibility of any higher education at all. It is the end of higher education, and it is the continuing victory of dualism over the notion, or reflection over philosophy.

Ironically this victory—the end of culture—has its representation precisely as the notion of culture *per se*.[4] Hegel defines culture as the general principle or form by which universality is produced. As such, culture is representation, for it represents universality to us that we might know it. As we have argued many times above, the relation of form to content that representation takes is itself determined by the misrecognition of the Idea that it seeks to represent. Culture is not representation; it is the representation of representation. This return marks the comprehension of culture as philosophy, but it is a return, currently, that is suppressed by the way illusion is determinative of culture's formalisation of itself.

It is ironic then that culture in fact repeats the illusions of natural consciousness whilst claiming to be their negation. In taking itself to be the identity of contingency, and thus the deconstruction of all identities, it dominates the conditions of its own possibility by forgetting or missing its determination within them. Our experience of the illusion that lies at the heart of contingency, formative for us, is the end of art and of religion in the sense that this re-presentation of representation is also re-cognition of misrecognition. But the substance of this experience awaits its own subject and substance in and as philosophy's higher education. However, this end of art and religion as formative political experience in their own right is not the end of culture *per se*. Far from it. At the end of art and religion lies the usurpation of contingency by culture as its own identity. This is the victory of abstraction over even the dialectic or education itself, a separation of formation from finality which marks the end of higher education. Freedom is now other than necessity, but is all possibility or freedom from heteronomy. Culture, once re-forming of natural consciousness, is now its most self-closing illusory being. Thus art and religion still have an advantage over culture *per se* for they do not entirely eschew their own negation and re-formation by philosophical experience.[5]

Culture in this sense is also a fate. To understand by fate a controlling providence is to repeat the illusion of culture outlined above. Subjectivity that re-presents its own freedom 'culturally' fails to re-present the necessity of its reformation within and by the totality of representation, or in and by its illusions. As such, necessity opposes culture as an externality or heteronomy when it takes the shape of fate. But for spirit, fate is self-determination, for Spirit's 'war upon itself' (1956: 73) is precisely the dialectical movement that constitutes its being in and for itself. The contradiction of culture, its self-negating activity, is our higher education regarding the significance of illusion as spirit. In this sense the philosophy of history in Hegel is the necessity that drives the *Phenomenology*. What the philosophical observer of the latter comes to realise is that all of the different shapes that the third party appears as when it knows illusion as constitutive of itself as spirit, are really the contradictions of culture *per se* become subject 'and' object. This is what the new form of pure culture refuses. It prefers to fetishise the 'and' of content and representation as 'difference'. Within the insights of philosophy's higher education this means that the self-determination of subjectivity and the substance of the Idea—which together are freedom—are become even more fixed within the property relation of illusion and the inessential object. As such, the 'and' of self and other, as of philosophy and education, is immunised from its determination in and by social relations.

This can be expressed another way. Reason is become culture as the form of its own universality. It re-presents itself not as art or religion or philosophy, which seek to re-present unity, but as culture *per se*, or the re-presentation of relation as the lack of unity. Thus reason here, as culture, is rational*ism*, turning diasporic reason into a reproduction of itself as self-satisfaction. It is a modern and therefore comprehensive form of scepticism. Above all, in claiming contingency in and for itself, it denies its relation to other as not me. Seeking to protect the other from an imperialism, in fact the culture of culture, or rationalism, relates to otherness itself as completely 'other'.

The Idea, here, has itself become 'thing' for culture. That it is often called 'post'-modern reveals the emptiness of the form for itself. To be after reason is rationally to be of reason but without reason. Here representation posits that illusion is known. But precisely therein it is *not* known. It is this lack of reason as the return of itself, or as spirit, that defines culture as the scepticism of an empty circle of rationalism. Rationalism is the grave of its own life and is despairing at its destruction of unity. In moments of bad faith it celebrates its despair, claiming the grave of life as heralding a new ethical relation.[6]

Reason as culture or as rationalism is therefore the zenith of bourgeois property relations. It is the triumph of the relation to other as thing over the work that sees relation to other as self. This is the master appearing without the slave, for all are equally for each other. But it is the suppression of the slave because the relation is granted no mind of its own. Abstract freedom is the positing of otherness as thing or property as universal law, and rationalism is the representation of that law as free or natural relation. Post-foundational culture expresses completely and comprehensively the illusion that defending contingency from unity means protecting the other from self-determining relation. In fact, such culture is relation robbed of significance, or is no substantial relation at all, and is thus the very essence of bourgeois freedom. It is philosophy's higher education which retrieves the significance of relation to other as free self-determination, or the absolute.

Is philosophy however not also a culture? And if it is, does that mean that philosophy itself has become rationalism, the representation and the suppression of actual freedom by abstract freedom? Is the slave still active for the master in philosophy, or is philosophy merely the culture or morality where form is all? Is there any higher education possible after the usurpation by post-foundational thinking of relation as all possibility and without a necessity or finality of its own? The answer is already in the question.

Hegel did not really explore cultures in modern bourgeois societies.[7] He expected philosophy to recognise in itself the vocation and the fate of representation as itself. As such, philosophy would represent relation not as pure form but as self-determination or freedom. Philosophy for Hegel should be the end of culture in the sense of *telos* as formative political experience, but it cannot be the end of culture in the sense of the elimination of all other forms of representation. To know culture is to know illusion, it is to know culture as a higher education than mere representation. It is to know representation as content even in its appearance as form. But this does not mean an end to culture, to representation, or to illusion. Philosophy does not eradicate culture, but in our higher education it 'spoils its own limited satisfaction... troubles its thoughtlessness and... disturbs its inertia' (1977a: 51). It is the fate and vocation of culture to be thought or known and philosophy 'is nothing other than the consciousness of this form itself – the thinking of thinking' (1956: 69).

Put another way, it lies in the nature of culture itself to be re-formed, that is, for form to be formed in being known. Culture exhibits for us the experience of higher education, the material for which 'is already prepared by general culture' (1956: 69). Philosophy, says Hegel, 'has indeed the condition of its existence in culture' (1956: 68) but it is a condition that is all too often suppressed. Where post-foundational culture takes its relation to philosophy as the condition of the possibility of philosophy and therefore the destruction of its pretensions to the absolute, philosophy knows *that* illusion *as* culture and knows illusion as free self-determination. Philosophy is not merely the representation of representation as pure form; it is its formation and finality, or the absolute as form and content. Culture is form, but experience is re-forming, and philosophy is this reforming higher education. Content for culture is arbitrary, as in possession made property. But content for philosophy is vocation and *telos*, its own end. This necessity is the only form of critique that does not re-impose universality as arbitrariness and suppress again existing relations of domination. It does not impose a new universality either, only a re-cognition of the one that is currently suppressed. Culture was always a learning experience, always a development and an education for it always enabled consciousness to think the relation of itself to itself, or to think freedom substantially. This is no different in post-foundational culture save that its relation now refuses freedom as object and claims all possibility for itself. This suppresses culture as learning and suppresses philosophy's higher education as the culture of learning and the learning of culture. Philosophy's higher education retrieves the educational significance of culture as its own being in and for itself. Indeed, it is what culture is for.

NOTES

[1] Rose argues that art has been more successful in avoiding assimilation than Hegel anticipated. See Rose, 1981.
[2] Like so many academic conferences.
[3] I have written about this in a previous book, see Tubbs (1997).
[4] I use the one term to 'represent' those aspects of current western theorising whose misrecognition of social relations and contingency is manifest as a critique of 'totalising' perspectives which supposedly impose

'closure' on and against openness and possibility. I draw a distinction between these (so prevalent, for example, in educational theorising) and the philosophically sophisticated explorations into aporia characterised by Caygill, discussed above in chapter 1.

[5] In one sense, Kant's *Critique of Pure Reason* could be argued to be a culture, for in setting out the doctrine of subjective freedom as lying within the conditions of its own possibility, it still posited the universal as other than the relation of the conditions. As with all modern cultures, Kant has his principle of subjective freedom re-formed by that very principle. Form presupposes content as other, and then dominates the truth it seeks to express. Relation is re-formed by the truth of relation. Culture which represents this modern relation does so without being able to represent its own re-formation. This belongs to philosophy's higher education and, as argued above, is the subject and substance of his *Critique of Judgement*. Only in philosophy's higher education is form also content and only in philosophy's higher education is illusion self-determinative and not suppressed.

[6] See for example, Rose, 1996, introduction.

[7] See Rose, 1981.

REFERENCES

Hegel, G.W.F. (1956) *The Philosophy of History*, New York, Dover Publications.

Hegel, G.W.F. (1977a) *Phenomenology of Spirit*, Oxford, Oxford University Press.

Hegel, G.W.F. (1977b) *The Difference Between Fichte's and Schelling's System of Philosophy*, Albany, State University of New York Press, trans, H.S. Harris and W. Cerf.

Hegel, G.W.F. (1985) *Lectures on the Philosophy of Religion Vol III*, Berkeley, University of California Press, trans. R.F. Brown, P.C. Hodgson and J.M. Stewart.

Hegel, G.W.F. (1988) *Lectures on the Philosophy of Religion, One Volume Edition*, Berkeley, University of California Press, trans. R.F. Brown, P.C. Hodgson and J.M. Stewart.

Hegel, G.W.F. (1993) *Introductory Lectures on Aesthetics*, Harmondsworth, Penguin, trans. B. Bosanquet.

Rose, G. (1981) *Hegel Contra Sociology*, London, Athlone.

Rose, G. (1996) *Mourning Becomes the Law*, Cambridge, Cambridge University Press.

Tubbs, N. (1997) *Contradiction of Enlightenment: Hegel and the Broken Middle*, Aldershot, Ashgate.

INDEX